GW00674886

# FIGHTER BOY

## JOHN WILLIS

From the author of
*Churchill's Few* (Mensch 2020),
*Secret Letters* (Mensch 2020),
*Nagasaki* (Mensch 2022)

# FIGHTER BOY

*THE MANY LIVES OF GEOFFREY PAGE*
*OBE, DSO, DFC, AND BAR*

## JOHN WILLIS

MENSCH PUBLISHING

Mensch Publishing

51 Northchurch Road, London N1 4EE, United Kingdom

First published in Great Britain 2024

Copyright © John Willis, 2024

John Willis has asserted his right under the Copyright,
Designs and Patents Act, 1988, to be identified
as Author of this work

A catalogue record for this book is available from the British Library

ISBN: HB: 978-1-912914-67-8; EBOOK: 978-1-912914-69-2

'Even in the context of the Battle of Britain
he was the bravest of the brave.'

*Air Chief Marshal Sir Christopher Foxley-Norris, 2000*


'We are the trustees of each other. We do well
to remember that the privilege of dying for one's
country is not equal to the privilege of living for it.'

*Sir Archibald McIndoe, 1944*

To

Sally and Robin in Kent

Michael and Pam in California

Ann in Australia

# Contents

# Prologue

12 August, 1940
Kent, England

The sound of the explosion was so loud Pilot Officer Geoffrey Page thought his eardrums would split. This was immediately followed by two more enormous bangs. A gaping hole like a wide-open mouth instantly appeared in the starboard wing of his Hurricane, and within seconds a huge fireball of flames began to engulf his cockpit. His initial fear turned to terror. As the young pilot looked down, he saw the bare skin of his hands shrivelling like burnt paper in a blast furnace. Geoffrey Page knew that the life was draining out of him. He had celebrated his twentieth birthday just a few weeks before. Now his Battle of Britain was over, his time as a 'fighter boy' finished. He accepted, with a calm that surprised him, that his life was over too.

Chapter One

# Beginnings

In the summer of 1939 two teenage girls were ambling along in a green field just outside Brighton in Sussex, chatting about school and friendships. They were suddenly distracted from their conversation by the sound of a small plane buzzing in the bright blue sky overhead. The little aircraft above was a training plane called a Hawker Hind, not that the two teenagers could tell one aeroplane from another. As they looked up, they saw the aircraft stutter, like a car stalling. Suddenly, it dramatically dropped as if it was being pulled by a magnet towards the earth. The young girls watched in horror as the Hawker Hind ploughed straight towards Honeysuckle Hill nearby and disappeared out of sight. Almost immediately the teenagers saw smoke curling upwards from the direction of the aircraft. They felt sure the little Hind was already a blazing inferno.

The pilot was Geoffrey Page, or Alan Geoffrey Page as he was christened, a science student at Imperial College, University of London. Imperial was one of the best science colleges in the world, but Geoffrey Page did not spend much time in the lecture hall or laboratory. He was much too busy flying with the University Air Squadron. As the eyewitnesses rushed towards the rising plume of smoke, they were relieved to see the young student standing defiantly by his smashed-up aircraft, He was very much alive. This was just the first of several life-threatening crashes Geoffrey Page would survive over the next few years.

*Geoffrey Page after his crash in 1938,*
*courtesy Brighton & Hove Herald*

A photograph exists of nineteen-year-old Page standing in a Sussex field following his spectacular crash. Geoffrey is wearing a light-coloured flying suit liberally spattered with dirt and blood. His right hand is heavily bandaged and in a sling. Underneath the messy flying suit, he is wearing a neat tie and shirt. Although he was now a university student Page looks so young and fresh-faced beneath his tidy head of brown hair, that he could have still passed for a schoolboy. There is a smile on his lips, perhaps of youthful innocence, or more likely an expression of relief.

The image simply looks like that of a young man who has upgraded his sports car for a plane and has endured what would be called in the officers' mess, 'a bit of a prang'. That day no one would have predicted that the young, bandaged pilot was destined to be one of the greatest and most courageous fighter aces of World War Two and would later be awarded the Distinguished Flying Cross (DFC) and Bar, and the Distinguished Service Order (DSO). Page not only flew in the Battle of Britain, but in the Battle of France close to Dunkirk, above the D-Day beaches, and at the Battle of Arnhem. He shot down or damaged at least fifteen enemy aircraft. On his appointment in 1944, he became the youngest Wing Commander in the RAF.

If his fearsome determination to fly is hidden in the photograph, the youthful smile beautifully captures Geoffrey Page's relaxed charm and sense of humour. The injured arm and dirt-covered flying suit also indicates a natural risktaker. What no image can reveal is the complexity of the man. Both Page's childhood and adulthood were more difficult than his easy manner belied. Later his natural courtesy and kindness camouflaged his wartime struggles with darker instincts, what he called 'a dormant lust for killing'.

The picture was taken by a photographer from the *Brighton and Hove Herald*. Geoffrey had flown from the RAF base at Thorney Island, where the London University Air Squadron was on a summer camp and headed towards Brighton. He told the *Herald*, 'I found the engine spluttering at about 100 miles an hour. I turned over from the main tank to the reserve tank but without avail.' The machine skidded along the grass, he explained, for nearly a hundred yards, before turning a complete somersault and landing upside down. The aeroplane was totally wrecked.

As the Hawker Hind hurtled into the ground, the joystick stabbed through Page's right hand. Although he was in significant pain, the young student described the incident with typically wry humour, 'I shut off the ignition and then managed to wriggle my way on my back between the cockpit and the grass. If I had not shut off the ignition, I should have had a very hot end.' The *Herald* noted that Page made his way towards the village where he was taken to the local school and treated by Dr Frederick Webb.

It was the *Brighton Evening Argus* that uncovered the real scoop of the day. It revealed that one of the first people to reach the crashed aircraft was the famous comedian, Max Miller, star of fourteen films and known on stage as The Cheeky Chappie. He told the paper, 'I found two girls who thought that the plane had crashed in flames, but the smoke they saw was from my garden bonfire. I went with the two girls to look for the plane which we found was almost two hundred yards away, and I took the pilot in my car to receive attention.'

At the time no journalist uncovered the real cause of the accident. Page had flown low over Sussex to impress a girlfriend. Unable to resist showing off, he decided to display his aerobatic skills above her house, but in mid- manoeuvre the engine stuttered and Page ploughed into Honeysuckle Hill. His life-threatening aerobatic display was completely wasted because the girl was not even at home when Geoffrey flaunted his aerial prowess. The girlfriend had a much more exciting rendezvous. She was at the dentist.

Like many boys growing up between the wars Geoffrey Page was entranced by flying. He avidly read the famous W.E. Johns *Biggles* books featuring a fictional pilot-adventurer, and as a little boy would sit on the floor in front of the fire with a poker between his legs pretending that he was flying an aeroplane. His ruling passion was not merely to fly but to emulate his hero, Captain Albert Ball VC, the legendary World War One fighter ace credited with shooting down more than forty-five German aircraft before he was killed in combat in 1917. Young Geoffrey knew every detail of Albert Ball's exploits in the air. At prep school he showed his talent for accidents when he wrote to his brother Douglas to tell him that 'I got hit on the head by a cricket ball, they say that I was unconscious for five minutes. I hope you have got me a nice birthday present. Another letter to his brother signalled his difficult lifelong relationship with money, 'I am nearly broke. I will send 9d soon.'

In the eyes of outsiders young Geoffrey looked as if he possessed every imaginable advantage. He had charm, intelligence, good looks, and natural talent as a pilot. In fact, his upbringing was short on joy, and sometimes painful. His own autobiography, *Tale of a Guinea Pig,* scarcely mentions his childhood, his parents, or his schooldays. The book plunges almost straight into his days at the London University Air Squadron, airbrushing out much of his life before then.

Page was born in Boxmoor, Hertfordshire, on 16 May, 1920. His father held a senior diplomatic position in Burma, which is where young Geoffrey spent the first three years of his life. Unfortunately, his parents divorced following his father's affair with a woman he met on the boat sailing out to his new post. As a result, Geoffrey Page returned to England as a small boy to live with his mother at Hove on the south coast. This was the beginning of an estrangement with his father. When he was old enough to understand Geoffrey found it hard to forgive him for leaving his mother.

For the rest of his life Geoffrey had very little contact with his father. They had a relationship but as his son Jamie put it, 'they never really knew each other'. Jamie Page recalls a rare visit to his grandfather as a little boy. By now he was living in a large but rundown house in Devon with his second wife and their children, 'The garden was overgrown and the bedrooms very sparse. I vividly remember a single naked lightbulb hanging in the room where I was to sleep and thinking how stark the room was…I think it was the only time I ever met my grandfather.'[1]

Page himself recalled that when he occasionally saw his father as he was growing up it was invariably at his 'rather dark and musty London Club. These tended to be somewhat stiff and monosyllabic conversations.' Geoffrey's father was a brilliant mathematician, who, not content with a First-Class degree from Oxford in Mathematics, took a further degree in History. However, he was clearly incapable of forming an emotional bond with the son of his first marriage. As a young boy at boarding school Page wrote to his father and criticised him for forgetting his birthday, adding a plaintive postscript pleading that 'a pound note would do'.

Perhaps that was too much to ask. The stark, dilapidated appearance of the house in Devon suggests that money was tight for a man with two families and a reasonably good fixed civil service pension being continuously eroded by inflation. Geoffrey's mother loved her son deeply and would do anything for him, but as he grew up funds were short. The two lived 'on a pittance from an ungenerous husband', as Geoffrey bluntly put it.

The young Geoffrey Page was not the only aircraft enthusiast in the family. His uncle was Sir Frederick Handley Page, one of the great aviation pioneers of the twentieth century. Sir Frederick was famous for manufacturing the Halifax bomber which the RAF flew on bombing raids to German cities in World War Two. Far from being an advantage in his chosen path as a fighter pilot, relations with his distinguished uncle were as strained as they were with his father.

Both father and uncle were fiercely opposed to Geoffrey's flying ambitions. His father insisted that pilots were commonplace and that aeronautical engineers were much more valuable. He made it

---

1    Jamie Page unpublished notes 2013

plain that Geoffrey's flying ambitions were foolish, and that if his son trained as a pilot, he would have to pay the fees for himself. Uncle Freddie promised young Geoffrey a job in his aircraft business, but only if he trained as an engineer not a pilot. No doubt he saw the clever, aircraft-obsessed, nephew as his natural successor at Handley Page. Uncle Freddie was even blunter than Geoffrey's father. He told his nephew that if he trained to become a pilot, 'I will never speak to you again'. And Sir Frederick Handley Page was true to his word. He also never spoke to his daughter after she married a man he disapproved of.

Page's mother had no money to support her boy's ambitions and, more importantly, was frightened that she would lose her precious son if he became a fighter pilot. Geoffrey was deeply disappointed but knew he was in a hopeless position. He reluctantly gave in to his father and uncle and was accepted to study Aeronautical Engineering at Britain's leading science college, Imperial, part of the University of London. He was still only seventeen. In a commitment to his newly chosen path of engineering, Geoffrey even worked at Handley Page for a few months in 1938. This largely involved sweeping the floor which was not much of an enticement to join the family aviation business. It was only later that Page divined a more compelling reason for the family's opposition to his fighter-flying ambitions. His father and uncle's younger brother Herbert had been killed flying for the Royal Naval Air Service in World War One.

If relations with both father and uncle were strained, Geoffrey Page's school days are also scarcely mentioned in his autobiography. Strangely, he indicates that he attended Cheltenham College when in fact he was educated at another public school in the same city called Dean Close. It may have been less well-known than Cheltenham but still produced some remarkable pupils, among them poet Rupert Brooke, painter Francis Bacon, and Rolling Stone Brian Jones. Page's school locker was full of aircraft brochures. Perhaps his obsession with fighter aircraft or his lack of money isolated young Page but, as his son Jamie, noted, 'I do not recall him ever talking much about his time there, nor ever mentioning friendships that he had formed.' His daughter Shelley added, 'He absolutely loathed it.'

A handful of surviving letters to his sister Daphne, who was clearly an important support for Geoffrey during his unsteady childhood, give us the only glimpses of his school days, 'I was second in the house junior swimming last Friday. Coming on aren't we!!' he wrote from Brook House at Dean Close in June 1935. Little did he know how useful those swimming skills would be during the Battle of Britain. Another letter to his brother showed the early signs of Page's lifelong struggle with money, 'I am nearly broke. I will send you 9d soon.' He joined the Officers' Training Corps and in March 1936 received his certificate. In 1937, close to leaving school, he wrote to Daphne, 'When are you going to send me that picture of Ginger Rogers?'

The conflict between the demands of Page's family and his own fighter pilot dream was resolved by Adolf Hitler. As the Nazis threatened the security of Europe, the RAF belatedly realised more planes and pilots were urgently needed. After World War One the number of RAF squadrons had been shrunk from a wartime peak of 181 to just 12. So, at Imperial College free RAF flying training was offered to anyone fit enough to enter the University Air Squadron. The plan was to develop a pool of student pilots who could quickly be made operational in the evermore likely event of war. This was the escape clause Geoffrey had been desperate for. He somehow persuaded his reluctant mother to sign the parental papers he needed to start flying. From that moment he spent more time learning to fly at the Air Squadron at Northolt than he did in lectures or writing essays.

In May 1938, the month in which he turned eighteen, Page completed twenty-two training flights. By July he had spent over seventy hours in the air. *His Summary of Flying and Assessments* for the year, signed by Wing Commander Thompson, the Chief Instructor, rated him 'exceptional' as a pilot. His next *Summary of Flying and Assessment* which no doubt reflected his reckless crash in Sussex was more cautious. The Wing Commander rated him as 'above average' and noted 'Must check overconfidence and rashness.'[2]

By the end of his second year Geoffrey was a good pilot but a terrible student. He spent so much time in the air that he failed his exams. As a result, his father demanded that he either gave up flying, or he left Imperial College. It was Hitler who came to Page's rescue a second time. The German leader's evident territorial ambitions and the RAF's increasingly desperate need for trained pilots made Page's choice simple. He waved goodbye to Imperial.

Geoffrey Page was fundamentally still the aircraft-crazy small boy who read Biggles and pretended to fly a fighter plane. His view of war was still heroic, 'I also thought I knew about war in the air. I imagined it to be Arthurian-about chivalry. Paradoxically, death and injury played no part in it.'

He later reflected, 'I had not yet seen the other side of the coin, with its images of hideous violence, fear, pain, and death. I did not know then about vengeance. Neither did I know about the ecstasy of victory. Nor did I remotely suspect of the presence within my being of a dormant lust for killing.'[3]

---

2    Geoffrey Page, *Pilot's Logbook*, Royal Air Force Museum, London
3    Geoffrey Page, *Tale of a Guinea Pig*, Pelham, London, 1981

Chapter Two

# First Flight

Geoffrey Page's chance to experience what he called 'the other side of the coin' would come soon enough, but for the moment he was still in the romantic phase of his long fighter pilot's journey. In September 1939, just after Hitler had marched into Poland, he received his call-up papers. A month later he joined several hundred other hopeful young pilots from University Air Squadrons at the new Aircrew Receiving Centre at Hastings in Sussex. Geoffrey was just 19-years-old, and he was extremely proud of both his new RAF uniform and his new rank, Acting Pilot Officer. He was, he acknowledged, not special or unusual, 'I was just one of a cross-section of young Englishmen. We were full of joie de vivre, being nineteen. We loved fast cars, fast girls, and fast aeroplanes. I don't think I was anything different from any young man then, or at any time.'

For the high-spirited trainee pilots Hastings was an extension of the universities they had so recently left. At night the bar of the Grand Hotel was the hub for endless discussion about aircraft and sex. There was little or no examination of their motives for fighting. They just wanted to fly fighters, and as they became drunker, confidence in their own prowess both in the air and in bed grew in equal proportion to the amount of alcohol consumed. Back in the harshness of daylight any bravado was sharply drilled out of the young pilots by the NCOs, who were never going to allow a bunch of soft university-types to have an easy ride. In time, Geoffrey Page and his new colleagues realised that they were more disciplined than when they arrived, and physically fitter from the endless marching along the promenade as the NCOs harshly barked out their orders.

At first, it was difficult for the trainers to spot in Geoffrey the man who would shoot down or damage so many German planes before the end of 1944. The NCOs had serious doubts almost immediately when the Acting Pilot Officer fainted during his routine medical injections. Page had made the basic mistake of looking at his arm as the needle was jabbed in. One medical orderly was heard to say, 'What happens when he sees real blood?'

His commanding officer, Michael Maw, who was only a little older but married with a child, took his unsteady charge by the arm, and sat him down by the sea. Bravado was easily replaced by under-confidence in many of the young pilots-to-be and Page was feeling ashamed. Maw reassured him that fainting at the sight of a needle did not mean he would not be a good pilot.

Even if they fainted at the sight of blood, the RAF could not afford to lose any of their new recruits who, thanks to their University Air Squadron experience, at least understood the basics of flying an aeroplane. By 1939 Britain was producing about two hundred pilots a month but Germany's well-oiled machine was training closer to a thousand pilots over the same period, five times the rate achieved by the RAF. Every half-trained student needed to be swiftly transformed into a pilot capable of flying in combat.

The leadership in Hastings must have detected something more in the fresh-faced young man from Imperial College than an ability to faint. Geoffrey was just one of twenty-four former students selected for flying training at RAF Cranwell. This was where it had always been his ambition to study, until his father and uncle bullied him into becoming an engineer. With characteristic modesty, Geoffrey later wrote that he 'drew' Cranwell, but selection for such an elite institution, the equivalent of Sandhurst and Dartmouth to the Army and Royal Navy respectively, was a question of being chosen for his potential rather than randomly 'drawn'.

As he headed to Cranwell on 6 November 1939, Geoffrey Page was in a joyful mood, and as excited as a puppy. Ever since the outbreak of war he had been desperate to get into action and Cranwell brought him one step nearer, 'When you're nineteen, you can't wait for it to start. Not everyone would agree with that point of view, but if you're young and hot-blooded and you can fly an aeroplane, you want to get at the enemy, if that's the right expression.' [4]

Page arrived at Cranwell on a typically grey November day; the atmosphere was dank, perpetually on the edge of rain, and mist curled up from the earth. But the dismal British weather did nothing to diminish his excitement. Cranwell had been his dream since leaving school and now he had arrived. Cranwell's elite status was underlined by its elegant hallway, and the civilian batmen on hand to help the youthful new arrivals with their cases. Geoffrey's batman even brought him tea in bed each morning. The brutal war that had already been fought in Poland and Czechoslovakia had clearly not reached Cranwell.

Most Cranwell training was carried out in Hawker Hind biplanes, which had no flaps nor a retractable undercarriage. Fortunately, Page had flown Hinds with his University Air Squadron, although he had managed to wreck one when he crashed into Honeysuckle Hill. Page enjoyed flying them, but they were very distant cousins of the Spitfire or Hurricane. The camaraderie between young men of the same age, all of them entranced by modern flying machines, was some

---

4    Geoffrey Page, *Imperial War Museum Sound Archive* 11103, London, 31 January 1990

consolation. They could talk about Spitfires even if flying them sometimes seemed a remote prospect.

Geoffrey Page was deeply critical of the old-fashioned aircraft the fighter pilots of the RAF's future were trained on, 'they were hardly an adequate steppingstone to the aircraft in which we would actually have to go to war.' He blamed politicians for shredding the RAF after 1918 and failing to arm adequately for the next conflict, 'We paid the price-in the blood of those who died during the invasion of France in outdated Blenheim and Battle bombers.' [5] Even though Britain was now at war, Page was still one of only fifty pilots a year graduating from Cranwell.

For all the heady excitement of flying at this elite institution, Page was uneasy. He had an uncomfortable sense that something was missing. Perhaps it was just a lack of confidence? Or maybe he was nervous that some external event would divert him away from his chosen fighter pilot path? The divorce of his parents, his uncle's steely views on his career, and Hitler's European invasions, had all blown his life about like a leaf in the wind. He didn't have a sympathetic father with whom could discuss his anxieties. He was comforted that Michael Maw, his mainstay at Hastings, was also part of his Cranwell group.

Page soon settled into his new routine with daily training in all aspects of flying. The only time reality burst into the cloistered world of Cranwell was when one of Page's fellow cadets was killed flying at night. On 23 November 1939 Geoffrey Page qualified as a pilot in both day and night flying, even though his night experience had been confined to just one solo circuit. He received his Certificate of Qualification as First Pilot. Early in 1940 Page's cohort on No 6 Course moved up to the Advanced Flying Training School. They were

---

5    Geoffrey Page, *Tale of a Guinea Pig*, Pelham, London,1981

on a firm war footing now, but the training aircraft were still Hawker Hinds. They were just better armed than the more basic version. Page was learning important skills but even a Hind armed with a bomb rack and a fixed machine gun, was a far cry from the Spitfires and Hurricanes he would fly in combat.

Once again, the tutors recognised something special in Geoffrey Page. He was naturally talented, quick to learn, and confident in the cockpit. He qualified as a pilot with an exceptional rating. He was a proud young man when his Wings were pinned on his chest at the Wings Parade. But for Geoffrey Page passing out as 'exceptional' was a disaster rather than a triumph. He was horrified that instead of a fighter squadron he was drafted to Training Command, which was the last RAF Command an ambitious fighter pilot wanted to join. When he desperately tackled his commanding officer, Wing Commander 'Speedy' Holmes, at a farewell cocktail party he was told that only the 'exceptional' could train others. The RAF needed those with high-level assessments to develop future pilots and not waste their valuable skills by being killed. Further salt was rubbed into the wound when Holmes added that talented flyers did not always make the most successful fighter pilots, 'a fighter pilot needs to be very ham-fisted on occasions and you're just not made that way. Sorry!' Page's roommate Derek Dunn played the system more cunningly and was drafted to his first choice, Bomber Command. He was killed four months later.

Page left Cranwell on 9 May 1940 and moved north to No 1 Flying Practice Unit at RAF Meir near Stoke-on-Trent. His lack of experience on modern fighter aircraft was frustrating but by the time he left Cranwell he had already amassed 239 flying hours. Towards the end of the forthcoming Battle of Britain new recruits were trained for just a few brief weeks before being thrust into the frontline to replace pilots who had been killed or injured. Many of these undertrained young men only lasted for a few flights before they too died or were badly hurt.

The RAF just could not afford to lose either fighter aircraft or pilots because in the interwar years the service had been reduced to almost nothing. In 1918 the RAF could field 22,000 aircraft. Just two years later they were down to 371. Neither politicians nor military leaders imagined another conflict so soon after what was called the war to end all wars and acted accordingly. The RAF salvage store near Croydon was crammed with unwanted machinery, including 30,000 engines and a third of a million spark plugs. It was only in 1936 that the RAF attempted to rectify this desperate shortfall. Flying training schools were almost doubled, university air squadrons were encouraged, and opportunities were rapidly opened for short-service commissions. Air Chief Marshal Sir Hugh Dowding, leading Fighter Command, was relieved when the Supermarine Spitfire was commissioned, following hard on the heels of the Hawker Hurricane. Some in the Air Ministry even thought that the outdated Boulton Paul Defiant, which did not even possess forward-firing guns, would suffice against the Luftwaffe. Dowding knew better. Britain needed aircraft that could match the Messerschmitt 109, with its sharp acceleration and good diving speed, if the nation was ever going to survive a potential invasion.

In a flagrant breach of the restrictions laid upon them in the Treaty of Versailles, Germany had rebuilt the Luftwaffe into a force of 2,000 aircraft with 20,000 men to fly and service them. In addition, their pilots had been battle-hardened in 1936 during the Spanish Civil War, gathering valuable flying experience in modern fighter aircraft. Even the horror of bombing to death so many civilians at Guernica in 1937 was lost on most Germans in the heady excitement of Luftwaffe success, mixed with the crude outpourings of Nazi propaganda. At the same time, the RAF were desperately playing catch-up.

Geoffrey Page was desolate about his move to Stoke-on-Trent, but his posting to Training Command was cut mercifully short. His salvation once again come from the enemy. On 10 May, Winston Churchill became Prime Minister. As a welcome present Germany invaded Holland, Belgium, and Luxembourg. Now the RAF needed pilots even more urgently, including those with no combat experience. Almost as soon as Geoffrey arrived in Stoke, his Training Command posting was abruptly cancelled, and a relieved Page was finally dispatched to 66 fighter squadron based at Horsham St Faith, Norwich. He had been in Training Command for less than a week.

His excitement at this move to Fighter Command was soon overtaken by anxiety. On arrival at Norwich station on 21 May 1940 there was no one to greet him. When he telephoned the squadron adjutant, he was appalled to discover that he was not expected. The adjutant thought the posting must be a mistake, but young Geoffrey re-read his orders, and 66 Squadron was plainly typed in black and white. Finally, he was picked up at the station and taken to Horsham St Faith where it was clear that the arrival of a new pilot was a complete surprise. When the commanding officer, Squadron Leader Leigh, realised that his newly arrived recruit had been trained on Hawker Hinds and had never even sat in a Spitfire, let alone flown one, he was appalled, 'Christ. Whatever will they be sending me next?'

Next day Page's confidence plummeted further. He was quizzed about his training and his new commanding officer was shocked that this young man had never flown an aircraft with a retractable undercarriage or one that flew faster than 120 mph. He said, 'Damned disgrace sending along a young boy who's never flown anything more advanced than a Hind. If you get killed it will be Group's fault. I've done my best to warn them.' At least, thought Page, I am not the one being blamed for this total mess. He was not to know that of the eighty-seven Cranwell-trained pilots who flew in the Battle of Britain twenty-four were killed. There was more than a one in four chance that Geoffrey Page would not survive the next few months.

The Norwich base was still being built; scaffolding adorned the control tower and builders were working on the hangars, but the grass runway looked smooth. Page looked on in wonder at the beautiful, sleek, Spitfires lined up like thoroughbred racehorses at the airfield. He was desperate to fly one, even sitting in a Spitfire would be exciting. But for a young man who had only flown small, slow planes this seemed a remote prospect.

Then his luck turned. The training aircraft at 66 Squadron was out of action and Geoffrey could not believe his good fortune when a reluctant CO added, 'Page you're about to fly a Spitfire. But if you break your neck, don't blame me.' Half an hour later he was sitting in the cockpit of the elegant machine he had dreamt about for so long. He was taken through the basic procedure. One minute he was told he was an unwanted and undertrained liability, the next he was at the controls of a magnificent fighter aircraft. It was confusing but Geoffrey did not care. He was excited and terrified in equal measure. So, it was an anxious young man who clambered into the Spitfire. Could he even get this beautiful machine airborne? He was dripping with sweat as he tried to remember all the instructions he had been hurriedly given. For a moment he froze as he looked at the large number of unfamiliar dials and knobs in front of him. He was too nervous to notice that a small crowd of ground crew had gathered to watch the inexperienced novice's inaugural flight.

As he eased the aircraft towards take-off Page noticed that his glycol coolant temperature was very high. Would his engine fail? The CO had warned him about this and added that if the glycol boiled the CO's blood would too. But, if he was ever going to get airborne, Page couldn't worry about that now. The coolant temperature was rising inexorably. So, he cut his cockpit checks short and turned the Spitfire into the wind. He hammered down the runway and eased the stick forward. The Spitfire soared gracefully into the air. It was as if a pilot was not needed, and the plane could fly on its own. As another Spitfire pilot put it, 'it was like pulling on a tight pair of jeans. It was a delight to fly.' Geoffrey was exhilarated, but just as he was admiring his own take-off the plane started to lose height. As he locked his wheels in the up position, the inexperienced young pilot had accidently pushed his control column forward. He was now so low he could see the trees above him as the Spitfire dipped. I am going to crash into the ground on my first, and now probably only, Spitfire flight, he thought. Page desperately pulled the stick back, and the Spitfire rose majestically once more. His life as an RAF fighter pilot had begun.

Page was relieved to see that the glycol temperature had finally fallen to normal. Now he could relax and enjoy the wonders of flying a Spitfire. It was only on his return that a second wave of panic hit him. He could not find his home airfield. Page circled the Norfolk sky several times, peering down in growing anxiety. He was relieved to finally spot the distinctive landmark of Norwich Cathedral pointing up to the sky above the city. He could find his way now. Pilot Officer Page almost surprised himself when he successfully eased his undercarriage down. Then he hovered above the ground before gently squeezing the beauty down on the grass. Geoffrey Page had never been so happy in his life.

The following days were bliss. With a fellow new arrival, Maurice Mounsdon,[6] he was tutored, not by the senior pilots in 66 Squadron, but by the Sector Medical Officer, Wing Commander 'Doc' Corner. This unconventional arrangement worked beautifully. The Doc was much more passionate about flying than medicine, and each day the

---

6    Page calls him Mark Mounsden in his autobiography, but he was Pilot Officer Maurice Mounsdon. He died in 2019 aged 101 years.

three men took to the air in their Spitfires as the waters of the Broads and green fields of Norfolk sped beneath them. Doc was a careful tutor who responded to any uncertainties in his young charges with sympathy. To his surprise and elation, Wing Commander Corner recommended that Geoffrey Page became an operational pilot.

Within minutes of hearing this thrilling news Geoffrey's dreams were crushed. As he emerged from the hangar, he heard the station commander angrily telling an officer from 66 Squadron, 'They've made a mistake with Mounsdon and Page's postings; they should have been sent to 56 Squadron instead.' As the senior officers ranted about Bloody Command and their hopelessness, the unwelcome news that Geoffrey was leaving his newly-found piece of heaven in Norwich quickly sunk in. He realised how much he would miss the comradeship of his newfound friends in 66. His tutor, 'Doc' Corner,[7] noted ruefully that this was, 'Command running true to form.'

The disaster swiftly turned into a full tragedy for Page when he learned that 56 Squadron did not fly Spitfires but Hurricanes. Geoffrey knew Hurricanes were sturdy and resilient aircraft, but they lacked the sleekness, and romance of the Spitfire. To Page this was like being told that you were banned from seeing the beautiful young woman you had just fallen in love with. A typing mistake had changed the course of Geoffrey Page's war. The only consolation he could find to soothe his aching heart was that 56, known as The Firebirds, was a legendary squadron.

The Firebirds had been the only squadron to produce two Victoria Cross winners in World War One: Major James McCudden, and Page's personal idol, Captain Albert Ball. In an echo of Geoffrey Page's feelings later in the war, Ball wrote to his father in May 1917, 'I do get tired of always living to kill and am beginning to feel like a

---

7    Corner was killed over the Channel in a Spitfire later in the war.

murderer. Shall be so pleased when I have finished.' The next day he was killed. McCudden died in a flying accident the following year, but not before he had shot down fifty-eight enemy aircraft. Within a few short months Geoffrey Page's wartime peregrinations had already taken him to Hastings, Cranwell, Stoke, and Norwich. Now his journey led him south to RAF North Weald in Essex.

Chapter Three

# 56 Squadron

North Weald was opened in 1916 as a landing field close to Epping Forest on the eastern approach to London. On 3 June 1940 when a down-hearted Pilot Officer Page arrived from Norwich it enjoyed an air of rural tranquillity. The airfield had been hastily converted for military use when another world war beckoned and RAF North Weald was well appointed, with a large flat grass strip and a solid Officers' Mess. On special occasions a glass case containing the tunic and gloves of Page's great hero, Albert Ball VC, was displayed in the Mess. It was a reminder to him that 56 was a famous squadron with a warrior reputation from World War One.

Page's arrival at North Weald was as dispiriting as his confused welcome in Norwich. The buildings were deserted. The young pilot headed to the main camp where it was touch and go whether an officious sentry would let him enter. Finally, his paperwork was approved, and he found a nervous looking adjutant who explained that the absence of pilots in this RAF ghost town was because the squadron was at RAF Digby in Lincolnshire on gun practice. At least Page had been expected this time, even if the adjutant was surprised that the young replacement pilot had been trained on Spitfires not Hurricanes.

Pilot Officer Geoffrey Page was one of just a handful of pilots who flew both Spitfires and Hurricanes in 1940, in his case due entirely to administrative error rather than deliberate planning. This rare experience gave him an insight into the two fighters, 'The bulldog and the greyhound. The bulldog being the Hurricane and the greyhound being the Spitfire. One was a tough, working animal, and the other a sleek, fast dog...they were both delightful aircraft with the same Rolls Royce Merlin engines.'[8]

The total absence of pilots heralded a bleak welcome, but it also gave the young man, who had turned twenty just a few weeks earlier, an opportunity to investigate his new home. It was a bright sunny day and the smell of fresh grass hung in the air. In one corner of the aerodrome stood some old-fashioned Blenheim night-fighters. On the south side of the airfield, he spotted a solid phalanx of Hurricanes. The Hawker Hurricane possessed a top speed of 320-340 mph depending on altitude. The Mark 1 Hurricane was armed with eight .303 Browning machine guns which carried 2,600 rounds. He located the Officers' Mess which stood eerily silent. He looked for the hut that housed B Flight, the unit he was about to join. The rows of empty iron beds and clusters of wooden chairs gave the place an unreal, ghostly quality. Playing cards sat on a dilapidated little table, as if the pilots had left in a hurry.

On the tarmac between the hangars sat two gleaming new Hurricanes minding their own business. He thought he might just hop into one, absorb the atmosphere, and study the cockpit layout, as any eager pilot-to-be would want. The squadron engineering officer had other ideas. He made it quite clear that no pilot could even sit in a Hurricane without permission of the commanding officer. Page continued his dispiriting exploration of the airfield. When he returned to the Officers' Mess there was a message to see the inflexible engineering officer for a second time. Luck smiled on him once more. The two new Hurricanes needed testing urgently, he was told. As Page

---

8    Geoffrey Page, *Imperial War Museum Sound Archive 11103*, London, 31 January 1990

was the only pilot available the job was his, despite never ever having sat in a Hurricane, let alone flown one.

To his surprise he took an instant liking to the Hurricane. The cockpit was roomier than the Spitfire and with good visibility. The propeller was of the latest constant speeding type, and the undercarriage could be automatically controlled. To Page's delight, the starting mechanism was the same as in the Spitfire. As the war progressed, Page always felt vulnerable when his Hurricane was climbing but once at the optimal height and speed its manoeuvrability, steady gun platform, and solidity could not be matched.

Geoffrey Page sped down the grass runway and smoothly eased himself up into the bright Essex sky. The young pilot felt instantly at home as he headed towards the North Sea, 'I had the immediate sensation that here was a lady with very few vices…below the wing tip shimmered the broad reaches of the Thames as they ran the course to meet the distant sea. Contentment filled my soul.'[9] Such was his happiness that Geoffrey was so confident, or arrogant, that he rolled the brand-new Hurricane on its back and completed an elegant loop.

His new Squadron had already endured a difficult time in this war. In the very first days of the conflict back in September 1939 two of their Hurricanes were shot down in what was called the Battle of Barking Creek. The 'enemy' attacker was not German but a Spitfire from 74 Squadron, RAF Hornchurch. This catastrophic friendly fire saw 56 Squadron lose P/O John Hulton-Harrap, aged 19, with F/O Tommy Rose bailing successfully out of the second aircraft. Hulton-Harrap, an eager young man who had only just joined the Squadron, was the first Fighter Command casualty of World War Two, and a self-inflicted one at that. Only a few days before, the adjutant had given the pilots blue forms to make their wills. The pilots roared with

---

9    Geoffrey Page, *Tale of a Guinea Pig*, Pelham, London, 1981

laughter as they willed their worldly possessions like tennis rackets and golf clubs to each other. Their laughter rang hollow now.

On 16 May 1940, while Geoffrey Page was still learning the ropes in the RAF Flying Practice Unit at Stoke and celebrating his twentieth birthday, 56 Squadron was dispatched to the frontline in the Battle of France. The Germans had pushed through Belgium at lightning speed and the Dutch had capitulated in just a few days. The advancing enemy were punching holes in the French defensive line with ease, hitting civilian targets including defenceless refugees straggling along the roads.

The old-fashioned Fairey Battle and Bristol Blenheim planes flown by several RAF squadrons in France had no chance against technically superior modern aircraft. Just a few days before, forty Battles and Blenheims had been shot down in just one attack. It was no wonder that aircrew called the Battles 'flying coffins'. Prime Minister Winston Churchill faced a difficult decision when it came to husbanding aerial resources. How many precious fighters should be sent to France and how many held in reserve?

Air Chief Marshal Dowding was clear that rationing of modern fighter aircraft was essential, especially the Spitfires that carried so many of the nation's hopes. He was nicknamed 'Stuffy' Dowding because of his humourlessness but he didn't need to be as charismatic as Churchill to understand that losing too many fighter planes defending France would leave the RAF short of aircraft in any forthcoming Battle of Britain. The Air Council had calculated that fifty-two squadrons were needed to defend Britain against a German attack and Dowding's strength was now down to just thirty-six. Dowding was clear that without sufficient modern aircraft Britain 'would be overpowered. Defeat would have entailed not only the destruction of all our airfields and our airpower, but of the aircraft factories on which our whole future hung.'[10]

The War Cabinet agreed to dispatch the equivalent of four more RAF squadrons to France even though it was against Dowding's advice. That decision left Fighter Command down to the bare bones to defend Britain. 56 Squadron's B Flight from North Weald was one of the half-squadrons to receive new orders to move to France and form a makeshift unit with 229 squadron. That afternoon, 16th May, Winston Churchill, flew to Paris for urgent meetings with the French Prime Minister Paul Reynaud and other senior political and military figures. He saw government documents being burned on a bonfire outside the Quai d'Orsay by his French allies and realised that plans were being made for the imminent evacuation of Paris itself.

On the day Churchill was in Paris, Air Chief Marshal Dowding wrote to the Air Council bluntly expressing his profound concern about aircraft shortage, 'The Hurricane Squadrons remaining in this country are seriously depleted, and the more Squadrons that are sent to France the higher will be the wastage...If the Home Defence Force is drained away in desperate attempts to remedy the situation in France, defeat in France will involve the final, complete, irremediable, defeat of this country.'[11]

As Dowding sought to avoid this bleak outcome, it was a tired B Flight of 56 squadron who landed at Vitry-en-Artois in Northern France. Geoffrey Page was so hungry to get into action he would have been desperate to join them, but he was still miles away in England, heading for the wrong squadron by mistake. The flight consisted of six Hurricanes supported by sixteen groundcrew, and their mood was an uneasy mixture of excitement at the prospect of

---

10    Winston Churchill, *Their Finest Hour*, Cassell and Co, London, 1949
11    Air Chief Marshal Hugh Dowding, *Letter to the Under Secretary of State for Air*, 16 May

combat and anxiety about the challenges ahead. Vitry was a large airfield about five kilometres from the town of Douai. A smashed-up RAF Blenheim sat ominously in the middle of the aerodrome. On arrival at Vitry a sentry heightened anxieties when he told the men of B Flight, 'There were six killed on Sunday and more the next day. They're all getting killed.'[12]

21- year- old Pilot Officer Fraser Barton 'Barry' Sutton was a tall, lean young man who had worked as a junior reporter for the *Nottingham Journal* before the war. He was to become good friends with Geoffrey Page. His daughter Caroline described him as not the classic clench-jawed pilot running determinedly out to his Hurricane but as 'a dreamy, diffident, and funny man, floating rather than striding through life.' During his Squadron's stay in France, Barry Sutton kept a diary. B Flight were up at 3am on the next day, 17 May, and airborne two hours later. They quickly ran into anti-aircraft fire near Lille, 'Shells were bursting all around us but miraculously no one suffered a direct hit. Something burst directly underneath me, and the blast lifted poor old Charlie (his Hurricane) as if by an invisible hand. But Charlie appeared to be still undamaged. Frankly I was a little bit frightened, but I could get used to this sort of thing.'[13] Despite the heavy enemy fire 56 Squadron shot down five German aircraft that morning.

In mid-afternoon Luftwaffe bombers smashed Vitry airfield, driving anxious aircrew into trenches. Immediately, 23-year-old Flight Lieutenant Ian Soden and Flight Sergeant Taffy Higginson, set off in vengeful pursuit before the pilot could make a second bombing run. This chase was described by Barry Sutton as 'the most thrilling spectacle I have ever seen while standing on solid earth.' Soden fired relent-

---

12    Alex Revell, *Fighter Aces!*, Pen and Sword, Yorkshire,2010

13    Barry Sutton, *Fighter Boy*, Amberley Publishing, Gloucestershire,2010 (original-ly published 1942)

lessly at the offending bomber, finally bringing it down in a field. He landed alongside his victim and realised there were no survivors. He picked up an ammunition pan from the wreckage as a trophy.

Despite these early successes, 56 Squadron's few short days in France were chaotic. The only contact with operational control was a field telephone in a small wooden hut. A second hut was the privy. Frederick 'Taffy' Higginson concluded, 'Our whole external operation was hopeless. We had no radar, limited communication with whoever was controlling us. The telephone itself was unreliable. On some occasions we took off on sight of enemy aircraft rather than being warned about them.'[14]  It was, said another pilot 'like operating blindfolded'. Telephone calls had to be routed through the local exchange and the swarms of enemy fighters already over Vitry when the RAF took off led them to conclude that the French telephone exchange was either passing on information or was extremely insecure.

The inadequate or leaky communications proved fatal. On 18 May as the Squadron took off about twelve Messerschmitt 109s were already lying in wait. 24-year-old F/O 'Tommy' Rose, a popular and experienced pilot, was hit. The ground crew below watched in horror as Rose's wounded Hurricane smashed into the ground between the airfield and the village with a thunderous explosion.

F/O Barry Sutton was injured in the same attack, 'Bullets began blasting and rattling all over the machine-one must have hit the glycol pipe in the cockpit, for steam began to shoot everywhere,' he recorded in his diary. On landing, the ground crew found him still in his aircraft, pale and motionless. Sutton realised his Hurricane N2553 was not fit to fly. Blood was beginning to ooze from the heel, where there was a neat bullet hole, but he bravely got airborne again in another

---

14    Frederick Higginson, *Imperial War Museum Sound Archive* 15111, London, August 1994

Hurricane even though it was widely regarded as unserviceable. He wore no shoes because of the pain.

On landing a second time, Barry Sutton, his wounded foot even more bloody, was placed into an ambulance. With him was Flt/Lt Fred Rosier from 229 Squadron who was so badly burned that his face was swollen beyond recognition. They were driven for seven hours through roads choked with refugees and were finally operated on in a tented hospital near Arras before being evacuated home.

That same evening the little aerodrome at Vitry was bombed from just a few hundred feet by several Dornier 'Flying Pencils', supported by a huge pack of about sixty Me109s. Once again, by the time the RAF pilots were scrambled it was too late. Nine British aircraft were destroyed, as the enemy picked off the Hurricanes at will. Unhesitatingly, 23-year-old Ian Soden jumped out of his trench and 'borrowed' an aircraft to defend the aerodrome, despite not even knowing if it was fuelled or armed. He was never seen again.

The Operations Record Book noted, 'Flt Lt Soden took off after the bombers and has not been seen since; a Hurricane which might have been the one he borrowed was reported shot down a few miles from Vitry. This was a very brave action as there were un-exploded bombs about.' He was awarded a rare posthumous DSO (Distinguished Service Order). The *Daily Mirror* reported, 'RAF pilot takes on 60 single-handed'.

In London, Churchill finally recognised the wisdom of Dowding's desire to preserve his best fighter planes and pilots for the Battle of Britain that lay ahead. Although he did not like letting the French down, Churchill agreed to send no further squadrons across the channel and those that were already in position were summoned home. But for 56 Squadron it was already too late; in a futile attempt to defend the undefendable the damage had already been done.

On 19 May what was left of a battered B flight spotted a mysterious man riding a donkey towards them. It was an Indian soldier in a British uniform. He was shouting that the Germans were only eight kilometres away. That same evening the shattered airfield at Vitry was evacuated to Norrent-Fontes about fifty kilometres distant. As they left, the men could hear gunfire from German tanks. On arrival at Norrent, Taffy Higginson was sent back to Vitry by car to destroy any remaining aircraft and stores. He managed to set all the petrol tanks ablaze as thousands of gallons went up in smoke, but the aircraft stubbornly refused to be set alight. When he heard the Germans close to the other side of the airfield, Taffy rapidly abandoned his arson attempts and speedily headed back to his Squadron. The few remaining Hurricanes were ready to fly back to England, and Higginson even had to physically evict a fellow pilot from his own aircraft to make it home. Six B Flight pilots had left for France and now two were dead and one badly injured.

It was tired but relieved men who headed back to England. Some even had bottles of French wine and champagne hidden in their Hurricanes. When 56 Squadron landed safely back at RAF North Weald Taffy Higginson described the past few days, 'It was just sheer bloody hell and terror from start to finish.' The survivors looked at each other. There were fewer of them now, but it was good to be home.

Chapter Four

# Dunkirk and St Valery

The experiences of 56 squadron encapsulated the predicament of the RAF. The Squadron had shot down several enemy aircraft but, in the process, three experienced pilots had been killed or injured and several precious Hurricanes destroyed. Defensive capabilities for the future had been weakened and to what end? The desperate position of British forces had not improved, as the Germans continued to relentlessly drive them into a small coastal corner of Northern France

The Squadron desperately needed reinforcements, but Pilot Officer Geoffrey Page was attached to the wrong squadron up in Norwich. In North Weald they had no idea where their latest recruit was. Geoffrey's daily flying was in complete contrast to the brutal war raging in Northern France. The tutoring of Doc Corner was as gentle as the Norfolk countryside they practised over. Page's days were full of contentment as his love affair with the Spitfire deepened. While 56 Squadron had lost so many Hurricanes in Northern France, there were enough spare Spitfires in Norwich for Page to practise flying a fighter aircraft to his heart's content. While his future colleagues moved exhaustedly from one sortie to the next, up in Norfolk there was plenty of time for Geoffrey Page to grow more confident as hours of regular flying passed. By the end of a week, he was looping and rolling as if he had been flying Spitfires all his life. The death and chaos his future squadron were experiencing in Vitry-en-Artois was a world away.

A few days after their hasty departure from Vitry, 56 Squadron was back in action over France. The dramatic and famous rescue of more than 330,000 troops from the beaches of Dunkirk in boats large and small was beginning. For the next few days 56 flew regular patrols over Calais and Dunkirk, usually in tandem with 151 Squadron, their stablemates at North Weald. They escorted Blenheim bombers tasked with attacking railway junctions and other strategic targets, and then flew defensive patrols aimed at deterring the Luftwaffe from attacking the desperate troops huddled in and around Dunkirk.

As 56 Squadron peered out of their Hurricanes, Dunkirk was an appalling sight below. The dock area was in ruins, and smoke billowed out in black clouds from the oil tanks the Germans had already hit. Below, the town was littered with abandoned vehicles, and ruined buildings. Through the smoke the RAF pilots caught glimpses of men like thousands of ants on the beaches below. An RAF Intelligence Officer arriving at Dunkirk described the scene, 'Dunkirk appeared on the horizon like an ugly bit of black lace, but the black cloud above it across the sky did not seem natural. The cloud suddenly changed into a huge serpent of smoke creeping above the factory chimney. It came from an oil tank which the German bombers had set on fire with a direct hit. Red flames were licking the tail.'[15]

56 Squadron was frustrated by the impossibility of fully protecting the men below from bombing and strafing. They were handicapped by fuel capacity which limited flying time over France to around thirty minutes from a forward base on the Kent coast and even less when they flew from RAF North Weald, fifty miles away from Dunkirk. After a fierce dogfight over Dunkirk one senior pilot landed back at the airfield with only five gallons of fuel left.

15    Geoffrey Myers in John Willis, *Secret Letters*, Mensch, London, 2020

Nonetheless, 56 Squadron tasted some success at Dunkirk. Minny Ereminsky, Taffy Higginson, John Coghlan and Ronnie Baker were among those who shot down enemy aircraft during what was called Operation Dynamo. On the other hand, the evacuation came at a heavy price for 56 Squadron. Flying Officer Michael Constable-Maxwell[16] was shot down by Belgian flak on 27 May. His mother was told he was dead, but he had managed to board a trawler which landed at Deal. Two days later 23-year-old Flight Sergeant James Elliott was killed defending Dunkirk. Three other pilots from 56 were shot down during Operation Dynamo and were badly hurt but managed to survive.

151, the sister squadron of 56 at North Weald, had experienced an equally grim time in the Battle of France. Squadron Leader Teddy Donaldson's views on the French were blunt, 'I had a grave dislike of the French at that time. I thought they were cowards. I've never seen anyone run so fast.'[17] He was appalled when the French Commanding Officer in Rouen helped the Germans by refusing to let the RAF refuel their Hurricanes, 'I would have liked to have shot the French colonel but did not have time to do so.' The squadron siphoned petrol from damaged aircraft into the serviceable ones and crept back to North Weald.

At the end of May, 56 Squadron was rotated out of the frontline and moved to RAF Digby for firing practice which is where they were when Pilot Officer Geoffrey Page arrived at a silent and ghostly RAF North Weald on 3 June. The two wrongly-posted Pilot Officers, Geoffrey Page, and Maurice Mounsdon, had finally been dispatched to the correct squadron and now replaced those killed or injured during the Squadron's endless sorties over France. At last Geoffrey

---

16    Geoffrey Page calls him Bob in his autobiography
17    Edward Donaldson, *Imperial War Museum Sound Archive 12172,* London, 7
       August 1981

Page was in the right place. He had missed the action but would soon make up for that.

Following Ian Soden's death in France, Flying Officer Leonid 'Minny' Ereminsky (or Ereminski) was promoted to become B flight's acting commander. It was Minny who welcomed Geoffrey Page into B Flight when the pilots returned from Digby. Page was relieved to see his future colleagues back at base and for the ghostly silence of an empty aerodrome to be replaced by the sound of chatter and laughter. Minny demanded to know where the hell Page had been, but as soon as the RAF's error was explained, Ereminsky relaxed. Geoffrey thought that Ereminsky resembled a Nordic god, although he was in fact a White Russian from Hampstead, North London. His father had been a Colonel in the Russian Army who was killed in the revolution of 1917. Despite his tumultuous background Minny was a reassuring leader who intuitively understood what Page and the other young pilots were thinking.

The arrival of replacement pilots was a relief to 56 Squadron. Young Geoffrey Page did not fully understand the catalogue of death and injury his new colleagues had just endured. Why would morale be low? Wouldn't every pilot be happy? They were all young and had a fast aeroplane to fly, he reasoned. Pilot Officer Barry Sutton's injury in France had made him more realistic than Page whose recent flying had only been over the peaceful fields and waterways of Norfolk. Barry was keenly aware that confidence was thin, 'When you've been bashed about a bit, like a dog that's been whipped, you went away and brooded a bit, but you soon got over it. I certainly knew I was never going to be a hero; I wasn't a hero...I was a bit worried I was running out of spirit.'

In Sutton's poem, *The Summer of the Firebird*, he captured this melancholy mood when he returned to North Weald after recovering from his injuries sustained in France,

*Now there on the edge of Epping Forest*
*The tide of the killed and missing had left its rim*
*Around the hangars and the messes*
*Motor cars with flattened tyres cobwebbed under gathering dust.*[18]

For Sutton, Geoffrey Page immediately lifted the mood in 56 Squadron, 'He was new blood, he was keen, he was a good flyer, and I think people liked him; two or three came at the same time and put heart into people like me. Geoffrey was obviously mad keen to get on with it. He was the sort of chap one needed.'[19]

Sergeant Pilot Frederick *'Taffy'* Higginson from Swansea was famous in the Squadron for both his flying skills and luxuriant whiskers. Higginson felt a similarly positive response to the new arrival, 'He was a very pleasant, charming character, handsome, good looking...he fitted into squadron life very well indeed. He was full of life and enjoyment, a typical young product of this country.'[20] One of the ground crew at North Weald, Eric Clayton, described Page in similar terms, 'He was typical of Dowding's 'fighter boys'-boyishly young, fair haired, smiling, and full of life.'[21]

Barry Sutton concluded that the arrival of Flying Officer Page and other replacements, 'Put heart into people like me that had been shot down once and had a long period of waiting when your nerves could get frayed.'[22] He was encouraged that 'the new blood was good'.

By 4 June, the day after Page's welcome arrival at North Weald, 338,000 Allied troops had been triumphantly evacuated from Dunkirk. This was a miraculous escape, a victory in defeat. Although

---

18   56 Squadron were nicknamed the Firebirds. Sutton's poem was transmitted by BBC Radio,15 September 1980
19   Barry Sutton, *Churchill's Few,* Yorkshire Television, Leeds 1983
20   Taffy Higginson unpublished author interview, 1983
21   Eric Clayton, *What if Heaven Falls,* Wye College Press, Kent,1993
22   Barry Sutton unpublished author interview,1983

vast numbers of military vehicles, equipment, petrol, and ammunition had been left behind, there were now 338,000 more troops,
most of them combat ready, who could fight in defence of Britain
over the next few months. The German commander of the panzer
divisions smashing through Belgium and France, Erwin Rommel,
noted, 'A miracle took place here! If the German tanks and Stukas
had managed to surround the British here, shooting most of them
and taking the rest prisoner, then Britain wouldn't have any trained
soldiers left. Instead, the British seem to have rescued them all-and a
lot of Frenchmen too. Adolf can say goodbye to his Blitzkrieg against
Britain now.'[23]

That day, Churchill addressed parliament, the nation and the
whole world and concluded with his famous words, 'We shall go on to
the end. We shall fight in France, we shall fight in the seas and oceans,
we shall fight with growing strength and confidence in the air; we
shall defend our island, whatever the cost may be. We shall fight on
the beaches, we shall fight on the landing-grounds, we shall fight in
the fields, we shall fight in the hills; we shall never surrender...'

The RAF's absence directly over Dunkirk and elsewhere along
the coast sparked a wave of fury from the soldiers even after their evacuation. They had looked hopefully to the skies from the beaches below
and asked angrily,' Where the hell is the RAF?' Geoffrey Page's answer
was that the RAF was almost invisible because they trying to defend
the soldiers from Luftwaffe strafing and bombing a few miles inland
*before* they reached the beaches. The RAF flew well over 2,700 fighter
sorties during the Dunkirk phase but Luftwaffe numerical superiority,
limited flying time because of fuel capacity, and some tactical errors,
ensured that the protection offered to the troops was limited.

---

23    Max Arthur, *Last of the Few*, Virgin Books, London,2011

The anger of the soldiers could turn ugly. One pilot who was shot down at Dunkirk tried to jump on three different destroyers only to be turned away, 'The navy said that all accommodation was reserved for the army and that the airforce could go f*** themselves...'[24] On returning to England anger against the RAF at Dunkirk and elsewhere in Northern France continued to boil over. Geoffrey Page heard of fisticuffs between soldiers and RAF ground crews in local pubs.

Operation Dynamo was not the end of the Dunkirk story. Around 41,000 men were left behind in France. Many had simply not reached Dunkirk before the last transport had departed on 4 June. They had been delayed in their retreat by enemy action, or by the total chaos of the refugee-choked roads in Dunkirk and the surrounding area. Some brave troops held defensive positions for precious hours to enable others to be evacuated from Dunkirk, and as a result missed the last boats out of the town.

Others had been captured by the Germans before they could reach their destination. Major William Anderson from the Royal Engineers was typical of the men who never reached Dunkirk. Anderson had already earned a Military Cross and his company had worked tirelessly demolishing bridges to slow the German advance. Most of his company made it safely from their defensive position on Mont des Cats near the Belgian border to the Dunkirk beaches, but Anderson and a small group were slowed down because they were looking after a wounded man. Halfway to Dunkirk they were captured by the Germans and spent the rest of the war in German prison camps.

Some of the British troops who fought tirelessly to keep open the corridor between the retreating troops and Dunkirk for a few precious days paid an even heavier price. Those unlucky enough to fall

---

24  Tony Bartley letter to his father, *Smoke Trails in the Sky*, William Kimber, London 1984

into the hands of the SS rather than the regular army faced execution. There were several massacres during the retreat including the murder by the SS of 97 soldiers of the 2nd Battalion, Royal Norfolk Regiment at Le Paradis. They were machine gunned to death and those who survived the bullets were bayoneted or had their skulls crushed by rifle butts.

The largest unit of troops left behind was the 51st Highland Infantry Division which was composed predominantly of Scottish regiments, men of the Black Watch and the Seaforth Highlanders, the Gordon Highlanders and the Cameron Highlanders, amongst others. They were joined by some English regiments including the 7th Battalion Royal Norfolk Regiment. The story of the 51st was to ultimately be one of brave failure which did not fit neatly into the uplifting narrative of Dunkirk. Their story was overshadowed by the heroic tale of the little rescue ships and thus became known as the Forgotten Dunkirk, or the Other Dunkirk.

These Highland soldiers were the men Geoffrey Page and 56 Squadron were dispatched to defend. For Page's friend, F/O Michael Constable Maxwell, this was a very personal mission. He had been in the Cameron Highlanders before the RAF and had recruited and trained some of the men he was now being sent to save. On 9 June over breakfast Minny Ereminsky instructed B Flight to get ready for action over France. Their role was to sweep the French coast to keep the enemy away from troops like the 51st Highland Division still on the ground. Geoffrey Page flicked nervously through the morning newspaper to get a better picture. It was clear that the Germans were smashing all before them, and that those left behind in France were being forced towards the small port of St Valery.

Page's mind moved in two completely different directions. On the surface he appeared confident, but privately he was very nervous. Any interest in breakfast disappeared with Minny's announcement.

He would soon be in combat against the Luftwaffe for the first time. As Page waited anxiously, he tried to write a letter to his mother, but he really had no idea what to say. He was unable to scribble more than the first three words, *My Darling Mother*. At dispersal Page was allocated the number three position, with the reassuring figure of Ereminsky in the lead. He was comforted to be flying the same new Hurricane he had trialled on his first day. The messages were simple; mind your tail, watch the sun, and with only thirty minutes' worth of fuel, check the level carefully to be sure there was enough juice to fly home to England.

Page concentrated on not forgetting any vital piece of equipment. He pulled his Mae West lifejacket on and carried his parachute out to his Hurricane. Maps were slipped into the side of his flying boots and a tiny compass was placed into his pocket. You never knew what would be useful if shot down over enemy territory. Out at the aircraft he suddenly felt an overwhelming desire to urinate. There was no going inside now, and it was an embarrassed young pilot who peed on the Essex grass. He was comforted to see that the grass was being watered by most of the pilots in the Squadron at the same time. He realised that a last-minute nervous urination was par for the course.

Bladder happily emptied; Geoffrey Page swung his Hurricane around to take off into the wind. He could see Minny Ereminsky give him a thumbs-up sign and Page returned the readiness signal. The White Russian's number 2, 'Dopey' Davis[25], did the same. Simultaneously the three Hurricanes opened their engines and sped along the grass, before easing upwards in unison and heading for France. Geoffrey's first wartime combat would not be taking place over the familiar fields and villages of the Home Counties.

---

25  In Page's autobiography he refers to a pilot called Davis in 56. Presumably this was F/O Peter Davies

His initial nervousness was swiftly submerged under the excitement and adrenalin. At nineteen or twenty years of age the young pilots believed they were immortal. The ever-present risks of being killed or badly injured were not yet apparent to them. But Geoffrey Page instinctively knew that this was serious, the busy sky above Northern France was no place for carefree young men. Survival would necessitate growing up fast and becoming old before his time.

Page was soon too busy to contemplate death. He scanned the clear blue skies searching for the enemy and at the same time tried to maintain the neat formation required. As he saw the narrow strip of water that was the Channel speed beneath him, Page realised that wearing a collar and tie was a painful encumbrance on an operational sortie. The endless movement of his head in his starched collar was rubbing his neck sore. Clearly, it was not practical to look smart and spot enemy aircraft at the same time. He desperately pulled his collar off, ripping his shirt in the process. He opened the hood of his Hurricane and threw the collar off into the roaring wind.

Minutes later they passed the French coast and flew over the town of Abbeville. In front of them appeared a giant, dark cloud. It took Geoffrey a few moments to realise that this deep-black mushroom was a giant fire blazing from the huge oil tanks below. Fear seized him when he heard the cry, 'Look out! 109's above'. For a moment his panicked mind went blank. Then his Hurricane jolted dramatically. He had accidently flown through the slipstream of Minny's aircraft. Relief surged through him when the next message revealed that the 'enemy' aircraft were not Messerschmitts, but Hurricanes from 151 Squadron, also based at North Weald. A few minutes later the Squadron flew in tight formation into the thick black smoke hanging ominously over the town of Dieppe. When Geoffrey Page emerged on the other side of the billowing smoke he was on his own. 56 Squadron had disappeared. Utterly alone, the 20-year-old dived down towards the ocean, levelled out, and crept back towards the safety of England just a few yards above the waves. His first sortie over enemy occupied France was over.

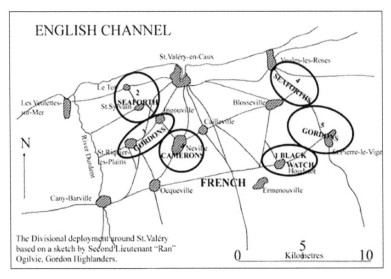

*From sketch by 'Ran' Ogilvie, Gordon Highlanders*

On the ground General Victor Fortune, commanding the 51st Highland Division, knew his troops were seriously outnumbered and outpowered, but they were not giving up an inch of ground without a fight. Days earlier, while thousands of soldiers were being scooped up from the beach at Dunkirk, they had bravely defended a line near the Somme against overwhelming odds. Once their own potential escape route from Le Havre had been cut off by the encircling power of Rommel's 7th Panzer Division, their only alternative was to head north to the small fishing port of St Valery-en-Caux. This was an unpromising town for a large-scale evacuation of troops. The quay and the port were just too small to allow deployment of the larger ships that had carried so many thousands to safety from Dunkirk. The

Other Dunkirk was about to begin, and the Germans were going to throw everything at stopping a second embarrassing evacuation.

As the 51st Highland Division and the French 9th Corps were being driven back, 56 Squadron was in a state of perpetual readiness. In the early hours, they sat in their dark cockpits warming up the engines so they could become airborne quickly. In the same afternoon as his first taste of wartime flying, Page flew a second sortie. He escorted Blenheim bombers to the French coastline before, once again patrolling behind enemy lines. His desire to be in the thick of the action was reflected in his logbook, 'AA (anti-aircraft) fire encountered. 12 Me 109s sighted **but they would not stop to fight!** Returned to Manston to refuel.'

Meanwhile the German grip round the throat of the 51st Highland Infantry Division tightened. Yard by yard their soldiers were pushed back towards St Valery. Progress was slowed down by the streams of refugees on the roads, as Sergeant Hurbert Tuck observed, 'German fighters found these wretched columns easy targets. Seeing the bodies of dead children was the worst scene one can witness and you try hard to forget but never do.' When they finally reached the fishing village of St Valery the 51st attempted to hold a bridgehead despite heavy casualties from the mortar and shellfire, 'I still wonder how we carried on as we did. Many of us had not slept for days yet they still fought on, it was very stirring. There were so many brave acts performed that I personally witnessed during the St Valery battle, but we were all far too busy to note names for medals, but then you don't receive medals for failure.'[26]

On 10 and 11 June the little port came under savage enemy fire. There was a constant sound of shellfire and bullets as the German pummelled the 51st Division from the cliffs above the port and

26   Sgt Hurbert Tuck, *BBC WW2 People's War*, 10 Feb 2004

Stukas strafed the troops on the ground. Sgt Tuck was one of them, 'You never forget the sound of lead striking bone. It was a sound I was to carry with me for the rest of my life. It was indeed Hell. You had to be there to realise the madness that was happening around you. Arranging burial for the fallen, and there was a great many of them, was very harrowing for me. I instructed burial details to wrap the bodies in ground sheets as I felt covering an unprotected body with earth was too heathen and barbaric. They were heroes and deserved to be buried as such. With the greatest respect.'

The hopes of a dramatic rescue by sea were fading under the enemy onslaught. On 11 June General Fortune received a message from the Royal Navy in Portsmouth saying that fog had prevented navy ships arriving off St Valery but 'will make every effort to get you off and additional ships are being sent to arrive tonight.'

Up in the air the pilots could see the perilous position of the army, but they had neither the numbers nor the flying time to put up a strong showing. Geoffrey Page and the rest of 56 Squadron operated in tandem with 151, their sister squadron at North Weald. On 12 June 151's Intelligence Officer reported, 'The strain was beginning to tell on the pilots, several of whom were reporting defective vision.' That same day, Page flew two sorties over St Valery-en-Caux where a desperate scenario was being played out below. He was on the lookout for enemy dive bombers aiming to strafe the Allied troops, 'Self and section leader dived to attack 2 aircraft flying low over the sea but lost sight of them over the sea.' [27] Page reported that the aircraft was a Ju87 Stuka dive bomber but that haze over the sea meant he lost it.

General Fortune and his men were now totally trapped and virtually out of heavy ammunition. Despite the presence offshore of over two hundred British ships, from Royal Navy vessels to small

---

27   Geoffrey Page, *Logbook*, RAF Museum, London

domestic craft, a combination of bad weather and the massive enemy bombardment from cliffs above the little fishing port spelt doom. As one of the Adjutants, Derek Lang, later Lt Gen Lang, put it, 'We were still hoping to be evacuated into the wide open arms of the Royal Navy. But things went wrong. The weather was against us. The tide was against us. They simply couldn't get in to take us off.'

Down below, the trapped men cheered when Hurricanes flew over them. These were the first friendly aircraft some of the soldiers had seen in days. They tried to attract the attention of the pilots but there was no response. Five pilots and aircrew were killed supporting the attempted evacuation from St Valery. By the time Page had flown his second patrol of the day over St Valery, the French had capitulated.

Soon after the 51st Highland Infantry Division accepted the inevitable and General Victor Fortune surrendered to General Major Erwin Rommel. More than 8000 soldiers were condemned to spend the next five years in German prisoner of war camps. Over 1000 of their colleagues had died and many more were wounded. A few soldiers escaped from the hell of St Valery. Thirty-one men from the 7th Battalion Royal Norfolk Regiment commandeered a small fishing boat and using shovels as paddles eventually made it to the safety of a Royal Navy vessel waiting out to sea.

The surrender at St Valery did not signal a full stop to Geoffrey Page's sorties over France. Other troops were still trapped, including the injured. On 14 June, two days after the capture of the soldiers, Page flew sorties in both the morning and afternoon over Northern France and Belgium, interspersed by a swift refuelling at RAF Manston just across the channel. These were nerve-shredding flights. Page craved combat with the enemy but not on a sortie over France because stopping for a dog- fight would leave him desperately short of fuel to fly safely home. The pattern of constant flying from the darkness before dawn until late continued for the rest of the month. In this period of Dunkirk and its aftermath, Geoffrey Page concluded that the protection he could offer the soldiers waiting so desperately for evacuation 'bordered on the pitiful'.

Soon after Geoffrey Page's first anxious sorties over France what little was left of his romanticised view of war was shattered. Standing outside dispersal at RAF North Weald he saw three Hurricanes flying low over the airfield in poor visibility. Page spotted the lettering of their sister squadron at North Weald, 151. As the aircraft began to pull away, the right-hand pilot attempted what looked like a victory roll. When the Hurricane was inverted its nose dropped rapidly and the aircraft smashed into the ground with a huge explosion. For a moment, the pilots and ground crews on the airfield were frozen still, as they processed the horror of what they had witnessed.

Then, as the plume of black smoke curled silently upward, men ran wildly through the long grass from all corners of the airfield towards the wreckage. Overhead the two surviving Hurricanes continued to circle, anxiously surveying the tragic scene below. On the ground, Geoffrey Page instinctively knew there was no hope, and hesitated, but driven by some inner emotion he did not fully understand, he then kept on running towards the burning aircraft. The silence was broken by the heavy breathing of the rescuers overlapping with the insistent sounds of a clanging ambulance and fire engine.

Page knew the pilot, 24-year-old Pilot Officer Jack Hamar, but he was in their sister squadron and not a close friend. The ambulance raced unsteadily across the uneven ground before halting beside the wreckage. Breathless, Page joined a small circle helplessly watching what was now a funeral pyre. Firemen and medics kicked the smoking pieces of metal to reach the burning remains of a man who a few minutes before had been a young and enthusiastic pilot just like Geoffrey,

'Suddenly there was a fine young man and he was no more, just a gaping hole in the ground.'[28]

Fresh from a combat success, Hamar had performed his customary victory roll as he came into land, but in the poor visibility failed to appreciate that he was only 100 feet above the ground. He was an experienced pilot who had been awarded a DFC just the day before and had flown with distinction in the Battle of France. Now he was dead because of a silly accident. At the scene Page was staring at his first dead body of the war. Looking at the white face of his friend Dopey Davis standing next to him Geoffrey realised that he possessed a strange immunity from this horror, 'I was aware of two definite reactions to the scene before me. The first was one of nausea from the combined smell of the wreckage and the burnt flesh. The other sensation was more powerful than that of a queasy stomach. I realised with surprise that the death of a recent companion did not disturb me very much. It was as if a wave of shock radiated out from the mangled debris, but just as it approached, the wave passed on the other side leaving the sense high and dry on a little island erected by nature to protect the occupant from the drowning effect of the horror of the event.'[29]

Suddenly, Page felt older than his years, much older. With a casualness that surprised him, he said to Dopey, 'How about a drink?' With one swift glance back at the crackling fire, the two young pilots led each other away from the wreckage so that they might, in the time-honoured way, anaesthetize themselves from the horror they had witnessed.

---

28  Author interview, North Weald, 1983
29  Geoffrey Page, *Tale of a Guinea Pig*, London, Pelham, London,1979

Chapter Five

# The Battle of Britain

For self-preservation Geoffrey Page pushed the vivid image of the flaming wreckage out of his mind and settled down to flying with 56 Squadron. Days in the air followed relentlessly, one after another and Page was soon used to the new pattern of his life. The early starts; the piercing shriek of the telephone before a scramble; the flights over endless water to and from France; and the sky studded with enemy aircraft before combat. Each day was much the same as the last, except all too often a pilot or two was missing from the day before.

Prime Minister Winston Churchill set the scene for the next phase of the war in stark terms, 'I look forward confidently to the exploits of our fighter pilots - these splendid men, this brilliant youth who will have the glory of saving their native land, their island home and all they love, from the most deadly of all attacks… What General Weygand has called the Battle of France is over; the Battle of Britain is about to begin.'

For 'this brilliant youth' in 56 Squadron, the different phases of the war, the demarcation between events as recognised by historians and politicians, largely passed them by. The Battle of France, the Dunkirk evacuation, and defence of St Valery, blended seamlessly into a single phase. The Battle of Britain followed swiftly on, and the endless rounds of patrols and sorties gave Page no time to pause and take stock.

The final hours of darkness were usually spent anticipating the next flight over France. Geoffrey Page sometimes waited in his cockpit, teeth chattering with the dawn cold, sometimes warming up his engine up in case of an emergency call. Tiredness was a new enemy. In one Squadron the emergency fire engine clanged its way hurriedly to an aircraft that had smashed into a boundary hedge on landing, only to find the pilot was not injured but had fallen asleep. Geoffrey Page was changing fast, stepping from being a schoolboy to manhood, with nothing in between. As he reflected, 'All that remained of youth in those swiftly moving Hurricanes were the physical attributes of our bodies; the minds were no longer carefree and careless. The sordid reality that our task implied, banished lighter thoughts for the time being.'

Faced with this relentless high-pressure, 56 Squadron needed a safety valve to forget the day's horrors, even if it reduced sleep further. After all, the pilots were not much more than overgrown schoolboys. Alcohol was the chosen remedy for calming nerves, even if was only for an evening. At the end of a hard day in the air they were aching for the excitement of the clubs in the West End, full of booze and beautiful women. Their favourite was the *Bag of Nails,* and if they were not in a club, the pilots of 56 could be found in the *Shepherds Pub* in Shepherds Market which was overseen by a Swiss gentleman called Oscar who, Geoffrey Page said, knew more about the RAF than the air force's own Intelligence Branch. For young men facing an uncertain and probably short future, these boisterous outings were a distraction. The battered old Squadron car, which was called Esmerelda, could sometimes be seen disgorging as many as a dozen pilots in the early hours of the morning, before they grabbed an hour or two's sleep ready for a dawn sortie. This wilful lack of sleep was, reflected Geoffrey Page, 'a self-inflicted wound', although no pilot was stupid enough to fly when drink made them worse for wear.

Geoffrey Page soon realised that a car was a vital asset for forays into Central London. Ian Soden's tragic death meant that his Ford V 8 car was available for a quick sale. Geoffrey Page was the lucky purchaser and inspecting the logbook he realised that Soden had recently bought his car from another pilot, now also dead. Soon after, Page was forced to sell the orphaned car to Maurice Mounsdon, largely because of a shortage of funds.

Like alcohol, humour was an important tool for survival. Unfortunately for Page, his mother gave his colleagues plenty of ammunition. She was an anxious and fretful woman, who sometimes telephoned the station commander at North Weald worrying about whether her beloved son had changed and aired his wet socks before he went out on a sortie. To the amusement of his colleagues and embarrassment to himself, Page would be greeted on landing from a sortie by wry smiles and the news that, 'Your mother has been on the phone again.' She also regularly nagged her son about wearing gloves when flying. A few weeks later he had good cause to regret not listening to his mother, as few 20-year-olds were inclined to do.

Page quickly became firmly embedded into his new squadron, this tiny and exclusive club. Friendships with his companions in the air and at the bar of the local pub deepened. Although a dog fight was solo man-to-man combat, teamwork in the sky was essential. Survival often depended on each pilot scouring the skies for the enemy and warning his colleagues of danger. In these early chapters of his flying career the senior pilots were key teachers in his aerial classroom. Sergeant Pilot Taffy Higginson was one of the very best, with several victories in France already to his credit. In the air the men flew alongside each other, and it was Higginson who owned the beaten-up Squadron car. So, it was unfair in Page's eyes that after an intense day's flying, he went to the Officers' Mess and Taffy disappeared into the

Sergeants' Mess. To Geoffrey Page they shared equal risk and should have lived in the same accommodation.

If the squadrons at RAF North Weald were ragged following so much non-stop flying over France, the overall Station Commander was the ideal man to steady the young men stationed there. Wing Commander Victor Beamish was a talented rugby player from County Cork with a friendly smile and steady blue eyes. At 36-years-old he was several years senior to the young pilots, so he was regarded as positively an old man. But they were impressed that despite his age and status he was not desk bound, and still flew regularly with both 56 and 151 Squadrons.[30] Pilot Officer Page was instantly won over by Beamish who was brave and efficient, charming and tough, at the same time. But even the Wing Commander's man management skills could not protect 56 Squadron from the next blow to crash down upon them.

Geoffrey returned to North Weald from visiting his mother and sister to hear the news. Just a month after his predecessor had died in France, the reassuring figure of Flying Officer Minny Ereminsky, Acting Commander of B Flight, had been killed. On 17 June 1940 Minny was returning to RAF North Weald after a routine patrol. The weather conditions were so poor that pilots had been forced to turn back from Northern France. Ereminsky, trying to thread his way through the terrible visibility, chose to fly low and smashed into the roof of a house at West Horsley near Guildford. He was 23-years-old and was buried on 21 June at Whyteleafe Cemetery, in accordance with the rules of the Russian Orthodox Church. Probate revealed he possessed the princely sum of £67.

Minny had been the most exotic but also the most respected pilot in B Flight. He had taken Geoffrey Page under his wing and

---

30    Beamish was killed in action over the Channel 28 March 1942

the young pilot had learned so much from him. It was, Page said, 'Another stab into the body of my own youth.' Minny's replacement was Flight Lieutenant Edward 'Jumbo' Gracie, who was physically the complete opposite to Ereminsky. Gracie's tubby frame invited an unflattering comparison from his fellow pilots to a small elephant. His image problem was compounded by piles, which made him grumpy and were his major topic of conversation. Gracie may have appeared to be the physical antithesis of the dashing, athletic, Battle of Britain pilot but mechanic Eric Clayton called him 'a brilliant leader, and an aggressive fighter pilot'. Michael Constable Maxwell was impressed by his lack of fear and thought he possessed the potential for greatness. Others were less complimentary about his leadership skills in the sky, including Page, who liked Jumbo but thought he was poor at spotting the enemy in the air.

On I July, 56 Squadron's commander, Edward Knowles, known as *Fuehrer* to the young pilots, was posted to a non-operational unit at the Air Ministry. Perhaps the authorities thought he was not the right man or the right age for the difficult job ahead. The gap was filled by promoting Flight Lieutenant 'Slim' Coghlan[31] on a temporary basis. John Coghlan was a short, sweaty, heavily-built man with a large moustache. He was friendly and unflappable. Coghlan had damaged or destroyed four enemy aircraft in France and was respected as a first-class pilot. His elevation meant that 56 Squadron headed into the Battle of Britain with a leader they trusted, but without a permanent commander.

The Battle of Britain started officially on 10 July 1940. The fate of the country was now largely in the hands of squadrons of 19- or 20-year-olds who a year before had been at university, in a civilian job, or even at school. Only a few pilots were married and, as pilot's

---

31    Geoffrey Page spells the surname Coglin

wife of just nine weeks Terry Hunt had a ringside view, 'It was a queer golden time. The world seemed full of lights. They were golden boys too. You met people once or twice, and then they were dead. Now they seem such little boys, such boys.'[32]

Despite his experiences over France and his aching tiredness, Geoffrey Page's view of the combat to come still echoed the past, a war governed by chivalry not brutality, 'Ours was the glorious prize of cleaving our way through the skies on flashing silver wings, killing and being killed in the manner of ancient knights tilting in the lists, reaping not the empty applause of posterity, but the excitement and thrill that made a short lifetime worth living.'[33]

Page was not alone in his romanticised view of aerial combat. His friend Barry Sutton, who re-joined the squadron three days before the Battle of Britain started, also described the Battle of Britain in sporting terms, 'I thank my stars that since it has been my destiny to fight, I have fought in the sky, for if there is any sport in modern warfare, it is in the air battle, and if there is glory in dying, it is in the knowledge that death comes only by the superiority of one's adversary in honourable combat. If the numbers are unevenly matched in favour of the enemy, death is only more glorious.'

Not that the prospect of honour in death made Sutton relaxed in the air. He was perpetually anxious when sunny summer skies offered no cloud cover. The sturdy Hurricane was not a fast climber compared to the Me109 and 'you seemed to be sitting there in a goldfish bowl wondering what was going to come out of the sun.' Other pilots described their feelings even more starkly, 'Anyone who says he was not frightened in the Battle of Britain was either a liar or an idiot.

---

32  Author interview, London,1981
33  Geoffrey Page, *Tale of a Guinea Pig*, Bantam, London 1981

One of the best reasons for choosing to be a fighter pilot was that you were only shit-scared for forty minutes at a time.'[34]

If 56 Squadron was ragged after Dunkirk and the Battle of France, Fighter Command itself was also in disarray. In just a few weeks the RAF had lost over 900 planes and 435 pilots, many of them experienced. Fighter Command was down to bare bones to defend the skies over England, and significantly below the battle strength that Dowding needed. It was easy to see why Stuffy Dowding had been so determined to ration deployment of Spitfires and Hurricanes in the Battle of France.

Across the Channel, the Germans, flushed with their rapid successes in the war so far, were optimistic. Feldmarschall Hermann Goering even gave assurances that the Luftwaffe could smash Britain's air force in a month. If he was right, and the Luftwaffe swiftly destroyed the defences of the RAF, the Germans could cross the Channel in large numbers with limited resistance. Plans were laid by the Nazis for six infantry divisions to land on the beaches between Ramsgate and Bexhill and three more further west between Weymouth and Lyme Regis. When the third wave of the planned Nazi invasion was over, 260,000 men would be ashore in Britain with more to follow.

Fortunately, at this moment of British military vulnerability the Nazis hesitated. Germany knew how to wage an impressive war on land, but the Straits of Dover represented a formidable obstacle. In addition, the Germans were short of both landing vessels and aircraft carriers in 1940 and had little experience in the use of amphibious craft on such a large scale. Key military leaders wanted to be sure the RAF were knocked out before beginning an invasion operation of such ambition and complexity. Hitler himself also wanted to pause before invading. The British had already seen Germany's military

---

34    P/O Alan Henderson, author interview,1980

might drive their army back across the Channel in a desperate escape. Surely, Hitler reasoned, Churchill would want to avoid the fate that had befallen the French. He thought that Britain, with its impressive achievements of empire and its racial strength, should be a natural ally rather than an enemy.

Around Calais, the Germans turned potato fields and meadows into airfields for their Messerschmitts. Over the Channel, 11 Group of Fighter Command, led by Air Vice-Marshal Keith Park, was also preparing right across the Home Counties of England. Park was an approachable but very focused New Zealander in his mid-forties who had been injured in World War One. The Germans had around one hundred and fifty more fighter aircraft at their disposal than the RAF but that was not sufficient advantage to give them control of the skies. The two air forces might have been more closely matched than often imagined, but it was Hitler who enjoyed the critical benefit of military momentum.

The German hesitation gave Britain the chance to rearm. The amount of money allocated to the war effort rose from £33 million in April 1940 to £55 million in June, with priority given to frontline fighters and bombers, beginning with an increase in Hurricane output. Repair capability was dramatically enhanced. Rolls Royce increased production of the Merlin engines that powered both the Spitfire and the Hurricane by nearly 70 per cent.

On the home front, a modest round of rationing began and a second wave of evacuation of children got underway. Road and rail signs were removed or obliterated to confuse any invader, and holiday beaches were covered with barbed wire. A Ministry of Information circular instructed citizens in the case of invasion, 'Do not give the German anything. Do not tell him anything. Hide your food and your bicycles. See that the enemy gets no petrol.' Lord Beaverbrook, Minister of Aircraft Production, urged the British public to support the aircraft industry by providing it with aluminium, 'We will turn your pots and pans into Spitfires and Hurricanes, Blenheims and Wellingtons.' Accordingly, thousands of saucepans were loyally sacrificed.

Fighter Command tossed more than saucepans into the battle. Pilots from the British Empire, many of them experienced; Australians, New Zealanders, West Indians, South Africans, and Canadians were amongst the many to respond to join the Few. The Poles and the Czechs, whose countries had been overrun by the Nazis, made a huge contribution. 'The Poles were mad men…they couldn't care less about orders from the ground…there was a burning hatred inside of them, very gallant men', observed Geoffrey Page.

In the first phase of the Battle of Britain, Germany focused on attacking Allied convoys in the Channel. They knew that starving Britain of food, oil, and other essential supplies would put an island nation under immediate pressure. At 56 Squadron Slim Coghlan put his exhausted pilots on full wartime alert. They were to be at readiness from before first light to half an hour after last light, with night flying practise mandatory for all. When a pilot plaintively asked about time off Coghlan replied with a laugh, 'You'll get time off when the war is over, or you're dead.'

Soon after, the Squadron was ordered to fly in darkness the short distance south from North Weald to a forward base at RAF Manston on the Kent coast. The enemy airfields nestled around Calais were only five minutes flying time from Manston. It was so close to the Channel you could almost smell the German breakfast sausages being cooked for the Luftwaffe pilots they would soon be trying to shoot down. Page watched the flames from the rear of the Hurricanes as they burst into life. Jumbo eased his Hurricane into the night air. Alongside him flew F/O Barry Sutton, now recovered from his injury received in France.

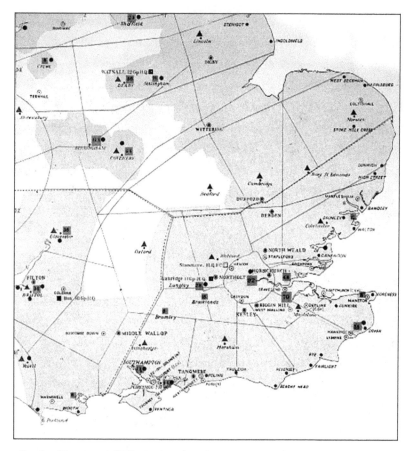

*Battle of Britain airfields, National Archives, Kew, London*

Then it was Geoffrey Page's turn, flying number two to 'Dopey' Davis. Here he was barrelling down the dark North Weald runway to war, he reflected, 'and I've never flown at night before'. His Battle of Britain was about to begin. To his relief, Page landed safely in the Kent darkness despite 'Dopey' leading the pilots on an unplanned tour of Kent. Although 56 Squadron had dreamt of a good, cooked breakfast to set them up for the day the best RAF Manston could offer was tea and baked beans, both lukewarm. Their welcome was as cold as the early morning chill. There was nowhere to sleep and so Page and the others kept warm by walking around their Hurricanes.

It was 13 July 1940, and the rising dawn sun opened the window on a bright sky with just a few clouds. It was a perfect day for a German attack on the vital convoys in the English Channel. Then the crack of the Verrey pistol sliced through the morning silence and cut to the marrow of Geoffrey's freezing body. The orderly shouted, 'Scramble B Flight, angels ten'. It took Page a few seconds to digest what he heard next, 'Ninety bandits over Calais'. There are six of us, he thought, fighting ninety German aircraft, that isn't fair odds. A flotilla of Luftwaffe bombers ahead was being escorted by a defensive shield of thirty twin-engine Messerschmitt 110 fighters. To make the situation even worse, sitting threateningly in the sky above them were about forty Me109 fighters. 56 Squadron's job was to hit this group of well-defended enemy bombers before they attacked the precious convoy in the Channel. Page was one of three pilots, led by Flt Lt Jumbo Gracie, who climbed up to attack the Messerschmitt 110s. His mouth went dry, 'I suppose with hindsight I should have been scared stupid, but I was too busy getting my aircraft ready for combat.' [35] There was no time for further reflection.

As Gracie launched his attack the scores of single-engine Me 109s still hovered above the tiny band of Hurricanes. The Me110s quickly formed themselves into a defensive circle, but Geoffrey Page dived right into the middle of the enemy. Page let rip, firing his eight Browning machine guns as if he was in a fun fair shooting gallery. His wild attack showed all the hallmarks of combat inexperience. In return the rear gunners in the Me 110s loosed off scores of bullets in the direction of Geoffrey's Hurricane. He was spellbound by the appearance of orange light bulbs suspended in the air, until he realised

---

35   Geoffrey Page, Imperial War Museum Sound Archive 11103, London,

that the hundreds of machine-gun bullets were aimed at him. He later recalled this defensive ring of enemy aircraft, 'I distinctly remember closing my eyes and coming out the other side. It was all a mass of German iron crosses, and I didn't know what I was doing. That was my first combat. I remember it well.'

To his complete surprise Page was not hit by the hail of bullets and positioned himself for a second attack. This time he was more measured, but inexperience still showed. He fired his bullets a fraction too early or too late. The Me 109s were never going to stand idly by while Page attacked the 110s escorting the bombers. Forty aircraft swooped down out of the sun and there followed what Geoffrey described as 'a nightmare'. Bullets criss-crossed the pure blue sky in pretty patterns as the Luftwaffe tried to finish off the British resistance.

Suddenly, for no apparent reason, the sky that had been thick with Germans only minutes before was empty and eerily silent. The combat had finished as quickly as it had started. This was a phenomenon that Page was to see many times. 'It is as if the Hand of God had wiped the slate clean and there is nothing else in the sky and I suddenly found myself alone.'

As he turned for home Geoffrey spotted a single Me109 in the distance. It was heading towards him. The air battle was not over quite yet. Page turned and headed straight towards the enemy. The two pilots closed in on each other rapidly, both firing every gun available. It was, Page reflected, the equivalent of tilting in a medieval tilt yard. Geoffrey had no idea if he hit the German but sensed that his bursts of fire were once again always a fraction too late. Page could see little white dots on the wings of the enemy's aircraft as he fired back. The fighters roared towards each other, but Page stubbornly refused to budge. He was sure that the two fighters would collide and end up merged into a single fireball. To his relief the planes missed each other by inches as the German pilot flashed just beneath him. Suddenly he was alone again.

The aircraft had disappeared, but he spotted another pilot dangling on the end of parachute. Page watched as the German hit the water. He wrote in his logbook, 'a 110 diving vertically with flames coming out of his port engine and one of the crew bailed out'. Attempts to radio for help failed and he headed back to Manston because he was now in urgent need of fuel. On landing, Page reported his valiant attempts to shoot an enemy aircraft down and was pleased to learn that 56 Squadron had damaged or destroyed five enemy aircraft.

In his autobiography Page's relates being told 'we got five for the loss of one machine'. That was Jumbo Gracie who eventually managed to land safely back at RAF Manston even though his glycol system had been hit. There was no mention that A Flight lost two Sgt Pilots that day, James Cowsill and Joseph Whitfield, both Yorkshiremen, who were shot down by the Me 109s over the Channel and lost.

Geoffrey was inwardly disappointed not to have hit an enemy aircraft but was also focused on the German airman he had seen parachute out of the Me110 before hitting the water. The controller requested the high-speed rescue boat be launched from Ramsgate. Page hurriedly refuelled and joined the rescue effort because he knew exactly where the German had plunged into the sea. On the way he spotted the rescue launch leaving Ramsgate. He located where the crash had taken place and hovered above the spot, but there was no sign of a pilot. He circled round several times over the next half an hour, peering anxiously out of his Hurricane, but the German had been swallowed by the sea.

Geoffrey wanted to tell the rescue launch of his failure to locate the enemy pilot. He also needed to warn them of the danger of two German aircraft still lurking menacingly overhead. However, his radio system was not working. No ammunition, no radio; what a mess.

So, he had to find another way of warning the little launch steaming out of Ramsgate.

Then he had a brainwave. First, he freed himself from the strait-jacket of his equipment and straps. He thought his escapology skills would have done credit to Houdini. Then he located his precious pencil. Flying with one hand he scribbled a few hasty words on the inside of a cigarette packet. But how was Geoffrey going to drop his crucial message into the safe hands of the rescue boat? Then he had a second brainwave. Trying desperately to avoid hitting the water that was ominously close beneath him, Page raised his leg and wrestled off his flying boot and sock. The Hurricane was vibrating unnervingly close to the sea. He popped the message into his sock and threw it just ahead of the Ramsgate rescuers. Miraculously, they retrieved the sock with the message secreted inside it. The men in the boat waved gratefully. Geoffrey wiggled his wings in acknowledgement. He was sweaty and exhausted, but he had overcome all the problems he had been confronted with so far that day.

His concern for the life of a Luftwaffe pilot was not rewarded. As he started heading home, Page spotted the two enemy aircraft now speeding purposefully in his direction. He swiftly dived down and turned his Hurricane towards Dover. He could not risk a dog fight. There had been no time to reload his guns during refuelling. He was completely out of ammunition. As he swooped low over the sea, the fast enemy aircraft were catching him up. He put on the super-boost to make the aircraft go faster, but the Germans were menacingly close. Page desperately pointed the aircraft's nose towards the well-fortified harbour at Dover. Page knew what he was doing, but this was a risky strategy. When the defence batteries saw three aircraft approaching, they assumed they were all German, and about to attack. The British guns thudded out rapid fire with every round of ammunition they could muster. Page twisted and turned away from the not so friendly fire. Finally, he coolly pulled steeply back on his stick and roared merrily over the white cliffs of Dover. His pursuers, fearing with good reason that they would be shot down by the British defence batteries, circled swiftly round and made their disappointed way back to France. What a warm welcome home, Geoffrey Page reflected.

Back at RAF Manston Page thought once again about the Messerschmitt that earlier had almost hit him head on before disappearing into a cloud. Had his attack been successful? It took him fully twenty-seven years to find the answer, when a book about Luftwaffe pilots revealed, 'Sergeant Dau had seen a Hurricane turn in towards him. It then came straight at him, head-on and at the same height. Neither of them budged an inch, both fired their guns at the same instant, then missed a collision by a hair's breadth. But while the German fire was too low, that of the British pilot, A.G. Page of 56 Squadron, connected. Dau felt his aircraft shaken by violent thuds. It had been hit in the engine and rudder and he saw a piece of one wing come off. At once his engine started to seize up emitting a white plume of steaming glycol. 'The coolant temperature rose quickly to 120 degrees', he reported, 'The whole cockpit stank of burnt insulation. But I managed to stretch my glide to the coast, then make a belly landing close to Boulogne. As I jumped out, the machine was on fire and within seconds ammunition and fuel went up with a bang.'[36] Although it had taken him decades to discover the truth, Sergeant Dau's aircraft was Page's first confirmed success of the Battle of Britain, his first blooding, as he called it.

In a speech a few days later Hitler made what sounded like a final offer of negotiation for peace. After accusing Churchill of warmongering, he said, 'I feel it to be my duty before my own conscience to appeal once more to reason and common sense in Great Britain...

---

36    Cajus Bekker, *The Luftwaffe Diaries*, London, Macdonald,1967

I can see no reason why this war must go on.' Hitler's vague overtures were ignored. Churchill was not going to open peace talks with an untrustworthy Nazi like Hitler. Britain's defensive position was precarious, but she was still more formidable than most of the countries Hitler had trampled over. Fighter Command might be smaller than Dowding wanted but was still intact. The Army had regrouped and rearmed after Dunkirk, and the Royal Navy was an impressive force. The British island fortress was surrounded by a giant sea-moat that had to be crossed. Realising Churchill was unwilling to negotiate a peace, Hitler intensified his invasion preparations for what was called Operation Sealion. The Luftwaffe moved a huge force of aircraft along the French channel coast.

In his autobiography *First Light,* Spitfire pilot Geoffrey Wellum summed up the rhythm of Battle of Britain life, 'My impressions of the last two months or so revolve around dawns. Pink dawns, grey dawns, misty, rainy, and windy dawns, but always dawns; first light.' In these dawns, the pilots of 56 Squadron took it in turns to fly in the very early hours down to a forward base on the Kent coast. If they were lucky, they grabbed half a cup of soup which had been held back from the previous night's Mess dinner. To their irritation all too often the soup was cold. Already tired and hungry, they flopped on straw palliasses in a bell tent that was their temporary home. Luxuries like chairs or a table did not exist. If they were lucky there was time to play cards or flick aimlessly through the newspapers, but minds were pre-occupied with what challenges the day would bring.

Not that the young pilots always slept when they should have done. On 19 July, after a hard day's flying, they spent the night drinking and flirting at the *Bag of Nails* in Regent Street. It was not until just before first light that the drunken pilots clambered into Taffy Higginson's car Esmerelda and chugged sleepily back to North Weald. They had hardly been to bed when the telephone rang at dispersal, and they were off into combat once again. It was 5am. As soon as he was airborne Geoffrey Page noticed that although he had managed to wearily pull on his flying boots, he had neglected to wear his flying suit. Instead, he was going into war dressed in thin summer pyjamas and without socks. He was soon freezing cold.

As the first fingers of dawn smudged the night sky on 20 July, he saw the purple flame spurting from Jumbo Gracie's Hurricane as their leader headed into the darkness. Barry Sutton was next in line and then Geoffrey Page followed almost blindly. He was immediately roused from his robotic torpor when he saw the masts of the local radio station right in front of him. He was so close he was forced to wrench his Hurricane violently onto its side. It was a very near miss. Page was just inches away from another disaster. His pyjamas offered no protection against the early morning chill and he was already soaked in sweat from his close shave.

At 18,000 feet a wide-awake Page spotted a Junkers 88 of KG4 on a photo-reconnaissance trip as it emerged from a cloud. The German pilot made the strange decision to try and outrun the faster Hurricanes. Jumbo Gracie swooped down for the first attack on the enemy. The Junkers was still flying despite Gracie's attack, and now it was Page's turn. He fired his eight machine guns before the German disappeared into the apparent safety of another cloud. Page could see a very faint outline of the Junkers as he drew closer. Then he heard a thump and realised his Hurricane had been hit. Furiously he pressed his firing button until there was no ammunition left.

As he wheeled, and headed home, Geoffrey Page had a deep sense of failure. He might have hit the German, but he wasn't at all sure. After all, the Luftwaffe pilot had disappeared into the cloud never to be seen again. What a useless pilot I am, he thought, not even able to hit a lone weather reconnaissance Ju88 at close quarters. This gloomy self-doubt was interrupted by the voice of the controller.

Page was astonished to hear that the Ju88 had crashed in flames off St Osyth, near Clacton. Four Germans had been taken prisoner. The rear gunner died from his wounds. Page or one of the other pilots from 56 had shot his arm off. Surprised though he was, Page had scored his first shared 'kill' dressed in his pyjamas. When he landed Page saw that he had been hit in his port wing. It was still only 5.45 am. Later he reflected that he had learned something new about himself, 'I enjoy killing. It fascinates me to see my bullets striking home and the Hun blowing up before me. It also makes me sick.'

Geoffrey Page grew to understand both the skills and the strategy needed in aerial combat. He learnt not to fire his precious ammunition too early, and he knew to aim at the engine because if that was hit it was likely that the pilot would be taken out of action too. At the same time, he also appreciated the old-fashioned rules of engagement. Although there were rumours that the Luftwaffe had shot RAF pilots who had bailed out and were dangling vulnerably on the end of a parachute, he never saw this himself. He believed there was a high level of chivalry between pilots.

The most difficult part of the day was return. Although 56 went off in a formation of threes that shape was soon disrupted by dog fights, and they often landed back at the airfield singly. It would take about fifty minutes for the stragglers to make it safely home and only then could the pilots firmly establish if any of their colleagues were missing. Even then, there was the hope that a missing pilot had bailed out or forced landed elsewhere. But if a comrade had not shown up by evening, he was probably dead or badly injured. The pilots did not dwell on death, 'We had to be quite callous and put it out of our mind. You just couldn't afford to think of it,' said Barry Sutton.

In these tentative early days, the enemy was not the only danger. Parachuting down in southern England was a risky business. When Barry Sutton bailed out of his Hurricane over Kent he was met by an angry-looking woman armed with a rolling pin. Sometimes the home guard could not tell the difference between RAF and Luftwaffe pilots dangling on the end of a parachute. One Fighter Command pilot was mistakenly shot at by the Home Guard as he floated down. They destroyed his parachute, and he was killed when he hit the ground. It was reported that when another RAF pilot parachuted down, harvesting workers, 'killed him with pitchforks and farm implements. He didn't have a Royal Air Force suit on, and he was chucking money down and papers to try and convince them, but they wouldn't have it. We took that very bad.'[37]

On 21 July, 56 enjoyed a quiet morning in the air before refuelling at RAF Hawkinge which, like Manston, sat on the frontline that was the Kent coast. It was an altogether friendlier forward base than Manston, with decent food. As usual Slim Coghlan was leading the Squadron, with Jumbo Gracie responsible for B Flight. That afternoon the twelve Hurricanes were ordered to patrol the French coast near Calais keeping about three miles out to sea. Page saw nine Stuka dive bombers heading from Calais towards England. Flying confidently above them was a protective glove of a dozen Me 109s. Strangely, it looked as if the enemy had failed to spot the Hurricanes. Slim Coghlan's first attack sent a Stuka spiralling down in a ball of flames. Now the enemy realised they were being pursued. Hurriedly, they dumped their bombs and headed down towards the sea in a vain attempt to evade the speedier Hurricanes.

Geoffrey Page soon had a Stuka's tail in his sights. He fired at the German, and a large piece of metal flew off the enemy aircraft 'Take that, you dirty bastard, for Minny', he shouted angrily to himself. He was unable to assess the damage and circled round again looking for another target. There followed a cat and mouse game with the Me

---

37    Joshua Levine, *Forgotten Voices*, Ebury Press, London, 2006

109, a much more equal adversary than a vulnerable dive-bomber like a Stuka. The 109 benefited from the extra firepower of cannons in each wing. Suddenly he realised that a second 109 was close on his tail. Streaks of white tracer bullets tore past his Hurricane. Page turned tightly time and again to avoid enemy fire. With his fuel getting rapidly lower and two Messerschmitts now waiting to pounce, he took the brave decision to head for the outline of a large ship in the distance. He prayed that it was a Royal Navy destroyer which was for some unknown reason close to the enemy shoreline. The wrong call and he was a dead man. He was relieved when he saw the White Ensign. The German aircraft were no match for the heavy guns of the Royal Navy destroyer and backed away. Page rolled his Hurricane in thanks to the sailors below and headed home.

The next day Colonel-General Franz Halder, Chief of the German General Staff confidently wrote, 'Britain's position is hopeless. The war is won by us. A reversal in the prospects of success is impossible.' Whether Halder believed this or was just acting as a cheerleader is not clear. But he would have known that, despite sturdy defence from Fighter Command, the Luftwaffe was enjoying success with attacks on channel convoys carrying vital supplies to an island nation.

The only relief from the constant preparedness in the early weeks of the Battle of Britain was a visit to North Weald by the King who was due to award two DFCs (Distinguished Flying Cross). The fixtures and fittings on the base were hurriedly polished and the tired pilots lined up for a simple but affecting ceremony. As he walked down the line King George the Sixth shook Page's hand and asked him how many enemy aircraft he had shot down. It was not a question the young pilot wanted to be asked but he muttered that he had shot no aircraft down but had a share in one. The King kindly reassured him that there was plenty of time left.

A few days later, 25 July, 56 Squadron was sent south to protect another vital Channel convoy, codenamed C.W.8., but they were dispatched too late. The Luftwaffe had already sunk Royal Navy ships in the minutes between two Fighter Command patrols. Below Page's Hurricane the sea was ablaze. It looked like a fiery carpet dotted with the wreckage of sinking ships and downed aircraft. A dozen German Stuka Ju 87 dive bombers, protected by a large formation of Messerschmitt 109s, were attacking the remaining Royal Navy vessels. The Navy lost 65,000 tons of shipping that day. 'It is the most sickening and awful sight, seeing these angels of death diving upon the ships,' noted Michael Constable-Maxwell. Page described them as 'predatory birds'.

56 Squadron disrupted the attack, but not before one more ship had been hit by the bombers. 56 Squadron screamed in, with Page's B Flight taking on the Stukas and A Flight dealing with the Me 109s. Soon the sound of bombs and machine-guns echoed across the sky. With his customary understatement Page described this in his logbook merely as 'a scrap off Dover'. He added that the Hurricanes had neatly interlocked with the Stukas 'like flicking [shuffling] a pack of cards...musical comedy procedure'.

There was no time for Page to reflect fully on the fate of the sailors below. As the Luftwaffe formation headed low across the sea back to France anger again welled up inside Page. Maybe this was for the casualties amongst the sailors? Or perhaps it was for Minny Ereminsky? In any event, rather than heading home himself, Page set off in pursuit. Page targeted one of the Stukas as he closed to within a hundred yards of the enemy. The rear-gunner fired back, and orange tracer rounds whizzed past Page's Hurricane.

Geoffrey was close now. The two aircraft were only ten feet above the sea. He fired a long burst into a Stuka and a large piece flew off the enemy aircraft as his bullets smashed into it. Seconds later the whole aeroplane was transformed into a ball of fire and plunged help-lessly into the Channel. It was a very calm day with scarcely a ripple in the water. Page circled round just above the surface. All he could make out was one solitary tyre bobbing on the ocean, and a patch of burning oil. He registered a mix of fascination and anger. Then he remembered the two men he had killed.

As Page flew like a robot back to base, the image of the Stuka as a funeral pyre hitting the sea replayed in his mind several times, 'I was right behind the Stuka. I could see the rear gunner firing at me. Then, as I fired, I saw the rear gunner slump and his gun pointed straight up into the air and so I knew he was finished. Later in the war it felt like you were just firing at another bit of metal flying through the sky. It was impersonal. This was the only time I felt a personal relationship between myself and the other aeroplane. It was so close it made me feel that I had killed another human being.' [38] Two men, young like him, had died in his attack,[39] 'Twenty minutes later, physically, and mentally exhausted, I landed and taxied to the dispersal pen, a differ-ent person. I had taken off from the same airfield an innocent, and returned a bloodied fighter pilot, or was it a murderer hiding behind the shield of official approval?'

In private, unpublished notes in 1959 he added, 'I felt a bastard at having done it - but soon got over that feeling.'

Richard Hillary, author of the famous wartime pilot's memoir *The Last Enemy* and who later shared a hospital ward with Geoffrey Page, described his own feelings on shooting down the enemy, 'He came right through my sights, and I saw the tracer of all eight guns thud home. For a second he seemed to hang motionless; then a jet of red flame shot upward, and he spun to the ground…then I had a feeling of the essential rightness of it all; it could easily have been the

38  Author interview, Henley on Thames,1983
39  Geoffrey Page, *Tale of a Guinea Pig,* Pelham, London,1981

other way round; and that would somehow have been right too. I realised in that moment just how lucky a fighter pilot is…he is privileged to kill well. For if one must either kill or be killed, as now one must, it should, I feel, be done with dignity.'

For Geoffrey Page not being able to 'kill well' had been unsettling. Stukas were relatively simple targets for a Hurricane or Spitfire, 'There was just one poor rear gunner with just one little popgun to defend his aeroplane. We were sitting there with eight machine guns. It was a pretty easy target. I'm not proud of the fact we just knocked them off like skittles.'[40]

His friend, Pilot Officer Barry Sutton, who was flying alongside Page that day, was also surprised to find himself with a Junkers 87 Stuka dive-bomber in his sights. He could not miss. The damaged Junkers headed dramatically towards the water before plunging into the channel. In his 1942 memoir, *Fighter Boy*, Sutton wrote, 'As I watched something wound up in my stomach. It was my first Hun but there was no immediate feeling of elation. For a moment I was aware of a sickly, nauseating wave of sympathy for the wretched men I had sent to their doom. It was a sensation which, thank God, I never had again.'

Sutton described the conflicting emotions of shooting down the enemy in his 5,000-word poem *The Summer of the Firebird*: -

*My Hurricane once more trembling*
*As it spews out his cone of lead and fire.*
*Smell again the tangy cordite*
*As pinpoints of flame stitch into the fishy shape:*
*See it writhe and raise one wing up*
*To fall in despair.*
*Hear my breath sobbing into my oxygen mask and microphone*

---

40  Geoffrey Page, Imperial War Museum Sound Archive 11103, London

*Feel something cold leap in my chest*
*As I watch my handiwork's havoc.*
*They found the wreck near Colchester*
*And offered me a prize I would have wished not to see:*
*A thin wallet in which there were two green banknotes*
*Two tickets to a theatre in Paris,*
*And a snapshot of a young woman*
*Whose eyes condemned.*[41]

The manufacturing of Spitfires and Hurricanes moved forward at great speed. In July the RAF lost around 145 fighters but manufactured nearly five hundred as replacements. Fighter Command possessed less combat experience than the enemy, but the RAF enjoyed the advantage of fighting over home territory. It was summer and the days were long and bright. Below them as they flew were the green and brown fields of Kent and Sussex, covered with hop fields and hay bales, orchards and oast houses. The pilots could see small villages dotted with pubs and churches, and sometimes a cricket field. It was a daily reminder of the country they were fighting for. More than that, it was also comforting for a pilot to know that if he bailed out, it would be over the green fields of Britain. Men and planes could be patched up and thrown back into the fray. On the other hand, if a German bailed out over England, he would be condemned to spend the rest of the war as a prisoner.

In their tents or farmhouses on the coast, the Luftwaffe were miles away from the comforts of home. The lack of an additional fuel tank to boost combat time, tactical errors by the Nazi leadership, and the quality of the RAF defences, all added to the growing stress the pilots across the Channel were feeling. But it was the deaths and inju-

---

41    Barry Sutton, *The Summer of the Firebird*, BBC Radio, London 15 September 1980

ries that undermined morale most. German ace Major Adolf Galland wrote, 'We saw one comrade after another, old and tested brothers in combat, vanish from our ranks. Not a day passed without a place remaining empty at the mess table.'[42]

Geoffrey Page knew that the RAF's other significant advantage was the developed radar network, or Radio Direction Finding (RDF) as it was called then. High-masted Chain Home radar stations were necklaced along the south coast, with smaller units detecting low flying aircraft in additional support. This early warning system gave Fighter Command precious extra minutes to intercept the enemy giving Fighter Command an edge over the Luftwaffe. Dowding was an enthusiastic advocate of radar but fearful that the Germans would work out the British secret. Despite the overall number of stations totalling as many as fifty-two, the enemy never fully fathomed the extent and effectiveness of the RAF's early warning system.

The occasional intervals between sorties gave Dowding's 'boys' a chance to enjoy the splendid British summer. Lying on the grass as the day came to its slow, sunny end, Geoffrey Page felt deeply content. It wasn't just the symphonic bird song or the smell of the freshly cut grass, it was the intense comradeship, the bond between the men in 56 Squadron, a bond that could only be forged in the chaos and horrors of war. At twenty years of age, every experience, every emotion, was distilled to its essence for Geoffrey Page. He was popular in the squadron, and friendships with Barry Sutton, Michael Constable Maxwell, and others blossomed. But for self-protection every pilot kept a part of himself hidden. On 29 July 56 Squadron lost another experienced man when 26-year-old Sergeant Pilot Cecil Cooney was shot down near Dover. His body were never found. Geoffrey Page knew that any of his friends might not return from the next sortie,

---

42    Adolf Galland, *The First and the Last*, Methuen, London,1955

and no pilot could afford to dwell on unwelcome absences, 'the death of a friend or enemy provided food for a few moments of thought, before the next swirling dog fight began to distract the cogitating mind from stupid thoughts such as sadness or pity-remorse had long since died.'

For their part, 56 Squadron were impressed by Page. His sharp eyesight in the air was building his reputation. Michael Constable Maxwell thought he was 'the keenest member of the squadron. He hates going on leave and can only think of fighting. He has done well, getting several planes down and is very self-confident.'[43] Most of the time Geoffrey felt just the opposite. His relative inexperience made him underconfident. Instinctively, he knew that this period of contentment would not last long, that danger was all around him, that, given the ruthless efficiency of the Germans, survival was unlikely. In fact, of the men like Geoffrey who were stationed at North Weald throughout the war, twenty-five percent of all the deaths occurred during just four months of the Battle of Britain.

If life was going to be short why not live it to the full, thought Page. The art was to cheat Death for as long as possible. But for all this foreboding, Geoffrey was deeply happy, as happy as he had ever been. Sitting on the grass as the summer sun offered up its final rays of the day, Geoffrey Page knew he loved his fellow pilots and, in that moment, would be prepared to lay his life down for them. Despite the closeness of death, Geoffrey Page was content, 'It was absolute paradise, because I was young, I was given a lovely fast aeroplane to fly for nothing and paid the glorious sum of £5 a week to do it. If I had been the son of a millionaire, I would have paid them to allow me the privilege of what I was now paid for. It was tremendous.'[44]

---

43    Alex Revell, *Fighter Aces*, Pen and Sword, Yorkshire, 2010
44    Geoffrey Page, *Churchill's Few*, Yorkshire Television, Leeds, 1983

## Chapter Six

# Shot Down

The bright blue skies of August signalled the end July's early probing skirmishes. In Berlin, Hitler finally accepted that his invasion plans should move forward. On 1 August he issued Directive No17 which heralded an 'air and sea war against the English homeland in a more intensified form than before', and stated, 'The German Air Force is to overcome the British Air Force with all the means at its command, in the shortest possible time.' An invasion date of 15 September was set, but there was now anxiety in the German Navy about launching Operation Sealion in the unreliable autumn weather. The Navy's Admiral Raeder insisted that air mastery must be a pre-requisite for a successful invasion.

As a result, the Germans shifted their strategy from convoy attacks to drawing the frontline squadrons along the coast of Kent and Sussex into the air and then hitting them with huge numbers of aircraft. The Germans planned a decisive pre-invasion aerial offensive called *Adlerangriff,* or Attack of the Eagles, which would reach its pinnacle on 13 August, *Adlertag* or Eagle Day. This was to be the Battle of Britain at its most intense and brutal.

11 August saw the loss of thirty-two British aircraft, the highest daily number in the battle so far, and thirty-five German planes. One of those aircraft was a Heinkel 59 rescue plane, destroyed by Blenheims from 604 Squadron under the protection of Spitfires. Although the crew survived, the shooting down of a rescue plane

searching for German aircrew in the sea made the Luftwaffe furious. Dowding argued that ambulance planes were legitimate targets because they enabled German pilots to fly against Britain again. This was no longer the gentlemen's war Geoffrey Page had imagined when he left Cranwell.

On that black day for losses, 11 August, another of 56 Squadron's pilots was killed, but by his own side not the enemy. Sergeant Pilot Ronnie Baker, a married 23-year-old from Wolverhampton, was on a convoy patrol when he was shot down by a solitary Spitfire. According to reports at the time, the pilot had mistaken Baker's Hurricane for a German aircraft. The Sergeant Pilot managed to bail out with his parachute into the Thames estuary fifteen miles from Walton-on-the-Naze. Three of his colleagues circled above desperately trying to keep Baker's exact location in sight. By the time the rescue launch had pulled him out of the sea Ronnie Baker had already been in the water for seventy minutes. Despite attempts at artificial respiration, he was pronounced dead from drowning.

In just three weeks in July, two hundred and twenty men had been killed or were missing at sea, and yet the British still only had eighteen high-speed rescue launches, just two more than in 1936. No wonder Ronnie Baker was in the water for seventy minutes before a launch reached him. Crashed pilots were drowning needlessly and Ronnie Baker was just the latest waste of life.

The next day 56 Squadron was greeted with a clear blue cloudless sky. It was the day before the German planned attacks on *Adlertag*, or Eagle Day. In the world outside the Battle of Britain, life was disconcertingly normal. On 12 August twenty-seven readers wrote to *The Times* to commend the fine quality of the cuckoo song that year. Londoners queued in the West End to see Robert Donat in *The Devil's Disciple*.

Geoffrey Page had already begun to feel that he was growing old 'at about ten times the normal rate'. Perhaps he was unsettled by the needless waste of Ronnie Baker's life? He was so busy during the day that sombre thoughts never found space in his head. At night it was different. There was time to reflect, too much time, as he tossed and turned trying to sleep. A few mornings earlier, before the first fingers of dawn had stolen into the darkness, by the light of a torch Geoffrey Page wrote to his friend, Michael Maw who had been such a support when Geoffrey first arrived at the Aircrew Receiving Centre in Hastings at the start of the war. It was an indication of how tired and edgy he already was:

'I sometimes wonder…if the whole war isn't a ghastly nightmare from which we'll wake up soon; I know all of this sounds nonsense but I'm slightly tight and it's only an hour until dawn…to me it will mean just another day of butchery… maybe I am a bit sorry for myself at this moment, but, and it's a great big but, I enjoy killing. It fascinates me beyond belief to see my bullets striking home and then to see the Hun blow up before me. It also makes me feel sick. Where are we going and how will it all end? I feel as if I am selling myself to the Devil. If only you were here. I need someone to talk to who isn't tied up in this game of legalised murder.' The letter was never posted, and it would have been pointless if it had been. Michael Maw had already been killed in a training accident.

The Luftwaffe plan to hit Fighter Command hard before *Eagle Day* by smashing airfields and radar stations started well. The precision team of Experimental (or Test) Group 210, led by Walter Rubensdoerffer, did their job incisively. They quickly hit three vital radar stations at Rye, Pevensey, and Dunkirk near Canterbury. But, to German disappointment, the giant aerials were only out of action for a few hours, although a fourth radar station on the Isle of Wight was inactive for weeks. At lunchtime the Luftwaffe attacked the forward base at RAF Manston. They dropped 150 bombs which destroyed workshops, hangars, and left the runway looking like the craters of the moon. Some civilian workers and mechanics were so frightened by the avalanche of bombs they refused to come out of their shelters. Sir Keith Park, leading 11 Group, Fighter Command exclaimed, 'at least we now know what he's after - my bloody airfields.' To add to the carnage, that morning over seventy Ju88 bombers unleashed a massive air raid on the naval town of Portsmouth, killing ninety-six people.

That afternoon, 56 Squadron moved from North Weald to Rochford, near Southend, just a ten-minute flight away. On arrival Geoffrey Page promptly fell asleep on the sweet-smelling summer grass. He lay in the afternoon sun with a newspaper over his face. Rochford was a pleasant but basic grass airfield that had been used for private flying until being pressed into war service. Its only dispersal facility was a bell tent containing a single telephone, and the few solid buildings were of First World War vintage. Page was extremely tired that day, and although his spirit was still strong, his body felt very weak.

Page's sister Daphne had bumped into Geoffrey at a dance the night before and he had looked 'very handsome and debonair'. Perhaps all the Pages were accident prone because Daphne, a naturally bashful woman, had the misfortune on her honeymoon of being woken by an air raid. She and her new husband immediately fled their hotel room in panic, only to find the door quickly lock tight behind them. Aunt Daphne was left in the corridor of a smart London hotel completely stark naked.

For all the debonair appearance admired by his sister, Page's bone tiredness wasn't just from dancing. He was woken from his fitful sleep on the Essex grass by the jarring arrival of a waggon loaded with Thermos flasks full of tea and plates of bread and butter. Aroused from his sleep, he amused himself by aimlessly killing wasps in the jar of strawberry jam that accompanied tea and exclaiming 'bang, bang' with every victim. By the time he had killed ten of the striped army Michael Constable Maxwell laughed and said, 'You'll come to a sticky end, Geoffrey, just like those wasps.'

The single telephone rang ominously, interrupting Page's wasp killing. The shrill sound cut through him, and he felt physically sick. How he hated that telephone. The jam spilt from his unsteady hand. 'Scramble…seventy plus approaching Manston Angels fifteen' bellowed out the telephone orderly. RAF Manston in Kent was under attack from a large enemy force of seventy aircraft approaching at 15,000 feet. As he started running, Page's weariness disappeared as his aching body began to pump adrenalin. His fogged mind swiftly cleared as he raced the fifty yards to where his Hurricane, P2970, stood with its name, Little Willie, now painted proudly on the side. Once in the cockpit and strapped into his Sutton harness, with his mask firmly on and oxygen working, there was no time for further reflection. A last-minute fiddle with the switches, and then the thumbs up to the ground crew. The engines dramatically throbbed into life. He was away, and his Hurricane roared out along the Rochford grass.56 Squadron was short of aircraft and were flying two below their customary number. Only ten Hurricanes lifted steadily into the air towards the seventy incoming enemy planes. Odds of seven to one, no better or worse than usual, thought Geoffrey. It was 5.20 p.m.

Flt Lt Jumbo Gracie was flanked by Geoffrey Page on the right-hand side and PO Barry Sutton on the other. One Hurricane had an oil pressure problem and the pilot turned for home, worsening the odds still further. Page noticed that he had forgotten his gloves, although as they covered his wrists they were more like gauntlets. He shrugged this off as just a minor inconvenience because many RAF pilots had now abandoned gloves for a surer grip without them. As they climbed steeply at more than 2,000 feet a minute, Page saw what looked like a swarm of midges ahead. His Hurricane was at ten thousand feet. He looked again. The tiny midges had turned into wasps but marked with crosses and swastikas rather than yellow and black stripes. Above his Hurricane sat thirty Dornier bombers escorted by forty Messerschmitt 109s. Taffy Higginson was appalled, 'the bloody sky was full of them'.

Geoffrey cheerfully acknowledged Michael Constable Maxwell as his friend switched position to prepare for combat. Constable Maxwell was eager with anticipation, 'it is a wonderful sight. A huge black mass of three vics of nine each. It is an exhilarating moment. There is no chance of missing them; we will soon be in battle…' Page's Hurricane was climbing up towards the same level as the enemy aircraft where he could increase his speed. As the thirty Dorniers of Luftflotte 2, Flying Pencils as they were called, turned north over the sea the Hurricanes of 56 Squadron started their chase, rapidly gained on them like racehorses chasing cart horses. Page could see a swarm of swastikas and iron crosses ahead. The Luftwaffe fighter aircraft hovering menacingly overhead made no move.

Barry Sutton was acutely conscious of Flt Lt Jumbo Gracie's gung-ho approach, 'a most positive, cavalier character…he was a dreadful pilot, but he was extremely brave…Unfortunately, Page and I got the fag end of his rather bad leadership-Page getting the worse of the deal.' [45] Gracie's leadership flaws were immediately apparent as he decided to attack the leading bomber, and so risk attacks from the rear gunners of all the other Dorniers, 'He was a press-on chap whose one idea was to destroy as many Germans as he could. He wasn't very scientific about it, but he was desperately brave, and he led Geoffrey and me into a fruitless chase.[46]'

Page was also surprised at what he thought was an unwise decision by his flight commander. As the Hurricanes moved in on the

45    Max Arthur, *Last of the Few*, Virgin Books, London 2011
46    Barry Sutton, author interview, North Weald,1983

leading bomber, they ran the gauntlet of thirty German rear guns. On the starboard side, Geoffrey Page was nearest to the bombers and the most at risk from his leader's brave but foolhardy strategy. As was his habit, Page locked his sliding hood in the open position, just in case he had to bail out quickly. That proved to be a wise decision.

Page looked carefully behind him and then above; from six hundred yards, too far to cause any real damage, he fired on one of the leading Dorniers. The distance between the Hurricanes and the German bombers continued to close. There was even time for a brief glance at the bomber pilots. Then the rear gunners in the enemy bombers returned fire. One minute the sky between the two sides was clear. The next it was full of streams of gleaming white tracer from the cannon shell fired by the Luftwaffe gunners. He saw Jumbo Gracie peel away from the attack. The Germans responded with a well-coordinated response, controlled by a gunnery officer in one of the Dorniers. Michael Constable Maxwell was impressed by how controlled 'and perfect' the enemy gunfire was. Page had now been singled out as the German target as clearly as if he had a bullseye on his back.

Geoffrey Page was rapidly closing in on the leading German. The pencil-shaped bomber was only three hundred yards away now. In a desperate race to destroy before he himself was destroyed he fired his Browning guns at the port engine of the bomber. In return, what looked like electric light bulbs flashed past him in daggers of light. Seconds later Geoffrey heard a tremendous explosion from the murderous crossfire. His Hurricane shuddered in the sky. Then there were two more explosions, so deafening he thought his eardrums would burst. In horror he saw there was now an, ugly, jagged, hole in his starboard wing. He found it hard to process the idea that he had been hit.

The smallest of the Hurricane's three fuel tanks, which sat behind the instrument panel, was the only one that was not self-sealing.

When the German cannon hit it, the tank exploded like a bomb. Unfortunately for Geoffrey Page, it was positioned just above his lap. Next to him Barry Sutton had a grandstand view of the attack, 'There was a tremendous explosion on my right only about ten yards away and such a sheet of flames came out of his aeroplane that I thought he must be dead already. I was quite convinced there was no way he could have got out of that.' [47] He later added, 'It looked to me as if the whole thing was too final. The reason Page was shot down and I was shot up was, I think, that we had insufficient overtaking speed due to old Jumbo's rotten leadership.'

Page's fear turned to terror as flames engulfed the cockpit in a fireball that spread swiftly towards the draught from the open hood. He cried out in agony, 'Dear God, save me, save me Dear God.' A few minutes earlier, he had pushed his goggles up for a better vision, 'It was like a blast furnace just coming straight up at my face and hands. One hand was still on the throttle, and I could remember looking for a fraction of a second as the burning was taking place. But it was painless, violent burning is painless, because it is so acute it numbs the nerve endings.'[48] As he looked down, he saw the bare skin of his hands, which were gripping the throttle and the control column, shrivel like burning paper in a blast furnace. Momentarily Page stared in strange fascination at the fire that was consuming him. Flames licked up towards his head which he threw back in an act of self-preservation. If Geoffrey did not escape the flying inferno in seven or eight seconds, then his Hurricane would be transformed into a flaming funeral pyre as he was fried to death. He screamed and then screamed again. He was not ashamed to admit his fear and terror. Page knew that life was draining out of him, 'they say the temperature goes from 5 degrees to 350 degrees centigrade - which is fairly hot,

---

47    *Churchill's Few*, Yorkshire Television, Leeds 1983
48    Geoffrey Page, Author interview, North Weald, 1983

like a cooking oven - in about seven seconds. It's as if someone was putting an enormous torch on you. It was a crossroads in my life.'

Many pilots feared burning more than death. Most of them had witnessed fires in the air and had rehearsed in their minds what to do if it happened to them. Occasionally a pilot's radio was still on when the flames and screams echoed across the sky before the victim either parachuted out or was burnt to death. Suddenly, Geoffrey Page felt a strange calm and peace envelop his burning Hurricane. He accepted that death was inevitable, and now nature was protecting him from the fear of losing his life.

Fortunately, any thoughts of death were overtaken by training. There might be an inferno engulfing him, but Geoffrey was still able to instinctively put into practice the life-saving routine that had been endlessly drummed into him. With his tortured right hand, he groped through the searing flame for the release pin of his Sutton Harness. Then he half rolled his plane on its back and virtually kicked the control column. Now the aircraft's nose pointed upwards, and he popped out of the furnace like a cork out of a bottle. There was a snap as the plugged-in oxygen tube and radio communication line disentangled and jerked his head. Fresh air was suddenly streaming across his burning face as he somersaulted head over heels through space. Perhaps because death had been so close, so apparently inevitable, the terror of frying alive disappeared as quickly as the burning Hurricane behind Geoffrey Page.

As he tumbled through the sky, he could feel a weightlessness as he hurtled towards the earth below, 'I remember seeing my right arm extended. I looked at it and my brain ordered me to bring it in and pull the metal ring of the ripcord.' Geoffrey summoned up all his strength to try and pull the parachute's cord on his left-hand side by edging his burned right hand across his body. As it touched the cold chromium ring his mutilated hand was shot through with an unbearable pain 'like an electric shock'. He was unable to get a firm grip and the ring bounced uselessly away. He continued to tumble helplessly though the air. In despair, he recalled the RAF maxim, 'It don't mean a thing if you don't pull the ring.' Just one more try, he thought, as the ground appeared ever closer. He stretched his damaged hand once more. The pain seared through him as he finally grasped the chromium ring of the ripcord. The fear, the adrenalin, and his basic survival instinct gave Page a strength that he did not think he possessed. In total agony he pulled the ripcord. Miraculously the webbing of the parachute pulled tight beneath his armpits, and then the silken canopy opened with a big thump like a giant umbrella.

As he swayed gently from side to side, the young pilot looked up and was relieved to find that his parachute was not burning from the Hurricane's inferno. The initial numbness he felt after the aerial inferno was replaced by a permanent and intense agony. He had not worn gloves and was already regretting his mistake. His hands were badly burned. His oxygen mask had protected his mouth and nose, but the rest of his face had been hit by the fireball.

As he floated slowly down from ten thousand feet towards the sea below Pilot Officer Geoffrey Page quickly assessed his situation. Sixty percent of all air fatalities took place over the sea and pilots called the Channel 'the dirty ditch'. Ronnie Baker had drowned after parachuting out of his Hurricane just the day before. Page was in very poor shape as the shock from the extensive burns hit him. The pain in his hands was unbearable. His burned face was beginning to swell, reducing his vision. He knew the acute danger was not over.

Geoffrey was still alert enough to know that the closer he landed to the coastline the greater his chance of rescue. But from the lofty perch beneath his parachute, the Kent coast still appeared to be six or even ten miles away. He could only see a dark and empty expanse of water beneath him. It would be ten or fifteen minutes before he hit the sea, he thought, and now, feeling extremely cold, he noticed that his trousers had been completely blown off in the explosion, as well as one shoe. There were small burns on his legs. He was able to fleetingly smile at his predicament, a badly burned man tumbling towards the empty sea in his underpants with only one shoe on. Footwear would be a hindrance in the water, even one of them, and so he carefully eased off his one remaining shoe with the toes of the other foot. He watched fascinated as it whirled helplessly down towards the endless ocean below.

He was enveloped in peace, although in the far distance the distinctive sound of fighter combat echoed across the silence. Suddenly he spotted the glint of summer sun on wings as two fighters sped into view. Geoffrey Page had heard rumours of RAF pilots being shot to ribbons by German bullets while parachuting gently to the ground. He breathed a sigh of relief when he saw that the two aircraft were Hurricanes. Then he noticed a stench, the distinctive smell of burned flesh, his flesh. He looked at his hands as his blood drained away from the exposed flesh. He had an almost irresistible urge to vomit.

Page started to shiver uncontrollably, teeth chattering as the shock from his injuries gripped him. His shivers were so intense the parachute swayed violently from side to side. His burned face continued to swell, and his vision worsened. To have any chance of rescue he needed to hit the sea as close to land as possible. He tugged as hard as he could on the shrouds of the parachute with his bleeding hands. It was hell, but finally the white canopy he was dangling beneath arced in the right direction.

What had happened to him, and what was about to follow, was something Geoffrey Page would replay in his mind for years to come, 'I can picture the event in every detail whenever I want to. It's etched into my brain forever. But that's just the events. The beautiful thing about pain is that you can't relive it. Once it's over, it's gone. And for that I am grateful.'

As he headed towards the empty expanse of the sea, back at RAF Manston his friends and colleagues had already written him off. Barry Sutton had seen the fireball of Page's Hurricane from just ten yards away. He was in no doubt. His last sight of his friend was just a plume of black smoke as the aircraft hurtled steeply downwards towards the sea. He had no time to watch the aircraft spiral down any further because the rear gunners of the Dorniers were throwing everything at the remaining Hurricanes.

Suddenly Sutton's machine also shuddered from an enemy cannon strike. He had been hit in the radiator, and clouds of glycol immediately started filling the cockpit. It was almost impossible to see. Sutton pulled back the sliding hood and pushed up his goggles. Like the windscreen, they were covered in a thick film of glycol mist. He limped back to Manston and miraculously landed blind on the one serviceable section of runway that had not been cratered by the earlier German bombing raid. Either through modesty or lack of confidence, he claimed this successful landing was due more by luck than judgment. He told everyone that Geoffrey Page could not have survived the inferno and must be dead. 'Number 2 bought it, Number 2 bought it,' he kept saying.

Chapter Seven

# Rescue

As he looked down on his shoeless feet, Geoffrey Page was disturbed by how fast the sea below was coming up to meet him. It would not be long now. He needed to think through his next challenge. Page knew that if he failed to release his parachute within seconds of landing, the great white canopy would drag him down into the deep. Around his stomach area was a small metal release box with a circular metal disc attached. This had to be turned and then banged to release the parachute. With my mutilated fingers how on earth am I going to manage that, thought Page?

He braced himself as he plunged into the sea feet first. Although it was the height of summer, the water felt icy cold to his shocked body. Then the parachute which had come down on top of him dragged Geoffrey under, 'so I was really inside a tent with all the cords, shrouds as they call them, from the parachute, rather like octopuses tentacles.' He knew that the parachute would quickly become waterlogged and pull him down into a watery grave so he kicked wildly with all the strength he could muster. The parachute cords and harness held him as tightly as a Victorian corset. Unless he could free himself from the parachute, death was inevitable and his white silk life-saver would become a white shroud. He did not want to survive a fusillade of German cannon only to be dragged to his death by an RAF parachute.

He gripped the release mechanism with his burnt hand and tried to turn it. A functioning hand could move it easily, but with a hand this badly burnt it was nigh impossible. The pain was immense as he tried to thump it open. He just could not make the metal disc move. Perhaps the metal had been fused together in the fire of the Hurricane? In the water the smell of his burnt flesh was intense and sickening. He watched, part horrified, part fascinated, as strips of his own skin began to float around him.

Perhaps it was the sight of his own body disintegrating in front of him? Or maybe it was the impact of the icy cold water on his badly shocked body? Page's mind was suddenly alert and clear. He only had seconds now. I must try one last time to escape from this parachute, he thought. Blood poured from raw tissues, flesh flaked from his fingers, and salt water stung his face agonisingly. With extraordinary courage, he attempted to release the chute for a second time. Still kicking desperately in the water to prevent the canopy from dragging him down, the twenty-year-old grabbed the release mechanism. Despite the searing pain he managed to slowly turn the metal disc. Then, with a final act of determination, he banged the release button. The agony cut through to his inner core. Then suddenly the white silk tentacles of the parachute slipped away from him with his few final kicks.

I won't be dragged down to my grave by the parachute now, he reasoned in relief, but there are plenty of other ways I could die out here. At least I have a life jacket, the young pilot thought reassuringly. His training had drummed into him the essential sequence of actions for survival. Free yourself from your parachute and then inflate your life jacket so you can float in the sea until rescued. As the parachute drifted lifelessly away, Page trod water and tried to inflate the life jacket that was going to save him from drowning. He opened the valve with his chattering teeth and blew into the little tube over his left shoulder with all the breath he could muster. He could see that only bubbles were emerging from the other end. His first attempt at inflating his life jacket was a failure. He tried again with the same disappointing result. The inferno in his Hurricane had burned a hole in the lifejacket's rubber bladder. He quietly uttered some strong RAF expletives. Now he had two choices: to drown or to swim for his life. He had not survived a fireball and a precarious parachute landing to give up easily. From the position of the sun, he worked out in what direction lay the safety of the Kent coast, but it was far in the distance. It would be a long swim.

He was a strong swimmer, but his burns were so bad every stroke was agony. As the sea salt dried on the raw tissue of his face, what had started as a sting soon escalated into a searing pain. The strap from his flying helmet cut deeply into his chin causing more agony and impeding his progress in the ocean. He desperately tried to wrench the helmet off. No luck. The flames from his Hurricane had welded the buckle and leather together and it was impossible to remove the helmet.

Page had never felt more alone. All around him was silence, apart from the salty water lapping at his chin. His eyelids were swelling rapidly and his distant view of the safety of the English coast was growing more blurred by the minute. In his frustration a different and better thought came to him. He remembered the slim brandy flask given to him by his mother earlier in the summer. He carried it with him on every flight in case of an emergency. Wisely, as he now thought, he had repelled all attempts by his fellow pilots to drink the brandy during boozy nights in the Mess. At last, he thought, this is an emergency, a special occasion, I am entitled to drink it. A slug of brandy might revive me enough to reach Kent. My mother's foresight can save me, he thought. In great pain he undid the button on his tunic and breathed a sigh of relief. His legs kicking wildly in the water to stay upright. The punctured life jacket was an unhelpful obstacle. Inch by inch his mutilated fingers worked their way under the life jacket towards the breast pocket. The prospect of tasting the warm liquid overcame the almost unbearable agony. With one final effort he undid the copper button on his tunic pocket with his raw hands. The flask was in reach at last. He could almost feel the warmth of the brandy.

Geoffrey Page slowly eased the flask up out of the pocket to the surface of the water. He held the flask between his wrists, which he used as a clamp. It hurt, hurt badly, but it would be worth it. He raised the brandy towards his mouth. His burned hands and wrists were busy holding the flask, so the only way of tasting the life-saving brandy was to undo the top with his teeth. They were chattering in the icy water, but he could do it he thought. Geoffrey gripped the flask top as best he could between his teeth. Nearly there. The water was throwing his head backwards. One small turn and it began to loosen. He kicked wildly again to stay afloat. Another small turn with his teeth. Then another. Suddenly, the screw top was in his mouth. He spat it out into the sea. The smell of brandy was intoxicating. His work on the brandy had forced him to tread water. He was slipping down into the deep. He struggled up with what little strength his aching body still had. He tried to raise the flask to his lips.

At that moment a large wave swept over him. The flask slipped between his damaged wrists and was cruelly swallowed by the sea. Page looked on helplessly. No brandy. No life jacket. For a short moment he broke down and cried. Tears ran down his burned face. He was exhausted, freezing and alone. He was sure he would die. His fear and self-pity disappeared as suddenly as the brandy flask. His astonishing inner determination, his overwhelming desire to survive, resurfaced just as quickly. His flesh was aching, and his face was now so swollen he could hardly see out of his eyes. He was no longer able to make out the hazy coast of England, but he knew the general direction. He realised he could not keep going for more than a few minutes, but he started to swim again.

The burned airman had been in the water for half an hour now. He was determined but losing hope in equal measure. In his mind he reconciled himself to death once more. As he looked up at the sun through his swollen eyes something odd was obscuring it. It was a thin curl of smoke. He was so disorientated it took him a few seconds to realise the plume of smoke ahead must be drifting up from a funnel. Was this real, or a dream? Perhaps he was dead already? If this was a ship, would it pass by without seeing him, a tiny human dot in the sea? He thrashed around in the water and waved his arms with all the energy his spent body could muster. His efforts were in vain. The ship sailed serenely past the small figure of the burned airman in the water and moved on its way. All his hopes had disappeared as quickly as the plumes of smoke. Then he heard the unmistakable sound of a small engine. At first, he could not see anything because of his swollen face but eventually the chugging engine grew louder as a second boat appeared though the tiny slits that were now his eyes. It was a small motorboat with two merchant seamen aboard.

The boat circled as if it had all day to spare. Page kicked his legs hard to stay afloat. The sailors made no attempt to pick up the downed airman who knew he could not keep going much longer. He waved his arms wildly again. One of the men shouted in an unforgiving tone, 'What are you? Jerry or one of us?' Page's desperate reply was inaudible as he swallowed a mouthful of water which drowned out his voice. The boat continued to slowly circle for a second time. What are they playing at, he thought? He was growing weaker by the second and was in danger of drowning just as rescue was so close. He was angry at the terrible predicament he found himself in. The sailors probably had good reason to let a German drown. They shouted again, 'Are you a Jerry, mate?' The struggling airman desperately shouted back, 'You stupid pair of fucking bastards, pull me out.' As they finally hauled his limp body onto their boat, one sailor said, 'The minute you swore, mate, we knew you was an RAF officer.'

Page's first reaction after being pulled aboard was that he wanted to vomit. He mumbled to the sailors that he felt sick and needed help to get to the side of the boat. Altogether friendlier now, the merchant men told him kindly to vomit in the bottom of the boat and that they would clear the mess up. But Page had standards to keep. He thrust his head between his legs and held back the nauseous feeling. One of the sailors showed the airman a clasp knife and said, 'Better get this stuff off you, mate. You don't want to catch a death of cold.'

The irony of catching a death of cold having lived through a fireball thousands of feet in the sky was not lost of the young pilot. He chuckled for the first time in hours. His helmet was removed. Then the sailor with the knife skilfully sliced his way through the sodden clothes. He refrained from asking Page where his trousers were, before the two men wrapped up the naked young pilot in a warm blanket.

As they chugged back to the mother ship, an old Trinity House coastguard vessel, one of the sailors sat next to Geoffrey by way of comfort, but he was lost for words. Page could smell his own burned flesh strongly. He mumbled to the sailor a platitude about the summer weather. It was all very British. As they pulled alongside the mothership a voice asked if their passenger was a Jerry. 'No', replied one of the rescuers, 'one of our boys.' A gangplank was lowered, and sailors formed a hand chair to carry the injured airman aboard. When the elderly Captain of the Trinity House vessel offered a handshake to Page one of the rescuing sailors said, 'He can't Skipper, both hands badly burned.' The Captain offered brief words of consolation and ordered that the burned pilot be helped down into the warmth of the galley.

The heat down below came as a shock after the freezing sea, but welcome sips of warm tea brought life back to his shuddering body. The Captain radioed news of their find back to the mainland and then reappeared with a first aid kit. The blanket was removed, and Page stood naked in front of him as the man inspected his new charge for injuries, 'You got shot in the leg as well.' Page looked down to see blood flowing out of a wound in his calf. Using pink lint, the Captain cut out fingerless gloves for the survivor's raw hands and tied another strip of lint across his forehead. The crew did a good job with what little they had, but the burned pilot clearly needed specialist treatment urgently, 'The crew had seen burns before...but never had they seen the skin flake away like peel from an orange.'[49]

The temporary Margate lifeboat, the *J.B. Proudfoot*, had been summoned by Trinity House and was now alongside. The lifeboat crew led by Edward Parker had distinguished itself two months earlier at Dunkirk by rescuing more than six hundred men. Page's body was wrapped in more blankets, and soft coverings placed round his hands. His pride initially prevented him from wanting a stretcher, but he was finally persuaded of the good sense. He was gently placed onto the stretcher, and as soon as he lay down, he was overcome with the exhaustion from his ordeal. A sailor offered him a cigarette and he quietly lay on the stretcher in the middle of the boat while a Woodbine was placed between his lips. Page felt a conflicting mixture of sensations. On one hand, he was relaxed for the first time since his Hurricane had been hit. On the other, the warmth of the tea and the blankets had revived his body to such an extent that he was suddenly aware once more of the agonising, sharp pain in his hands.

The pilot's response to the searing agony was to lapse in and out of consciousness on the journey back to the Kent coast. Page

---

49    Richard Collier, *Eagle Day*, Hodder and Stoughton, London, 1966

was sitting upright wrapped in his blankets so he could see his own not-so-triumphant arrival. He was immediately aware of how deserted the town appeared. About a dozen onlookers were huddled on the quayside. Behind them stood a single white ambulance. Page knew who its passenger was going to be. For the third or fourth time that evening, the same rough sounding question was shouted, 'Is it a Jerry?' Whether it was at the time or later Page was not sure, but he wondered how a German pilot would have been treated by the men and women of Margate. The British were fundamentally kind, but this was the Battle of Britain, and the nation was fighting for its very existence. When they reached Margate, the twenty-year-old pilot was gingerly lifted out of the lifeboat and taken ashore.

The fact that he wasn't a German clearly changed the warmth of his reception. Through his eye slits, Page could just make out a tall figure looming above him at the top of the steps. He appeared to be wearing a top hat and chain. Was this yet another dream? In fact, it was the Mayor of Margate dutifully welcoming the burned pilot to his town. An hour before he had been in mortal combat with the enemy and now a man dressed in a top hat and tail suit was welcoming him as if he was a celebrity tourist to Margate. He laughed to himself for almost the first time since he had escaped the inferno of his Hurricane.

The official records show that Page was rescued by a Trinity House cutter called *Prudence* - not a virtue that Page was famous for - and was transferred to the lifeboat *J.B.Proudfoot* 'at 6.45 p.m. which arrived back at the station at 7.10 p.m., where a Doctor and an Ambulance awaited.' The lifeboat then conducted a wide but unsuccessful search for Page's parachute until darkness fell.

In his semi-conscious state, Geoffrey Page only had hazy memories of what happened next. Two policemen asked him for details of both his squadron and next of kin so they could be informed of his crash and subsequent rescue. The ambulance was waiting. Lying on his stretcher, Geoffrey asked the crew if anything was wrong with his face. He was reassured that he would be fine. Then he asked again, 'Tell me, what has the fire done to my face?' Once more he was reassured, but he instinctively knew the truth. His skin felt tight, and his face was so swollen that seeing anything clearly was difficult. As he drifted in and out of consciousness, he hazily recalled an ambulance ride and the imposing front of what he later learned was the Royal Sea Bathing Hospital in Margate. The Matron fussed over him. Then he was pushed down endless, dreamlike hospital corridors before he arrived outside an operating theatre. He was mortified to find that before the operation he had to suffer the indignity of an enema. 'To make matters worse', as Page himself put it, 'the enema was performed by a very pretty nurse, such was the price of glory.'

Indignity over, the operation commenced. The bright lights sparked him back into full consciousness. As the nurse and surgeon scrubbed up, he asked a doctor, 'Can I have a mirror?' 'No,' was the firm answer. It did not matter. As he lay on the surgeon's table, Page looked away from the needle the anaesthetist was about to insert into his arm. He caught a vision of himself in the reflector mirrors of the overhanging light. It was a ghastly sight. His handsome, fresh twenty-year-old face was now a hideous mass of swollen, burned flesh. Then the operation began.

## Chapter Eight

# Hospital

Pilot Officer Barry Sutton did not arrive back at North Weald until after tea, following his emergency landing between the cratered sections of the runway at RAF Manston. He had been so close to Geoffrey Page's burning Hurricane he could have almost reached out and touched his friend's aircraft. Sutton had been certain that no one could have survived that fireball, 'I was absolutely astonished. I heard that Geoffrey was alive that night. I couldn't believe it.' He added in his diary, 'One of the first surprising and pleasant bits of news was that Page was safe. He must have bailed out, for he had subsequently been picked up by a ship and landed at Ramsgate suffering with shock and very bad burns to his face and hands.'

At RAF North Weald a weary 56 Squadron took stock of that afternoon's combat. They had lost a talented and popular young pilot but at least he was alive, against all the odds. The rest of the squadron had made it back to base safely. They had shot down two Dorniers including the aircraft which Page, Gracie, and Sutton attacked before it burst into flames. The RAF pilots missed seeing the enemy plane crash, so no one claimed the credit.

In his hospital bed in Margate credit for jointly shooting down a German was the last thing on Geoffrey Page's mind; he was in too much agony. That night the fireball of his Hurricane shaped his nightmares. Vivid images of his two recently dead colleagues, Minny Ereminsky and Ian Soden, driving a car along the road at a crazy speed appeared. As they hurtled along, the two dead pilots waved cheerfully at Page to join them. A parachute magically opened and dropped him down neatly on their back seat. Minny and Ian welcomed him warmly to the car of death. Then their vehicle sprouted wings and took off into the clouds above an aircraft hangar. Perhaps he was already dead? Maybe this was heaven? Or hell? When the bonnet of the flying car jammed upright, he tried to close it with his hands. He was waking up now from his drug-induced sleep. His hands were stuck. He could not free them. The agony in both his hands was horrific. Then the dream disappeared. He was fully awake now, but his hands hurt like hell.

When Geoffrey Page woke up as dawn broke on his first day in Margate it was because of the tremendous thump of anti-aircraft guns right outside his window. With every bang his whole body would jerk, sparking stabs of intense pain. Page scarcely realised where he was or what had happened to him. He was just drifting along in a hazy cocktail of tiredness and painkillers. He was blissfully unaware that the doctors rated his chances of survival as very slim. Burns units were learning fast in this war, but they were still relatively unsophisticated. If more than a third of the body was burned, then death was certain. More than half of the skin on Page's hands was covered in burns.

After one of his nightmares, Geoffrey Page woke up in pain and sticky with sweat. He could just distinguish the vague outline of a woman in white standing by his hospital bed gently wiping his perspiring forehead. His lips and throat were so dry the only word he could squeeze out was 'drink'. The white shape gently lifted the injured man's head from the pillow and held a lemon drink to his parched lips. Even in his dazed state he caught a glimpse of the nurse's pretty face as a look of horror flashed across it. He lay wearily back on the bed hating that moment and hating the nurse for her look.

Later that morning the sharp prick of a needle, the welcome arrival of morphine, stabbed him out of a semi-daze. He was desperate for a drink again and once more his head was raised and lemon-tasting liquid poured down his desperate throat. A nursing Sister awkwardly but solemnly asked him for his next of kin and religion. He replied through his swollen lips, 'I'm going to disappoint you I'm afraid, Sister. I'm going to live.'

The letter to his father from the Director of Personal Services at the RAF two days after the crash, on 14 August 1940, played down the horror of his injuries, 'I am directed to inform you that your son, Pilot Officer Alan Geoffrey Page, has been admitted to Margate Hospital, Kent, suffering from slight burns as result of air operations on 14th August, 1940. As his injuries are not serious, no further reports are expected...' In his own logbook Pilot Officer Page wrote with similar understatement mixed with dry humour, 'Shot down in flames six miles north of Margate. Bailed out and picked up by an old tramp steamer (starts a small two-year session in hospital). Grouse shooting begins!!'

His friends in 56 Squadron might be concerned about a popular colleague being so badly burned, but there was no time to stop and think. The Battle of Britain was not going to pause for a medical bulletin about Geoffrey Page. Combat the following day matched the intensity of that experienced by Page. On 13 August, the day after his crash, three more Hurricanes were lost. P/O Charles Joubert was slightly injured, but F/O Davies [Dopey Davis] was described as 'badly burned'. Sergeant Peter Hillwood bailed out into the water and swam more than two miles before two anti-aircraft gunners waded into the sea off the Isle of Sheppey to drag his exhausted body to safety. Geoffrey Page's disaster was just one of 56 Squadron's early Battle of Britain casualties.

Page's first outside visitor was his sister Daphne. She thought he looked all blown up like a Michelin Man, but she was relieved to see him alive. But there was a look in his sister's eyes that disturbed the injured airman. It wasn't much more than a flicker, or perhaps a flinch, but it was unmissable. Daphne tried to mask her feelings but were these looks of revulsion that he saw in her? Something, he thought, must be very badly wrong with my face. Before he could find out, Geoffrey Page was on the move again. It was decided that Luftwaffe attacks on RAF Manston nearby made Margate especially vulnerable to bombing. To Page's relief, he was to be moved to the Royal Masonic Hospital in Hammersmith, away from the danger and the noise.

The five-hour journey was hell. Page was placed on the lower of two stretcher racks. Every bump in the road shot pain right through him. Despite liberal helpings of morphine from the nursing sister accompanying him, and supportive words from his sister, Daphne, who was also in the ambulance, Page was in agony for the full five hours. The two FANY (First Aid Nursing Yeomanry) drivers were hopeless. They giggled like schoolgirls most of the way and had no idea how to find Hammersmith. They were completely unaware that their useless meanderings had prolonged the journey, causing unnec-essary suffering to the young man on the bottom stretcher. When they finally arrived at the Royal Masonic after five hours on the road, Geoffrey Page thought that he had never suffered such severe pain, especially in his arms. When the hospital porter treated him like a carcass of meat, he finally lost control and let out a piercing scream, followed by a volley of RAF swear words. The noise echoed round the ward. Then all he could remember as he slipped into a twilight world of drugged sleep, were flashes of pain interspersed with vivid images of a burning aircraft.

Despite the endless rounds of hospitals and procedures Geoffrey Page was confident he would survive, 'I felt rough on occasions, but I never thought I would die. The worst thing was the nightmares. I saw myself in a burning plane and being trapped. Then I would wake up with a terrific jerk. It was very painful as my hands jerked. These nightmares were very unpleasant.'[50]

One family member who never visited Geoffrey in hospital was his uncle, Sir Frederick Handley Page, aviation pioneer and creator of the Halifax bomber. Uncle Frederick never forgave his young nephew for not joining the family aviation business. It was a strange lack of compassion after his nephew's horrific crash. As Page's son Jamie noted, 'After the war my father wrote to his uncle trying to reconcile with him, but he never wrote back. I think my father was quite embittered by this treatment even to the end of his life and he never really referred to his uncle, ever.'

Geoffrey had no idea how long he had been in Hammersmith when things changed. One day he emerged from his nightmare-like dream back into the real world. The haze that had surrounded people and objects dissolved, and their outlines sharpened. The nurse, who all the patients called Skipper, instinctively sensed the change. For the first time she pulled the heavy curtains back. Sunshine flooded into Geoffrey Page's room. He was ravenous, and a giant meal was brought, accompanied by half a bottle of champagne. Perhaps it was to celebrate that he was going to live? But Geoffrey only managed two sips because the alcohol set his hands off again. Under Skipper's tender but firm guidance, the young man began to slowly build his strength back. Page was still a long way from doing anything for himself, but Skipper gently fed him by spoon as if he was a baby. In this

---

50   Geoffrey Page, Author interview, North Weald, 1983

new reality, Geoffrey began to wonder how his friends in 56 Squadron were. Were any burned and injured like him? Or were they dead?

A few days later he had his answer. Although his vision did not stretch beyond the end of the bed, Page was now strong enough to be permitted visitors from his squadron. Three of his friends from 56 came to visit, Jumbo Gracie[51], Barry Sutton, and Michael Constable Maxwell. This was not as life-affirming as he expected it to be. His colleagues were delighted to see him alive and making slow but steady progress. Their tone was jokey and boyish, as if they were still sinking pints together in the Officers' Mess. They pretended that Geoffrey was not as badly hurt as they all knew he was. But underneath their boisterous camaraderie, Page detected tension and anxiety. He could see the strain in their eyes, the tiredness etched on their faces from the endless days of aerial combat. Gracie was in plaster from a suspected broken neck. Constable Maxwell had nearly been killed when he crash-landed from a sortie. Sutton had been wounded in the Battle of France. They tried not to upset their burned friend when they told him about the deaths of his former colleagues, but their hollow, flat eyes said it all.

Geoffrey Page was upset to hear about the death of one of the Squadron's warrior leaders. Flt/Lt John 'Slim' Coghlan was no longer in 56 Squadron but paid a surprise return visit on 17 August, five days after Page's disaster. Coghlan was flying a Lysander on his first clandestine Special Operations Flight dropping an SOE agent into France. He never returned. Both 'Slim' and the agent were captured and executed by the Nazis.

Eventually, the trio of pilots said their jolly farewells and headed back to the war. Geoffrey Page was quietly reflective for a few minutes. The real world had rudely barged its way back into his new,

---

51    Gracie was promoted to Wing Commander but was killed near Hanover 15
       February 1944

enclosed, life. Suddenly he sobbed helplessly in a way he had never experienced before. His crying went on for a long time. Tears rolled down his damaged face. Were these tears for friends now dead? Or was he feeling sorry for himself, no longer part of a close-knit squadron? Or was it just shock after such horrific injuries? Whatever the reason, Geoffrey Page felt better after his tears. Skipper assured him that crying was normal. He was cleansed.

On 28 August, a few days after his hospital visit to Geoffrey Page, 22-year-old Barry Sutton was the next pilot in 56 Squadron to be shot down. Sutton's fate was an uncanny echo of Page's own disaster, which he had witnessed from just a few yards. Barry was also badly burned, 'A blinding flash and the sear of flames on flesh, the long, swinging descent with nothing between this world and eternity except that merciful cushion of air in the parachute above; two and a half miles of space between the soles of one's feet and the solid Kent countryside; the stillness.' Sutton may have been a victim of friendly fire, shot down by a Spitfire, but this is not completely proven.

His uncle, the writer Lovat Dickson[52], immediately visited Barry in Canterbury Hospital. He was half-conscious, 'A black mask of tannic acid covered his face, his hands, and his legs. His arms hung in slings, suspended on hooks from the ceiling.' When he regained consciousness the two men talked of Barry's wife Sylvia and what their future might be. His uncle wrote, 'I felt most deeply moved in spirit, not only by the thought that Barry might die, but by the sense of universal tragedy.'[53] Later, Sutton's daughter Caroline added, 'My mother used to visit him in a ward full of young men, some of whom were so disfigured that their girlfriends screamed and ran when they saw them and never came back.'

---

52   Dickson wrote a Biography of Richard Hillary (1950)
53   Barry Sutton, *Fighter Boy,* Amberley Publishing, Gloucestershire, 2010(first published 1942)

In his poem Barry Sutton described his shooting down,

*Now, the fluttering of silk above*
*This swooning through space*
*In silence, except for the sound of a bird.*
*Unashamed, I babble and pray,*
*And hold aloft hands from which already hang*
*Long skeins of flesh*

He goes on, as he thinks about his life,
*Falling and blazing against the distant haze*
*I saw my shattered, spent, Hurricane, slowly writhe and smoke its*
*epitaph.*
*Never again, I swear, will I dare,*
*Or avoid, or complain, or lie, or kill or destroy.*
*So, please God: give me just one more chance:*
*I have so much to give, so much to love.*

Across the Channel the Luftwaffe suffered from their own crises. There were increasing cases of *Kanale Krankheit*, or Channel illness, which was how incidents were described in which pilots mysteriously developed engine trouble or radio failure to avoid combat. Tough leaders like Adolf Galland were having none of that. When one of Galland's pilots panicked over the radio that he was being chased by a Spitfire, Galland brusquely cut in and said, 'Then jump out of your plane, you bedwetter.'

The struggles of individual Luftwaffe pilots were not helped by major errors at the top of the Nazi party. On 4 September, just as the relentless bombing of the airfields in the Home Counties was succeeding, Herman Goering switched tactics and decided to bomb London. For sixty consecutive nights from early September the

Luftwaffe bombed the capital. Now Germany's precious fighter aircraft were reduced to flying as bomber escort, wasting the speed, and diving superiority of the Me 109s. This strategic mistake eased the pressure on Fighter Command and allowed it to husband the limited human and mechanical resources available. Letting the RAF off the hook showed how little tactical acumen Goering possessed, and how overoptimistic his expectations of the Luftwaffe were. It was no wonder Air Chief Marshal Dowding said after the war, 'I could hardly believe that the Germans would have made such a mistake…it was a supernatural intervention at that particular time, and that was really the crucial day.'

In the Royal Masonic Hospital Geoffrey Page was scarcely aware of how the Battle of Britain was going. He was still in too much pain. But he knew that he badly needed a sense of purpose, a target to aim for. For him it could only be one thing. He wanted to fly again. It was this compulsion that drove him forward. To him flying was an addiction and being unable to fly hurt him more than the pain of hospital treatment. Under Skipper's sympathetic but disciplined care Geoffrey Page began to improve day by day. But for every step forward there was another barrier to surmount. The biggest hurdle was when Skipper was joined by an assistant, a young VAD (Voluntary Aid Detachment) nurse. She was one of the most beautiful women Geoffrey Page had ever seen.

Her first meeting with the young pilot was disastrous. As soon as she looked at him, the new nurse could not mask her feelings. A look of revulsion was etched on her face as she saw his injuries. The twenty-year-old instantly understood just how much his young, boyish face had changed. His eyes followed the stare of the nurse's face down to his arms. They were a putrefied mass of pus-filled boils, a result of the condition of his blood. The hands from the wrists were jet black and shrunken. Soon after the crash, tannic acid had been smothered on his raw hands and face back in Margate. The acid was designed to coagulate any blood that was oozing from the burns and to lessen the risk of death from shock. Now the tannic acid had become baked as hard as concrete, and his skin was as thick as the hide of a rhinoceros.

'The black stuff's not your skin,' said Skipper, reading her patient's grim thoughts, 'It's only tannic acid.' Her understanding was not shared by the other nurse who dashed out of the room with the speed of an Olympic sprinter to be sick. Skipper gently reassured him. Geoffrey Page looked down again at his ghastly arms and hands, a mass of boils and blisters smothered in cream and tannic acid. If his hands and arms looked this horrific what on earth did his face look like? Fearful about the truth, he demanded a mirror from Skipper. 'No' she insisted. He asked firmly, almost coldly, again and again. 'You will be allowed to look in a mirror Pilot Officer Page when I see fit to permit it and not before,' she replied equally firmly.

Page was not to be deterred by Skipper, or anyone else. He had to know what he looked like, to see for himself. As soon as Skipper disappeared, Page thought, 'Right you miserable bitch, I'll look in the mirror even if it kills me.' Two steps from the bed sat a washbasin. There was a mirror temptingly hanging above it. It took five minutes of throbbing pain in his hands and arms just to pull the tightly tucked in sheets back. After agonizingly swinging his legs so they dangled over the side of the bed, he prepared for the big drop onto the floor. Suddenly he felt dizzy but eventually steadied himself. Here we go. He slid achingly off the bed down towards the floor. His knees buckled as he hit the hard surface, and he was forced to rest for a few minutes before restarting his slow move across the room. Sweating with fear, aching from just those two steps, he focused his watery eyes and stared at last into the mirror. A gargoyle stared back, its face swollen and ugly, and three times its normal size. He was horrified by the

Frankenstein monster he had become. From the mirror the monster stared back at him, and he collapsed helplessly onto the floor. As he fell, he was dimly aware of the hazy reflection of Skipper entering the room. On the way down his body crashed against the washbasin, driving still more searing pain through his ruined hands.

## Chapter Nine

# McIndoe

By the middle of September 1940 Geoffrey Page had been in his hospital bed for just over a month. In the world beyond his ward the Battle of Britain was building up to its climax and 15 September was later officially named as Battle of Britain Day. The German decision to blitz London with their bombs meant that even Hammersmith, which was on the other side of London from the strategic target of the East London docks, was no longer safe. It was decided to evacuate the patients at the Royal Masonic to the relative safety of the countryside.

Soon after this decision a stranger came to see the injured young pilot. The man was in his late thirties, squat, with dark hair, horn-rimmed spectacles, and a friendly smile. At first glance he was the double of comedian Harold Lloyd. This was Archibald McIndoe, the Consultant who headed up one of Britain's three maxillo-facial units for burned and injured servicemen. McIndoe was a New Zealander based at Queen Victoria Hospital, East Grinstead, Sussex. Through his pain and the fog of drugs Geoffrey Page could not have foreseen that this brief meeting was going to change the course of his life forever.

McIndoe was friendly but also crisp and business-like. Which plane was Page flying? Which tank was hit? How long was he in the water? How long before he received tannic acid treatment? 'Were you wearing gloves?' asked McIndoe. 'No,' replied the pilot. 'Clot,' said the surgeon, smiling; and he was right - gloves would have protected hands against burns. Geoffrey Page felt instantly that this was a man of empathy and understanding. 'See you again, young fellow,' said McIndoe, and was gone.

On the way back to East Grinstead Archibald McIndoe must have been fuming. The tannic-acid treatment given to Geoffrey Page was recommended by the authorities because it reduced deaths by shock, but for serious third-degree burns like Page's, tannic acid caused the fingers to curl into claws and the skin to thicken. Tannic acid or gentian violet were also used around the face with the result that skin stiffened, and eyelids shrank back, leaving corneas exposed. Before the war doctors had not encountered burns on this scale, and tannic acid was still the official treatment. McIndoe wrote in his notes, 'Down with Tannic Acid!'

Next day Geoffrey Page said a sad farewell to his favourite nurse, Skipper, as the hospital was decanted of patients. The destination was RAF Halton near Aylesbury in Buckinghamshire. Sensing Page's sadness, Skipper was reassuring, 'You'll get better more quickly in the country, and you can have a nice long convalescence.' Page was defiant, 'Convalescence be damned. I've got to get back to flying as soon as possible.' Skipper laughed, 'Silly boy, you'll never fly again.'

Page was relieved to see that his ambulance to Halton was driven by two male nurses and that the FANY drivers were nowhere in sight. He was delighted that a new uniform had been forwarded to him from his squadron's base at North Weald. His arms were slipped into slings and instead of a tie a silk scarf was wrapped over the bandages on his neck. The tunic was draped over his shoulders like a cloak. I look more like a scarecrow than a pilot, Page thought to himself. His eyes were watery as he held back tears. The bitter sweetness of sporting a new uniform to travel between hospitals rather than returning to his Squadron was hard to take.

This time the drivers packed him carefully into the ambulance where he was soon joined by two other pilots headed for convalescence at Halton. One of them had been shot in the neck and the other had suffered burns around the face and mouth. When the burns patient suggested they stopped at a pub, Page realised it was a good chance to try out his new Frankenstein's monster features on the public at large. When the three men walked into the pub, although in Page's case this was more of a stumble than a walk, they were a terrifying apparition to the regulars who were so shocked they even had to stop their game of darts. Page heard a pitying mutter from the landlord's wife.

The pilots ordered pints. Geoffrey Page's hands were so painful and stiff one of the other men had to pour the beer down Page's throat. A second pint was ordered and once again another patient lifted the glass and poured the amber nectar greedily into Page's mouth. The men were in weak condition and two pints were enough for them to arrive at RAF Halton singing merrily and significantly the worse for wear.

Halton was an undistinguished pre-war building which could have been mistaken for a barrack block or a prison. Indeed, the Sister in charge often treated her patients like prisoners. Geoffrey Page developed a deep distaste for this unsympathetic Ward Sister but was too preoccupied with his injuries to notice his grim surroundings. Over the following weeks the dire consequences of tannic-acid treatment became clear. Page's tendons contracted unstoppably, curling the fingers downwards. The thin skin hardened to a thick crust on top of his raw, burned, flesh. His fingers felt so immovable it was as if they were stuck in concrete. At the same time the tannic acid welded the fingers together so that they were no longer separate digits. For severe burns, Page called tannic acid 'the kiss of death'.

It was clear to the medical officer in charge at Halton, Wing Commander Stanford Cade, that Geoffrey Page's hands were more painful and less flexible than ever. The only answer was to remove the hard tannic-acid covering. After the acid had been removed, Page woke up from the anaesthetic astonished to see that his hands were no longer coal black but pink. His skin was as thin as tissue paper. The hands were so sensitive that even a gentle draft across the room caused a searing burst of pain.

To soften the hard skin, Geoffrey endured the agony of a hot-wax bath every day, but even this treatment failed to halt the negative impact of the tannic acid. Page's skin hardened even more, and his fingers slowly bent downwards until they touched the palm of his hand. Page was steadily losing the battle with his own hands. For three more months he faced the horrors of the hot wax bath but still his hands hardened and contracted. Geoffrey Page felt so despondent he wondered if life was worth living. Stanford Cade realised that the only answer was a skin graft. A place was found for Geoffrey Page in the Maxillo-Facial Unit (later renamed the Plastic Surgery and Jaw Injury Unit) at the Queen Victoria Cottage Hospital in East Grinstead, Sussex. The hospital was so small and cosy that it was not until 1943 that the word 'Cottage' was dropped from the name.

The hospital sat tranquilly on the edge of the town and was surrounded by orderly flower beds and lawns. The main building was less than four years old, a trim 1930s replacement for the original which had been built in 1863. This neatness was only disrupted by the wooden huts which had been hurriedly erected for all those servicemen who would be burned and injured in the war. Here, Page was destined to meet for a second time the friendly, no-nonsense New Zealander who had visited him in Hammersmith. The Queen Victoria Hospital Maxillofacial Unit was Archibald McIndoe's domain, and it was clear to everyone exactly who was in charge.

Chapter Ten

# East Grinstead

When Pilot Officer Geoffrey Page arrived at the Queen Victoria Hospital in late November 1940 it was like walking through a mirror. He was astonished to find the ward full of young men with ruined faces and hands just like his own. Some looked even more hideous. On his first day in the twelve-bedded Kindersley Ward, Page found three human gargoyles standing at the end of the bed to welcome him. They introduced themselves as Toby Tollemache, Roy Lane, and Richard Hillary. Two years later Hillary wrote his classic war book *The Last Enemy*.

Seeing Hillary now, that was hard to imagine. The young Spitfire pilot looked monstrous. There were two large bloody red circles of skin around his eyes. Each circle had horizontal slits in it, with an eye peeping out. His hands were wrapped in lint covers. A new pair of eyelids had just been grafted onto his face. He was courageous and heroic but bitter and cynical too. The voice from behind the mask called out, 'Another bloody cripple. Welcome to the home of the aged and the infirm.' Roy Lane[54], who was in the next bed to Page, reassured the new patient, 'Don't let him get you down. He's a conceited young man with a sharp tongue and a large inferiority complex. For years he

---

54    Lane flew again in Burma. In April 1944 he was captured and beheaded by the Japanese.

has been told by his mother what a wonderful boy he is, but in the Service, he's had his backside kicked and he's a bit mixed up.'

Kindersley was a small ward in the main building. The nurse in charge was Cherry Hall from Ireland, sister of the overall hospital Matron. Page knew instinctively that he was in the hands of an efficient nurse who was good at her job. But Sister Hall was not a woman you wanted to get on the wrong side of. Even a man as clever as Richard Hillary was no match for Cherry Hall. When he was overheard saying, 'Jesus Christ, what a hospital. It stinks like a sewer, it's about as quiet as a zoo, and instead of nurses we've got a bunch of moronic Irish amazons,' Sister Hall had him moved off her ward immediately. Boisterousness was acceptable, but not extreme rudeness.

The ward was divided into glass-partitioned sections with four beds in each. Despite the friendliness of Roy Lane and the competence of Sister Hall, the newcomer felt ill at ease. He was in a community but still alone, 'I was in too much pain to worry about my fellow human beings…we were a variety of shapes and sizes, but we all had one common denominator, and that was the colour red. Some people were blind, some burned about the hands. One poor chap had been immersed in salt water in a dinghy for ten days. His legs were amputated but he had no burns. There were all different sorts of injuries.'[55]

He was still only 20-years-old, and it wasn't surprising that Geoffrey Page was furious about the cruel blows of the world. This inner anger made him incapable of reasoned discussion and fuelled a negative attitude to everyone around him. When his mother visited, he was unable to see her because of his ruined eyelids. He could just hear her voice. He had hoped that as soon as the tannic acid came off, he would be back flying, but even Page could now see that was a fantasy. He believed he was a write-off, a cripple for the rest of his

---

55    Geoffrey Page, Author interview, East Grinstead, 1983

life, his flying career over. Just six or seven seconds in a flaming air-craft had transformed a bright, good looking, young pilot into one of McIndoe's patients for life. His only anchor was McIndoe himself who had warned Geoffrey that he faced many operations but that he would be all right in the end. The surgeon's confident demeanour gave him hope.

McIndoe's worst cases were treated in Ward Three, a long wood-en hut about fifty yards away from the main building. The ward was brightly lit with pastel colours on the walls. Fresh flowers adorned the room. A keen eye would have noticed that the beds lining each side of the ward were not the regulation iron structure found in most hospitals. One observer thought they looked more like hotel beds. They were separated by small lockers and were close enough to touch the next bed, although few had good enough hands to try that. In the middle of the room was a stove, a wireless, and an old piano. The dull, worn lino on the floor was the only clue to what Ward Three had looked like before Archie McIndoe had transformed it. When the New Zealander had first seen the Hut, it was being painted regulation cream and brown and the beds were all standard hospital issue. It was, said McIndoe, 'A bit of a shack'. He decided to 'tart it up', and he did not hang around changing things.

It was the patients in Ward Three who attracted far more atten-tion than the decor. VAD (Voluntary Aid Detachment) Nurse Jane Lyons was reeling on her first day in 1940 when she saw the face of her first patient, 'It was mashed to a pulp. There was a hole where his right eye should have been, the other eye was sort of lying on his cheek. The bottom half of his face had been jammed sideways and his teeth were smashed and sticking out at all different angles…I just turned around and went to the toilets and wept.'[56]

---

56    Liz Byrski, *In Love and War,* Fremantle Press, Western Australia, 2015

Another nurse arriving for her first night duty could not put the initial image of the ward out of her mind, 'The whole ward was blacked out except for lamps over the top of the beds. The light itself showed straight onto the faces of the patients...I thought I'd come into the chamber of horrors. I didn't know how I was going to stay there at the tender age of nineteen but in two or three days I was used to it.'[57] When she grew up the daughter of one East Grinstead nurse could never eat barbecued pork because it reminded her of the smell in Ward Three. Even the patients themselves described each other as 'grotesque' or 'horrific'.

McIndoe was not just concerned with the appearance of the wards. He was also mindful of how his 'boys' looked. To him the shapeless hospital uniform demanded by King's Regulations, the 'blues', as they were called, were demeaning for young men who had been flying Spitfires and Hurricanes just a few weeks before. He astonished the staff by ordering them to burn almost all the bright blue outfits which in McIndoe's eyes made his 'boys' look like convicts. He then kitted the men out in their RAF uniforms. This instantly restored their dignity and self-respect. Outside the hospital they would now be recognised first and foremost as RAF pilots, not as invalids.

It was a few weeks before Flying Officer Page was admitted to The Hut, as Ward Three was nicknamed, but before then he was encouraged to visit by McIndoe. Page soon met the most severely burned man at the hospital, a twenty-six-year-old South African called Godfrey Edmonds. Edmonds had crashed at night in his Hampden bomber which had been manufactured by Geoffrey's uncle Sir Frederick Handley Page's company. It was Godfrey's very first solo flight. He had fried for several minutes before being rescued.

---

57    Helen McAlpine, *Imperial War Museum Sound Archive 30261*, London, 2007-9

On admittance to East Grinstead, Edmonds scarcely appeared human. One patient remembered hobbling on crutches from Kindersley to Ward Three and meeting Edmonds, 'I had never seen anyone so badly burned. I was terrified. He looked literally like Frankenstein. His face was a grotesque mask. His hands were burned. His ears were just stubs and holes, he had no lips, just a hole for a mouth. There were no eyelids, just two holes in the face. He picked up a chair, and through his lipless mouth said, "Have a seat, old boy".'

Even Archie McIndoe was doubtful he could repair a patient who had 'the worst frying of any man I met.' It was only after the war that McIndoe revealed how shocked he was when he first saw Edmonds, 'when I saw him, I said to myself, "I hope he won't live". Now I wish I'd not thought that.'

Page's visit to the Hut had made him realise that, although his own injuries were terrible, others were even worse. He had nothing to complain about it, 'Godfrey Edmonds was one of the toughest individuals that God ever made and, funnily enough, it was the worst injured man who was always the most cheerful.' The uncomplaining nature of Edmonds and others was the perfect antidote to the self-pity that was bubbling inside Page.

Even Richard Hillary's cynicism evaporated when he was moved into the bed next to Edmonds. Hillary just could not understand how a human being could put up with so much pain for so long, 'He was completely cheerful, and such was his charm that after two minutes one never noticed his disfigurement...if ever a pilot deserved a medal it was he. He read little, he was not musical, but somehow, he carried on. How?'[58]

Geoffrey Page soon settled into the routine of Queen Victoria Hospital, but it was the echoes of the world outside that disturbed

---

58   Richard Hillary, *The Last Enemy,* Macmillan, London,1942

him. East Grinstead was close to the Sussex and Kent coasts, the frontline in the Battle of Britain. As he sat outside in the autumn sun, Geoffrey could hear Spitfires and Hurricanes overhead. He thought about what might have been if a German had not shot him down in a ball of flames. Geoffrey wondered how his friends in 56 Squadron were faring. How many of them were dead, or badly injured like him? He desperately wanted to fly again, to join the Hurricanes and Spitfires in the skies above as they headed home from a sortie, 'These days were hell...how my heart yearned to be one of them, and not just a burned cripple lying in a hospital bed.' But he finally understood that repairing his damaged body was going to be a long job. Flying a fighter plane again was a distant prospect.

This desperation to return to flying was shared by Richard Hillary. Beneath the cynicism Geoffrey Page glimpsed Hillary's vulnerability. Page realised the two young pilots had much in common, except Hillary was flying a Spitfire not a Hurricane when it was transformed into a fireball, 'I felt a terrific explosion which knocked the control stick from my hand, and the whole machine quivered like a stricken animal. In a second the cockpit was a mass of flames; instinctively, I reached up to open the hood. It would not move. I tore off my straps and managed to force it back.' Hillary was just able to open his parachute and when he hit the water,' I noticed how burnt my hands were; down to the wrist, the skin was white and hung in threads; I felt faintly sick from the smell of burned flesh. By closing my eye, I could see my lips, jutting out like motor tyres.'[59]

Page and Hillary also shared a similar background, public-school education, university air squadron, and a romantic view of fighter pilot combat. Like Page, Hillary had also been rescued from the sea by the Margate lifeboat before receiving early treatment at the Royal

---

59    Richard Hillary, *The Last Enemy*, Macmillan, London,1942

Masonic Hospital. At East Grinstead one of the nurses described Hillary simply, 'He was a very good-looking man. You could tell that from the back. He was a tall, slender young man but that face of his was a tragedy.'

These were the men who Archibald McIndoe had to repair both physically and emotionally. McIndoe was born into a family of Scottish heritage in Dunedin, New Zealand. Like so many immigrants, his grandfather had travelled to the other end of the earth to build a better life for himself and his family. McIndoe's father John was a successful jobbing printer, but it was his formidable mother Mabel who was the dominant force in young Archie's early life. Archie entered Medical School at Otago University in 1919 determined to become a doctor and over the next few years he displayed many of the talents that made him one of the greatest medical figures of the Second World War.

Archie was extremely clever and possessed a wide range of other skills which made him popular both on the dance floor and the rugby field. The humanitarian instinct that emerged at East Grinstead was evident in his student days. His final-year thesis focused on health care in the slum areas around Dunedin's docks. He was already imbued with an urgent restlessness that dictated the direction of his life. Soon after graduating he left New Zealand and headed to the famous Mayo Clinic in Rochester, Minnesota on a scholarship. Before he left for America, the penniless medical graduate found time to marry 18-year-old Adonia Aitken, a beautiful and gifted young pianist.

Within a few years in Minnesota, Archie was recognised as a talented abdominal surgeon with an apparently brilliant career stretching ahead of him. But there something about the steady advancement at the Mayo Clinic he found frustrating. McIndoe was at heart an innovator, a leader, rather than a talented cog in the well-oiled machine that was the Mayo Clinic. This gnawing unhappiness was not helped by strains in his relationship with Adonia. After seven years, the young New Zealander abandoned the prospect of a very successful surgical career in America to try his luck in England.

The red tape that he sliced through so incisively in wartime was harder to cut in peace. His American surgical qualifications were not recognised, and his medical sponsor in London was unhelpful and evasive. His saviour was a fellow New Zealand surgeon, Sir Harold Gillies, who was a cousin on his mother's side. The older well-established man warmed to his 'country cousin' and opened a door for him at St Bartholomew's Hospital in London. Gillies soon admired McIndoe's surgical talent, 'McIndoe's abdominal surgery was of a very high order. With a little encouragement it seemed to me he could become one of the greatest technicians in the country.'

Gillies himself had been a pioneer in rebuilding the faces of soldiers injured in the trenches of World War One. Bullets or shrapnel tore eyes, noses, jaws, and whole faces apart. The innovative work of Gillies on these injuries created a platform for McIndoe to meet the very different needs of a second war twenty years later. In the meantime, Archie McIndoe was too restless to wait for his surgical skill to be recognised in Britain. When Gillies suggested a cosmetic surgery partnership, McIndoe was both intrigued by the surgical intricacy demanded and attracted by the financial rewards of private practice. He had been living in tight financial circumstances for too long to turn this chance down. McIndoe swiftly showed his skill in lifting breasts, bobbing noses, or removing scars. His creation of a delicate snub nose became such a sought-after cosmetic operation it eventually became known as McIndoe's Nose. A handsome fortune, as well as an enviable reputation, was now within reach. The Gillies-McIndoe partnership was successful, although not without occasional tensions relating to both money and reputation.

McIndoe tried to ignore the growing threat from Hitler and focus on his own plans. Perhaps he would start his own practice and buy a villa in France with the profits? But eventually even McIndoe could not ignore the Nazi threat. The military authorities hurriedly prepared for the inevitable flood of injured men, and three primary treatment centres in England were established. Archie had already stood in for Harold Gillies as a Consultant in Plastic Surgery for the RAF, and in 1938 this arrangement was made permanent. McIndoe was one of only four plastic surgeons then working in England and, given his position as a Consultant to the RAF, he was earmarked to lead one of the new units. He was given responsibility for what was eventually called the Centre for Plastic and Jaw Surgery at East Grinstead. Harold Gillies[60] took charge of the Royal Navy unit in Basingstoke.

The choice of a cottage hospital in a small town with fewer than ten thousand inhabitants was deliberate; East Grinstead was well away from the larger cities that would be German bombing targets but close enough to the airfields of Kent and Sussex. At last McIndoe had what he most needed, the chance run his own show in the way he believed was right. He wrote to his mother, 'It is a nice little hospital on the outskirts of a nice little town, and I think something can be made of it.'

When the Battle of Britain started, he was nearly forty years old, although to his many patients in their twenties he seemed older. Archie had the solid build of a New Zealand front row rugby player, but this sporting image was undermined by chain smoking. His hair was plastered flat and parted in the middle. He had a warm smile and round owl-like spectacles. 'McIndoe had a magnetism', recalled Geoffrey Page, 'He could walk into a cocktail party and although he was quietly spoken, everyone would instantly gather round. He did

---

60    Pilot Officer John Gillies, son of Harold Gillies, was a pilot in the RAF. He was shot
down in May 1940 and became a Prisoner of War until 1945.

not show his emotions much, but his sense of humour often came through.'[61]

To avoid the risk from German bombs, McIndoe sent his wife and two daughters away from London to America. His old friends at the Mayo Clinic agreed to help his family settle into new surroundings. The family's absence allowed McIndoe to focus solely on his work and he moved into a cottage near the hospital. He wrote regularly to his wife, but his marriage would not survive such a significant geographical and emotional distance.

McIndoe had no template or manual for rebuilding faces and hands. Before the war little had been learned about the treatment of severe burns simply because, so few victims survived. Most burns patients died within two days of an accident. If they survived in World War One, wrote Harold Gillies, 'these poor burned patients were shoved into a dark smelly corner in the worst ward in the hospital to die or scar in their own serum and sepsis.' Twenty years later, modern fuel-laden fighter aircraft had huge potential to turn into fireballs, but their pilots and aircrew were more likely to survive. They would need to be repaired.

The design and technology of Spitfires and Hurricanes were dramatically different from the simpler fighters of the First World War. In the Hurricane, one unsealed tank holding twenty-eight gallons of high-octane fuel was directly behind the dashboard, almost in the pilot's lap. This was the tank that burst into flames when Geoffrey Page's Hurricane was hit. During World War Two about 3,600 aircrew suffered from burns to the face or hands, and usually both. These terrifying injuries were colloquially called Airman's Burn, or, more specifically, Hurricane Burn or Hurricane Rash,

---

61   Geoffrey Page, Author interview, Henley-on-Thames, 1984

Pilot Officer David Hunt from 257 Squadron was shot down over Essex in his Hurricane during the Battle of Britain. His experience was typical of McIndoe's Hurricane Burn patients, 'Immediately flame came through the instrument panel, filling the cockpit and burning my hands, legs, and face. The reserve fuel tank had exploded, and I had neither gloves nor goggles, which I had pushed over my forehead in order to get a proper view... I started to survey the damage. My hands were all bloody, like I was feeling, and they were covered with protective tissue; that was the skin; and all that was left of my sleeve was a charred ribbon of rank.'[62]

It was essential for Hurricanes to equal the German Messerschmitts in speed and manoeuvrability. A fuel tank sealant system would have added weight to the Hurricane, and so there was an inevitable design compromise between speed and safety. In wartime, range and speed were always going to win out against fire safety. As Tony Ditheridge, whose company has rebuilt more Hurricanes than anyone else, put it, 'A fighter is made for one purpose only. It is a tool to kill people. It was made to be very efficient, not to worry about the pilot.'[63]

Dr Emily Mayhew of Imperial College, University of London, pinpointed a second fire safety weakness in the Hurricane's design. The Hurricane also possessed wing tanks which were vulnerable to attacks from the side. The points where the aircraft's body met the wing (the wing root) were not closed by a sealing mechanism. This created a direct channel from fuel tank to cockpit. Geoffrey Page's friend from 56 Squadron, Flying Officer Barry Sutton was one of the first unfortunate victims of this design weakness, 'His port wing tank was hit and set on fire. He had the hood half open and yellow flames

---

62    Esther Terry Wright, *A Pilot's Wife's Tale*, Bodley Head, London, 1942
63    BBC Radio, *Hurricane Rash*, London, 8 May 2012

came into the cockpit from the wing tank via the web root end which was not sealed off from the fuselage.' [64]

It was left to Archie McIndoe to deal with the human consequences of safety compromises in aircraft design. But the Battle of Britain was as much a turning point for Archie McIndoe as it was for his young patients with Airman's Burn. Without it, McIndoe might still have been lifting breasts or reshaping noses full-time. With his Harley Street practice and wealthy clientele, Archibald McIndoe was not an immediately obvious saviour for these men suffering from Hurricane Burns, nor did he appear destined to be one of the great heroes of the Battle of Britain. As Emily Mayhew noted, 'there's nothing in his personal life that indicates he's going to be this kind of heroic figure who's prepared to take the risks that he does.' Perhaps it was his total control of this new unit that unlocked something in McIndoe, 'You have this incredible coherence of a patient group of unexpected survivors, a plastic surgeon who is prepared to take risks and do work that no one else has done, and a unit that is not very big but where he gets to decide everything. In a small town. And it all just comes together.'[65]

His young burns pilots were very different from an actress craving a new nose, but Archie McIndoe quickly formed a strong rapport with his patients. It helped that McIndoe's told his 'boys' at East Grinstead the truth about the many obstacles they faced. Geoffrey Page appreciated the candour, 'Archie bent over my crippled hands, turning them over slowly to examine the damage, "Long job, I'm afraid." I asked whether he would have to operate. This time his head went back, and his dark eyes looked firmly into mine. "Yes," he said, "many times, I'm afraid. But you'll be all right in the end." Somehow, I believed him.'

---

64   E.M.Mayhew, *The Reconstruction of Warriors*, Greensill Books, London,2004
65   Dr Emily Mayhew, *The Town That Didn't Stare podcast*.

Archie McIndoe's aim was to, 'within a reasonable time create order out of chaos and make a face that does not excite pity or horror.'[66] McIndoe took patients into his confidence, and he didn't use medical jargon. One patient was told frankly by McIndoe on first meeting, 'They made a bloody good mess of you…never mind, we'll fix it up.' When he first saw the extent of Richard Hillary's injuries he commented, 'Well, you certainly made a thorough job of that didn't you.'

In the early days of his unit McIndoe visited hospitals around the country scouting for cases, the more challenging the better. He found Jack Fleming, a fellow New Zealander, in the military hospital at RAF Halton where Geoffrey Page was also treated. Fleming was so severely burned he had been told he would die. So, he was in a black mood when a crowd of visitors were ushered in to see this human showpiece. Jack Fleming lost his temper, shouting that he was in a hospital not a circus. A New Zealand voice cut through the noise and told the visitors, 'The boy's got a point. You'd better go.' McIndoe sat down and invited Jack to become his patient,' I've got a wonderful wine cellar down in East Grinstead, so If I can't cure you, you'll at least die an alcoholic.'[67] McIndoe did such a good job on Jack Fleming he eventually returned to flying.

Geoffrey Page was surprised when he was given a bottle of champagne which was clearly not standard hospital medicine. He would have been less enthusiastic if he had realised that champagne gifts were reserved for the most badly injured to cheer them up. Champagne was the East Grinstead equivalent of Blind Pew handing out black spots, one relative remarked.

---

66   Archibald McIndoe, *Total reconstruction of the Burned Face*, Bradshaw Lecture, London,1958

67   Author interview, East Grinstead,1983

Page's initial skin graft was the first in a series that lasted two long years. As he waited for his operation to start Geoffrey was very nervous. His anxiety was not helped by the humiliating process of having his pubic and upper leg hair shaved. As he was wheeled into the operating theatre his last memory was John Hunter, McIndoe's amiable and skilled anaesthetist, introducing himself as The Gasworks. For five days after the graft, he was in constant agony, unable to sleep at night. His only relief was a regular injection of morphia. Page described the pain as, 'burning and grazing like falling off a motorbike at 60 mph'[68]. This was a semi-sanitised version of his original observation which was, 'as if many nails were being hammered inexpertly into the fingers…then pincers would wrench the nails out, after which the hammering would start again.'

McIndoe saw the agony Geoffrey Page was suffering from even a few days after his first graft. His twenty-year-old new patient was in tears. 'Hurts like hell doesn't' it?' said the surgeon sympathetically. Page tried to minimise his suffering, but Archie McIndoe returned later to find the young pilot still in acute pain. McIndoe slowly nicked the stitches with scissors, easing the pressure that had been causing Page so much agony. Carefully, the New Zealand surgeon lifted the blood-stained sponge. Underneath Page could see that his hand was disgusting, a swollen lump of raw, putrefied flesh, oozing with pus. The smell of his rotten flesh was overwhelming and filled Page with despair. But then he looked at McIndoe. He was astonished by how cheerful his surgeon's round face appeared. Archie's voice was equally positive, 'Luckier than I thought. That's about a fifty per cent take, I should think. Now we've got to get you fit enough for the next lot.'

As he did with all his patients, McIndoe explained the skin graft to Geoffrey Page. McIndoe had scraped the thick scar tissue from

---

68    Geoffrey Page, Author interview, Henley-on-Thames,1984

Page's hands from the knuckles to the wrist. He then replaced the 'rhino' skin on his hands with a paper-thin layer of skin taken from the inside of his thigh. Geoffrey now realised why his thigh hurt almost as much as his hand. This was called a Thiersch graft, named after its German inventor in the late nineteenth century.

Archie McIndoe explained further, 'This skin graft is sewn into position-in your case about sixty to seventy inches-and the long ends of thread are left hanging at regular intervals from quite a few of these stitches. After that a dry sponge is cut and placed to fit over the grafted area. The trailing ends of the stitches are then brought back over the back of the sponge and knotted together. The sponge is then moistened which in turn causes it to swell, but as the thread restrains it, it can only exert pressure against the hand, facing the new skin against the raw surface. That way the two surfaces join together.'

Next day an RAF surgeon in uniform was delegated to remove Page's stitches. He clearly lacked McIndoe's dexterity. On the seventh stitch Page let out a blood-curdling scream which echoed round the ward. A nurse at the other end of the room dropped a lunch tray. The surgeon was not best pleased and continued his snipping. Page was in such agony it was like a red-hot needle being shoved up his hand and arm. He screamed again. The pain was even worse. The surgeon was furious at his patient's apparent weakness, but Geoffrey Page was giving no ground and shouted, 'You swine…you bloody filthy butchering swine. Get away from me and stay away.'

The doctor had hit a nerve in Page's already badly damaged hands. It was left to Sister Hall to call a merciful halt to proceedings. Next day, on his rounds McIndoe instructed Sister Hall to give Page some morphia and take the seventh stitch out herself which she did painlessly. Why the RAF doctor hadn't bothered with a pain killer Page never knew. It was left to Richard Hillary, the ward cynic, to try and put Page in his place. As he saw the young pilot writhing with pain after the operation he said, 'Bloody fool. You should have worn gloves.' He was also addressing this brutal put-down to himself because Richard Hillary had also not worn gloves when his plane was torched.

Chapter Eleven

# The Hut

Brimming with youthful optimism, Flying Officer Geoffrey Page thought his stay at East Grinstead would only last for three or four weeks. In the end he was hospitalized for two long years. He endured fifteen painful skin grafts in the war, and around the same number in the years after. Most burns victims at East Grinstead endured ten to twenty operations. One McIndoe patient, Reg Hyde, eventually lived through over eighty operations and grafts.

McIndoe always welcomed the most difficult cases, and Squadron Leader Bill Simpson was certainly one of those. Simpson had the misfortune to be flying an old-fashioned Battle bomber over the Low Countries in May 1940 when he was hit, 'The pilot's cockpit was enveloped in flames. The flames streaked up-tongues of red and yellow thirty feet into the air. The air gunner and observer scrambled out of the cockpit near the tail and leapt up on to the right wing. They pulled out the pilot, who had become stiffened into a sitting position and was burning like a torch. They dragged him to the ground and rolled him in the long cool grass; then carried him to safety, fifty yards away from the flames that were rapidly consuming the Battle. I was that pilot...'[69]

Simpson was finally moved into the care of Archie McIndoe after eighteen months in French hospitals that did not have the experience

---

69   William Simpson, *The Way of Recovery*, Hamish Hamilton, London, 1944

to deal with such serious injuries. The whole of his face was badly burned, and his eyelids had been fried. His hands and fingers were charred stumps and were so stiff that he could not feed himself. He was not just a physical wreck, but his self-esteem was also at rock bottom.

Simpson was an insular man who was not naturally at ease with the boisterous behaviour in Ward Three. He was allocated the bed next to Geoffrey Page and was struck by how young Page looked, 'He had obviously been very good looking and was still, in a way, fairly good looking. He was kind, he was amusing in a facetious kind of way, and he was a very nice guy altogether. He was always popular.'[70] Then he noticed Page's hands which were 'as brittle as sticks with fingers locked at the joints and excessively tender', and his eyelids, which clearly needed renewing.

It did not take him long to see saw beyond the 20-year-old's looks and charm, 'Geoffrey was a good person to meet on arrival in Ward Three. He had a gaiety that never irritated and a sensibility that allowed him to get at your feelings without you taking offence at having them exposed.' As their friendship developed, he was most affected by Geoffrey's 'intention to get back to flying again. This was not wistful dreaming or extravagant optimism. It was a quiet, practical determination.'[71]

It was Geoffrey Page who boosted Bill Simpson's fragile confidence by telling him, 'You won't know yourself by the time the Boss has finished with you.' Page was right. Simpson, Page, and the others were lucky to be in the care of such a talented surgeon. His arms were variously described as like a 'butcher's boy' or 'plough boy' but his hands were as supple as those of the pianist he also was. One patient noted that 'his hands did not move they seemed to flow.'

---

70    Author interview, London 1984
71    William Simpson, *I Burned my Fingers*, Putnam, London,1955

Archie's wife, Adonia, had never been in doubt about how technically skilful her husband was, 'Here was a man who could open up a stomach and put right what was wrong inside it more speedily and expertly than any man I had ever seen. I know what I am talking about. I watched others and I watched Archie. He had no equal.'[72] Lady Gillies, wife of his mentor, cousin, and friend, Sir Harold Gillies, agreed, with one caveat, 'I have never seen another surgeon, apart from my husband, who cut so beautifully as Archie did.'

Medical colleagues were also in awe of his skill. One said, 'He stitched every face as it were the Bayeux Tapestry.' He had, said another, 'a gift in his hands which would smooth the handiwork of God and repair the ravages of the devil.' Another doctor who worked with McIndoe added, 'He was probably the fastest surgeon in the country, one of the most beautiful and rapid technicians I have ever seen...he moved so quickly it seemed as if he was operating on three people at once in three different operating theatres.'

Archie McIndoe was a risk-taker who was unafraid to venture into uncharted medical territory. It was no wonder his patients called themselves the Guinea Pigs. Reconstructing eyelids which had burnt off in an aircraft fire was a completely new challenge. When asked about how he learned this unique repair work McIndoe famously replied, 'I looked down at a burnt boy and God came down my right arm.' McIndoe trusted his surgical instincts to do the right thing, and then his skills with the knife to achieve a good result. Nor if he thought something was wrong would McIndoe stay silent. In 1940 he campaigned against the widely accepted practice of using tannic acid to treat serious burns until eventually the practice was stopped.

At one end of Ward Three was the Saline Bath Unit, which was rather more rudimentary than its grand name, and was one of

---

72    Leonard Mosley, *Faces from the Fire*, New Jersey, Prentice Hall Inc, 1962

the first in the United Kingdom. McIndoe had noticed that pilots who had crashed into the sea benefitted from the ability of salt water to ease and heal burns. Geoffrey Page was lucky, McIndoe said, to have crashed into the giant saline bath that was the English Channel. Every day men's bandages were removed, and they were gently lowered into a soothing bath of warm salt water. Wounds were carefully bathed until they were clean before they were powdered with an antiseptic and covered with a soft gauze, before bandaging again. This operation was run by RAF medical orderlies who the patients called the Bathroom Boys, although there was often a WAAF, Betty Andrews, on duty too. Bill Simpson noted that, 'The Bathroom Boys have a character, language, and method of working that is entirely their own...some patients are very trying; some who are extensively burnt take more than an hour to treat. This is a great ordeal for patient and orderlies alike... (they) have developed a particular blend of patience, firmness, and tolerance.'

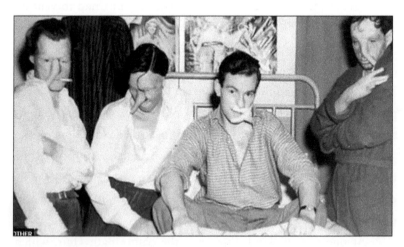

*Photo courtesy: West Sussex Record Office*

McIndoe also built on the tube pedicle technique used by Harold Gillies decades earlier in the First World War. These were skin flaps, often taken from the abdomen or leg, that were used to conduct a blood supply to areas needing to heal, especially the face. The tube construction used the patient's own skin to protect the live tissue inside from infection. Over a period of weeks one end of the tube was detached and 'walked' up the body from its original location to the burn injury site.

The most vivid examples are in photographs of McIndoe's patients with long, unsightly pedicles or tubes hanging from their faces, like elephant's trunks. After a few weeks lost tissues were replaced by the graft and the pedicle discarded. Other techniques were more basic. Geoffrey Page was surprised to wake up one morning to find a nurse above him with a garden watering can sprinkling water over him as if he was a bed of flowers. He was told that this was to keep his bandages moist.

Geoffrey Page's second skin graft was on his left hand. It was as painful as the graft on the right. At least Sister Hall knew not to let the grim-faced RAF doctor anywhere near him this time. Two nights later in the depths of his pain, Geoffrey heard a familiar sound overhead, a Junkers88. Then he listened to an unmistakeable noise as a bomb whistled its way down towards the hospital. As it thudded into the ground the building shook. It was only a few yards outside the window. There was no escape for Geoffrey Page now. He waited in tense anticipation. Then there was silence. The bomb had failed to detonate. A large, unexploded bomb just outside the building was not a comforting prospect, but at least he was still alive.

For Page, who was used to the discipline of service life, the Queen Victoria Hospital was an extraordinary place. In most military hospitals, the hierarchical structure of the British forces remained untouched, and officers were allocated their own rooms. McIndoe was having none of that. He was clear there was to be no division between ranks; a sergeant pilot could be in the next bed to an air marshal. Archie had learned that officers on their own did not recover as quickly as those in combined wards and so, like a squadron flying into combat, he ensured that the men were all together, whatever their rank.

Archibald McIndoe changed more than the traditional hierarchies of service life. McIndoe allowed his 'boys' far greater freedom than was permitted in any other hospital in Britain. After all, his patients were young and in his care for the long-term. They needed to live by a different set of rules. A Lt Colonel in the Irish Guards underwent a single operation in East Grinstead. Despite his seniority, the officer was treated with full Queen Victoria Hospital humour and the customary lack of respect for senior ranks. As he left the Lt Colonel said to McIndoe, 'I have never seen a place with discipline so low, and morale so high.'[73]

It was this human understanding that was valued as much by Geoffrey Page as the technical brilliance of the New Zealand surgeon. To Page, part of McIndoe's genius was his certainty that his work did not stop with surgery. It was equally important that he cared for the whole man, that he repaired the psychological damage just as much as the physical. McIndoe understood that successful surgery was only the beginning of the journey. He needed to build confidence in their new faces and hands, their new selves, if these young men were ever going to find a meaningful place in the world outside the narrow confines of the hospital.

To McIndoe these young men had damaged bodies, but they were not sick. Why shouldn't they still enjoy themselves? And why should they be locked away in a hospital ward as if they had leprosy? Surely, they would gain in confidence by enjoying the same fun as

---

73   Geoffrey Page, Author interview, Henley-on-Thames, 1984

any other twenty-year-old? So, a big barrel of beer at the end of Ward Three was never empty. The radio blared out. Visits from family and friends were not confined to a miserable single hour. Visitors were encouraged and could stay for as long as they liked. Nurses were chosen for their sympathy, cheerfulness, and good looks. The operating table was 'the Slab', being burned was 'Fried', and Ward Three was 'the Hut'. Any self-pity was corrosive and soon dispelled.

The staff treated the pilots not as cripples but as ordinary active young men. On arrival Alan Morgan noted, 'I had no idea where I was. It sounded like a nuthouse. I thought they were all a load of nutters. I just kept thinking-this is a bloody place and they are all bloody mad in here'[74] Geoffrey Page thought that the atmosphere in Ward Three was 'a cross between *Emergency Ward Ten*, the Bull's Head, and a French brothel'. Others saw the ward as more like 'a very jolly sixth form or an undergraduate common room just before Christmas.'

Freeman Strickland was one of nineteen Australian Guinea Pigs. He was shot down flying a Spitfire, 'I think I got a good roasting. It was assumed I wouldn't survive. I could smell roast beef and I kept thinking, 'God, that's me'. Strickland did survive and was sent to East Grinstead, 'The first time I entered Ward Three there was a tremendous party going on. There were girls draped over the beds with patients all bound up. There were crates of beer everywhere. I got the surprise of my life. This was supposed to be a serious hospital.' The barrel of beer had a subtler purpose than astonished newcomers realised. It was watered down to help dehydration. McIndoe and his staff had worked out that this cohort of young men would not bother to drink water but would be tempted by beer, even watered-down beer.

Despite the bawdy atmosphere there was still respect for those struggling with physical or mental challenges. The pain, the relent-

---

74    Quoted in Liz Byrski, *In Love and War*, Fremantle Press, Western Australia, 2015

less schedule of medical procedures, the failure of relationships, meant that sometimes patients were submerged in black days of deep depression. On those occasions they were allowed restful peace by the remainder of the ward and were not expected to drink beer or make jokes.

On one of his hospital trawls, Archie McIndoe found 24-year-old David Hunt, one of the worst burns cases in the RAF, at Billericay Hospital. In her wartime memoir *Pilot Wife's Tale,* David Hunt's wife Terry describes leaving her badly burned husband at Ward Three for the first time, ' We looked at the Hut where David was to be, and at the sister in charge: a lovely girl with hair and skin of two shades of honey; and I left the forlorn figure of David standing in the drive in the rain…I rang up the hospital in the morning and heard from the honey-coloured sister that I might come whenever I liked. The Hut had its own set of rules.'

When Terry Hunt hurried back to the hospital the next day, she observed the atmosphere in Ward Three, 'There were fifteen men in the Hut, and one woman; a girl who had been badly burned in a sweet factory. She wore a pink knitted cap at a rakish angle and was bright and familiar with all the men and no one appeared to find it odd at all.' The girl was called Joan and her accident had happened on her first day at the factory. She was just eighteen and had been covered from head to foot in boiling sugar. When she arrived from London her hair was still coated in toffee and was alive with maggots. Eventually her hair had to be completely removed under general anaesthetic. Joan was in and out of the Queen Victoria Hospital for five years.

On Ward Three a sense of humour was essential to survival. One young pilot was so badly burned that he had to be helped on to a bedpan by two nurses, one of whom wore a rather obvious wig of golden curls. On this occasion, as the patient was being moved off the pan for cleaning up, the second nurse stretched forward for the foal (a gold-coloured substance used instead of lavatory paper). 'She found some resistance,' her sister remembered, 'She went on pulling and found she'd pulled the other nurse's wig and was about to wipe the patient's bottom with a foal with a Red Cross hat on it. He laughed so much he had to have morphia. We thought he'd die of that. Still, it was a turning point.'[75]

One patient, Lieutenant Patrick O'Connor from the Highland Light Infantry, who was not a burns patient, was remembered by Geoffrey Page as 'pleasantly round the bend'. O'Connor returned from a heavy night's drinking and as he felt his way along the corridor trying to stay upright, he forgot that the corridor eventually gave way to a curtained area behind which was the saline bath. O'Connor crashed through the partition and landed in a bucket of highly concentrated disinfectant. Page recalled, 'I was awakened by his drunken screaming, as he dashed round the ward in a frenzy, clutching the seat of his pants...'My bottom,' he yelled, 'It's on fire!' The night nurse, Mary Rea, swiftly took the man's tartan trousers off and at the same time noticed that the wall was now a mass of blisters where the pure disinfectant had acted as a paint remover. She turned the drunken patient on his stomach and began treating him for first degree burns. 'What a bugger,' said the Lieutenant O'Connor, his naked bottom visible for all to see, 'I come to a burns hospital with a few broken bones and finish up getting my arse burnt.'

Amidst the drinking and the noise, it was possible to miss how professionally run the Unit was. Surgery was conducted with extremely tight discipline. Sam Gallop who had no legs described how well-run Ward Three was. 'There were very tight medical rules but at the same time a wonderful balance of being relaxed...it was a very

---

75   *A Fine Blue Day*, BBC Radio, London, August 1978

tight medical ship.' Theatre technician Bob Marchant is probably the last survivor of those who worked with McIndoe. Under McIndoe's leadership, the running of operating theatres was very disciplined. McIndoe was a stickler for both cleanliness and being on time, 'He didn't suffer fools gladly. He expected everyone to know what they were doing and to work to his own high standards. But he was always good with his juniors and at the end of the day he would always thank all of us working in the operating theatres.'[76]

McIndoe might work fast in the operating theatre, but he was also patient and would not operate until the optimal moment. Archie was prepared to bide his time, 'I can see little virtue in immediate excision and grafting of the burned areas in a facial burn. It is so difficult to tell viable from non-viable tissue…any failed graft in a facial repair is a major disaster to the patient whose confidence and trust is maintained by a steady succession of successful operations.'

Ward Three was not just a drinking den. The patients also enjoyed regular concerts of classical music. Famous pianists of the time would come to East Grinstead and sometimes play on the piano the patients used for rousing, often bawdy, singsongs. Weekly classical concerts were held in the hospital and broadcast to McIndoe's wards. Although these concerts did not involve drinking, they were still well received by the patients.

McIndoe set the tone for every aspect of hospital behaviour. He would laugh and drink with his patients, but he stood above the fray as well. To his 'boys' he was simply a god, bringing life back to their charred bodies. Archie even allowed his patients to watch him operate. McIndoe reckoned this would give his men confidence in the surgical team, and also better understand what they would face. It worked for Bill Simpson, 'I left the theatre with a thrill of satisfaction running up

76    Bob Marchant, Author interview, East Grinstead, 19 May 2023

and down my spine. I had seen a wonderful example of the marvels of modern plastic surgery. I was encouraged beyond words that the pair of firm skilful hands which I had just seen operating would continue to operate on others and on me.'[77]

McIndoe was supported by two key personnel he had brought with him from London. Dr John Hunter was a brilliant anaesthetist and a big, amiable, relaxed man who could drink any RAF pilot under the table. Geoffrey Page thought he looked more like a pork butcher than an anaesthetist. Others described him as looking like Mr Pickwick or Friar Tuck with a solid paunch and bald pate adorned by only a few wisps of hair. He had first met McIndoe at the Hospital for Tropical Diseases in London. In the language of the Guinea Pigs, Hunter ran 'the gasworks' and was known as 'The Knockout King'. He often used bawdy humour as he anaesthetised his patients. 'Just a little prick', he would say, as he injected a burned pilot. But underneath the jollity was an innovator who extended the boundaries of anaesthesiology. Face operations were tricky technically, but Hunter was able to keep the patient anesthetized for as much as seven hours even while the face was being operated on. McIndoe often acknowledged Hunter's importance, 'I couldn't have accomplished what I have done without his help. I've seen no one to touch him as an anaesthetist.'

The third member of what the Guinea Pigs called *The Immortal Trio* was McIndoe's surgical sister, a tall, slender, titian-haired nurse with green eyes called Jill Mullins. They first met at Bart's Hospital in 1931 and Archie quickly noticed her talent in the operating theatre as well as that 'she was the most beautiful nurse in the hospital'. From 1935 the two worked together constantly at Bart's, the London Hospital for Tropical Diseases, and finally at East Grinstead. Mullins was skilful and efficient, with light hands that were well-suited to the

---

77    William Simpson, *The Way of Recovery*, Hamish Hamilton, London, 1944

world of plastic surgery. She would anticipate McIndoe's every move in the operating theatre without words being exchanged. More than that, her warmth softened McIndoe's occasional toughness. Some patients were so captivated by her beauty that an operating theatre visit was almost a pleasure. Archie McIndoe knew the importance of surgical teamwork and Bill Simpson could see how intuitively they worked, 'McIndoe, Hunter, and Jill are a perfect team and to watch them together in the theatre is to see a marvellous example of teamwork.' McIndoe's was always quick to praise Hunter and Mullins for their vital roles in the team.

Once the operation was over the skills of the nursing team in keeping wounds safe and clean was vital. The post-operative care instigated by Jill Mullins was, said Archie Mcindoe, 'outstanding. Her knowledge of wound healing was uncanny and was based on the sound principle that cleanliness was next to godliness.' As Dr Emily Mayhew from Imperial College, London points out, 'Good infection management by the nurses was critical. After weeks or months in an RAF hospital these men would probably have died. But in a specialist unit like East Grinstead the nurses knew their job and did it well.'[78]

Moira Nelson joined as a nurse late on in the war. She had hated her time at a hospital in Harrogate. The Queen Victoria was different, 'East Grinstead was marvellous. You had the feeling that everyone was working together, although we were all very clear that Mr McIndoe was in charge, and he was a hard taskmaster. He was never rude or condescending though - I never called him Archie - but a lot of people did, and Archie was God.'[79]

The nurses might have been good looking, but they were also very effective at their job. Bill Simpson was hugely respectful of one nurse, 'The most impressive thing about her was her unobtrusiveness.

---

78    Author interview, London, 26 January 2023
79    Quoted in Liz Byrski, *In Love and War,* Fremantle Press, Western Australia, 2015

She was completely self-effacing…when I was feeling at my worst she would nurse me - as she would nurse all of us - gently and devotedly, knowing instinctively what the most urgent need was and how to supply it.'

Geoffrey Page was still in awe of the patients who were even more damaged than he was. He grew to know Godfrey Edmonds, the South African he had met soon after his arrival. He had no hair on his head and his face was a grotesque mask. Yet, there was not a drop of self-pity in Edmonds. When McIndoe needed to give him a new pair of eyebrows, Edmonds was so utterly bald that the surgeon was forced to use the only hair left on the South African's body, pubic hair. When McIndoe asked if he was happy with his new pubic eyebrows, Edmonds replied 'OK boss, but when I see a pretty girl in the street my eyebrows keep flickering.' Edmonds was, it was said, the worst burned pilot in the RAF to survive.

As the Battle of Britain marched on to its final days the number of burns patients at East Grinstead inevitably increased. There were many new arrivals, but discharges were rarer. Archibald McIndoe rose to the challenge by just increasing the number of hours he operated for. On occasions, the New Zealander could perform as many as seventeen operations in a day. When he first saw Jimmy Wright, who had been blinded, he could see the pain his lack of eyelids was causing. Although he had finished operating for the day, he asked Jill Mullins to reopen the operating theatre and the two of them operated on Jimmy Wright after their supper.

After his hands, Archie McIndoe then moved on to Geoffrey Page's face which was marked with burns from the helmet line down to where his silk scarf had been. There was a particularly vivid mark where his chin strap had sat. Page had a scar from ear to ear. Any treatment on his face felt like 'a fork had been stabbed into my cheek'. The scorching heat of the fire had caused a general contraction about

Page's eyes, with the result that the top and bottom eyelids could not meet for sleep. Although he could still blink a little 'when I woke up in the morning there was no lubrication and it felt like someone had shoved a bucket of sand in my eyes.'[80]

His operation left Page blind for three weeks. During this time, Geoffrey felt very lonely. One minute he was looking forward to further independence and the next the nurses had to do everything for him, including washing, teeth cleaning, and cutting up his food. When Page blindly tried to feed himself, he only succeeded in stabbing his own cheek with the fork. To complete the eye work, new eyebrows were created by taking hair from the nape of his neck and grafting them above the new lids. For the rest of his life his eyebrows grew rapidly and needed regular pruning. By now, Geoffrey Page was a fully paid-up member of the McIndoe fan club. Decades later he dedicated his autobiography to the man 'Whose surgeon's fingers gave me back my pilot's hands.'

A month after the Battle of Britain ended in October and with the German invasion plans successfully thwarted, the two key architects of that success, Air Marshal Sir Keith Park who skilfully ran 11 Group, and Air Chief Marshal Sir Hugh Dowding, were moved against their wishes from Fighter Command. Dowding sent a farewell message to his men, his Dear Fighter Boys.

In sending you this my last message, I wish I could say all that is in my heart. I cannot hope to surpass the simple eloquence of the Prime Minister's words, 'Never has so much been owed by so many to so few'. The debt remains and will increase…goodbye to you and God bless you all.'

---

80   Author interview, Henley-on-Thames, 1983

Chapter Twelve

# The Town That Didn't Stare

When Pilot Officer Geoffrey Page was cheerfully settled into the rhythm of life in this strange community, he noticed a slow, almost invisible, improvement in himself. It was time, he realised, to venture out. Archie McIndoe knew that once repairs to hands and faces were on the right path, the confidence of his young patients also needed bolstering. He said to his welfare officer, Edward Blacksell, 'Imagine how they feel. On Friday night they were dancing in a nightclub with a beautiful girl and by Saturday afternoon they are a burned cinder. A fighter pilot can't help being vain because the girls all swarm round him like a honeypot. He can take his pick. Think what it must be like for that young man to go back into the same circle with his faced burned to bits.'[81]

McIndoe also put this problem more formally, 'The impact of disfiguring injuries upon the young adult mentality is usually severe…they may be psychically lost, depressed, morose, pessimistic, and thoroughly out of tune with their surroundings…they believe that their former social status and facility of performance are at an end, that they are no longer marriageable, and must be objects for well-meant but misguided pity.'

McIndoe met this challenge head on by encouraging his patients out into the town of East Grinstead. He met with the local

---

81    Peter Williams and Ted Harrison, *McIndoe's Army*, Pelham, London 1979

community and urged them not to treat his patients as 'freaks', but as ordinary young men. In the local pubs he explained that the staff might have to pour drinks for his 'boys', hold their beer glasses, or even help do up their flies. Above all they needed to be sure to look his Guinea Pigs in the eye. East Grinstead rose to the challenge and the town was as welcoming as it could be. Mirrors were taken down in most of the bars and pubs so that McIndoe's army could not catch an unhelpful glimpse of their own faces. 'We loved the people of East Grinstead,' said one patient, 'they gave us heart.'

At first Geoffrey Page found safety in numbers and comfort in a group; an outing with half a dozen other badly burnt characters made him less self-conscious about his own scarred face and hands. Although sitting in the hospital minibus the Guinea Pigs were conscious of some passers-by staring in as if they were zoo animals, overall, Page thought, the public were understanding.

Making it to the pub by car was a challenge. If Geoffrey Page was driving for an evening's 'grogging', as he called it, he would press his feet on the pedals while his passenger compensated for Page's ruined hands by working the steering wheel and gearbox. On his way Page might pass a flotilla of wheelchairs from the hospital all heading for the same hostelry. At the beginning, it was embarrassing to have someone pour beer down your throat or handle your money. It was even worse to head off to the Gents with a friend whose job it was to do up your fly buttons.

Quickly, however, the burned airmen found places of safety where they could fully relax. Their favourite haunt was the Whitehall, a restaurant and entertainment complex in the centre of town, where the barmaids and customers grew so used to seeing young airmen with scorched faces and crippled limbs, they never gave the pilots the embarrassed look they all dreaded. Even the pedicles, the long tubes of flesh, were just called 'sausages' and one of the Whitehall waitresses recalled, 'Even with a sausage coming down from the nose and one hand bandaged up, they managed to eat and drink, though sometimes we had to cut their food up for them.' [82]

Terry Hunt and her husband David preferred the company of each other. Unlike the wives of other Guinea Pigs, Terry travelled with her husband from hospital to hospital, often acting as an informal or supplementary nurse. Her wartime memoir was subtitled *The diary of a camp follower.* One place the young couple did venture was the Whitehall where Terry was surprised by the responses of Archie's patients, 'In the restaurant near the hospital there would be gatherings of McIndoe's creations...I suddenly found they were real people, as I had only known before. They showed their new features off with pride.'

The 'creations' were not above adorning their ward with stolen road signs or belisha beacons after a heavy night at the Whitehall. They never lost the sense of humour that helped them survive. One patient advertised in the Lost and Found section of the local paper for, 'one blue artificial eye answering to the name of Joey, lost between the Crown and Blackwell Hollow.'

Bill Gardiner, who ran the Whitehall, instinctively understood the needs of the young patients from the Queen Victoria Hospital. He was amiable and supportive, dealing politely but firmly with any customer who did not understand the unwritten rules of Whitehall behaviour. Gardiner and his staff were so natural with this distinctive crowd of customers that a visit to the Whitehall made McIndoe's patients feel normal. At the Swan Hotel, another popular drinking spot, locals would help carry the East Grinstead patients in their wheelchairs up the stairs to the bar. Sometimes the surgical trinity

---

82    Peter Williams and Ted Harrison, *McIndoe's Army,* Pelham, London, 1979

of McIndoe, Mullins and Hunter would join the young men at the Whitehall in the evening. McIndoe would entertain on the piano, Hunter would tell jokes of questionable taste, and Jill Mullins was the person whose attention made everyone feel better. The Whitehall was a special place for special customers, and it was no wonder that East Grinstead later became known *as The Town That Didn't Stare.*

Geoffrey Page never noticed anyone in the town give his swollen, livid face a second glance. It was different when he went up to London in a gap between operations. When he arrived at the underground station, he was suddenly self-conscious about his huge bandages and ruined hands. His jacket was draped around him like a cape. It was impossible for him to reach into his pocket for the tube ticket because his hands were so inflexible and hard. He was forced to say to the ticket collector, 'Help yourself.' There were scores of people sleeping in the underground which served as a well-protected bomb shelter. As Geoffrey walked past them, he heard sympathetic mutterings of, 'Look at him' and 'God bless his heart.' On the bus, the conductor even suggested, 'You don't half look a mess mate, you should go and see one of those plastic surgeons, they can do miracles you know.'[83] Geoffrey Page was relieved to return to the anonymity of *The Town That Didn't Stare*, to the company of his new mates who understood him because they looked just as bad or even worse.

Tunbridge Wells was just a few miles from East Grinstead but there was uproar when two of McIndoe's patients stepped down from a bus to do their shopping in the town. One woman screamed in horror at the sight of the two 'freaks' and a second said loudly, 'They shouldn't be allowed out in that condition.' Outside the safety of East Grinstead nothing much appeared to have changed since World War One when disfigured servicemen were hidden away. When the pa-

---

83    Jamie Page notes, Devon, 2013

tients of Harold Gillies were convalescing in Burnham-on-Crouch between procedures, they were not wanted in view of the townsfolk, 'The good people of that place requested the home to keep us in, as we gave them the shivers.'[84]

Despite the reassuring comradeship in Ward Three, Geoffrey Page was missing his friends in 56 Squadron. How were they all? How many had been killed or injured? One day he jumped into his little sports car. He could only drive by strapping his burned hand to the steering wheel and the other hand to the gear lever. Then he headed for RAF North Weald on the other side of London.

On arrival, Page quickly unstrapped his hands from the car to appear normal. His fellow pilots were thrilled to see him but unsure how to react to his injuries. One pilot was uncertain whether to say, 'God, your face looks awful' or to treat Geoffrey as if nothing had changed. For 56 Squadron to see a popular colleague looking like a monster was hard to bear. Sergeant Pilot Taffy Higginson was immediately struck, 'He looked absolutely dreadful. He had no eyes, no eyebrows; just two slits in his horrid, ploughed flesh-nothing like the handsome young fellow we had known before.'[85]

Pilot Officer Barry Sutton had been flying alongside Page's Hurricane on the day his colleague was shot down in a ball of flame. He was astonished Geoffrey was still alive, 'I'd never seen a close friend so badly burned. He was a terrible sight. His face was really unrecognisable'. It was Geoffrey Page who made his friends feel more at ease, 'The moment he spoke his voice was cheerful, and I felt that Geoffrey hadn't changed.' In time-honoured fashion the small but excited crowd took Page into the bar and an impromptu, very drunken, party developed. Before he was too drunk Page took a slow look

---

84    Letter from Horace Sewell quoted in Lindsey Harris, *Facemaker*, Allen Lane, London, 2022

85    *Churchill's Few*, Leeds, Yorkshire Television,1984

round the squadron. There were several new faces, replacements for his old friends who had been killed or injured. The rest, like Taffy Higginson and Barry Sutton, looked older, wearier, than he remembered back in August 1940.

Unavoidably absent in hospital, Page had missed the arrival of a Squadron mascot. The Squadron Leader and the Adjutant had headed off to acquire a dog as a mascot. On the way they passed a zoo and instead of the dog they returned to 56 Squadron with a monkey who was swiftly named Me109. The plan, devised after copious amounts of beer, was for the monkey to sit behind the pilot facing backwards and to warn the pilot when he or she saw an Me109. This hare-brained scheme was never tested because the monkey wisely escaped into the woods, before being recaptured and taken back to the zoo.

The next day Page was much the worse for wear, although not from his operations. Once again, he strapped one hand to the steering wheel and the other to the gear lever. His return to his old squadron had been joyful. He was touched to receive such a warm welcome. But it also made him realise that the strange community in East Grinstead, this cult of Archie McIndoe, was where he now belonged. For all the warmth and drunken fun, the visit to North Weald was unsettling. Perhaps it was the initial hesitation he saw when his friends saw his burned face for the first time? More likely, it was staring at his own 'ploughed flesh' every time he looked in the mirror of his little car. This disturbing vision, and the sharp burst of pain in his hand every time he changed gear, was a reminder of how improvement was needed before flying again was possible.

Page was not the only Guinea Pig whose visit back to the RAF proved unsettling. When Richard Hillary visited RAF Hornchurch to see Ronald Berry, an old colleague now commanding a squadron, Hillary was not even allowed to meet the young pilots. Berry decided that 'he was terribly badly burnt and with my young flock I'm afraid I denied him the pleasure of going round the squadron...one or two of the young pilots would have found it hard to take...that young chap was utterly brave...an outstanding young man.'[86]

It would have been no consolation to know that his horrific injuries may have saved Geoffrey from something worse. In the most brutal phase of the Battle of Britain 56 Squadron lost eleven aircraft in just five days. Two weeks after Page's crash, on 24 August, the Germans dropped more than two hundred bombs on RAF North Weald smashing buildings and aircraft and killing nine people. A second attack in early September killed five more and injured thirty-nine. Finally, another attempt to bomb North Weald just a few days before the end of the Battle of Britain in late October resulted in six more deaths and forty-two further injuries. In all 56 Squadron lost fifty-eight men in the few short months of the Battle of Britain, including forty-one pilots.

Back in Ward Three Page experienced a renewed sense of purpose inspired by the visit to his Squadron. His determination was remarkable. He bought himself a rubber squash ball and for hours on end squeezed it until his hands were raw with pain. To straighten his crooked fingers, he made a nurse strap four splints tightly to his hand. The fingers remained stubbornly bent, but finally the hard work made them supple enough for him to tie his shoelaces. This was triumphant progress. Alongside his determination, Page was dimly aware that there was another parallel emotion competing in his brain. Hatred was growing inside him, hatred for the Germans, hatred for the men who had burned and disfigured him. 'Right, you bastards,' he said to himself, 'Let's see how many of you I can knock off.' Revenge was a powerful survival tool. He resolved to shoot one

86    Ronald Berry, *Imperial War Museum Sound Archive* 11475,London, 15 August 1990

German down for every operation he endured. Fifteen operations would mean fifteen 'kills'.

Although he did not show emotions easily Archibald McIndoe had grown very fond of the young man in his care. Maybe he admired Page's astonishing will-power? Perhaps he was the son McIndoe never had? The two became like a father and son, observed other patients. Certainly, McIndoe was a father-figure to Page, whose relationship with his own dad scarcely existed.

Archie McIndoe was also fascinated by Richard Hillary, 'He's a strange bloke. The boys in the ward don't like him. He has a sharp tongue and an intellectual approach that gets them on the raw. He mixed them up so much recently that they bombarded him with their precious egg ration, and this quietened him down for a time. But, like all of his type, he soon bobbed up again.' Geoffrey Page was, of course, one of the instigators of the egg attack on Richard Hillary.

By 1941 McIndoe's unit was overflowing. Bomber crews rather than fighter pilots began filling the beds in East Grinstead. Archie no longer had to go on recruitment drives hunting for patients because they were now being sent directly from several feeder hospitals. He wrote to his wife in America, 'All three theatres were going full blast all day. The hospital is now so full of new cases and the old ones returning for their repair that we shall have to ask for another extension.' By the end of Archie's reign six hundred and forty-nine men had become McIndoe's Guinea Pigs.

Between procedures Geoffrey Page and other patients were given short breaks at the RAF Officers' Hospital in Torquay. The Torquay medical report in early 1941 illustrated just how far away Geoffrey Page was from full recovery. It recorded, 'Scar extending from ear to ear beneath his chin-there is considerable facial disfigurement' and in his hands 'a severe degree of flexion deformity of both hands…range of movement restricted to a few degrees only.' A few months later the Medical Board noted that movement in his fingers was 'still very limited' and his face was still scarred with only one eye able to close. The Medical Board reported that his progress was satisfactory, although they had no idea that Page measured his own steps forward by how close he was to flying again.

One day in Torquay Geoffrey was astonished to see his old car from North Weald whizzing through the streets. Ian Soden had bought it when a fellow pilot was killed, and Page acquired the vehicle after Soden himself was shot down in France. In turn Page sold it to Maurice Mounsdon for £5 when Page himself was in the burns ward and short of funds. Although Mounsdon lived to 101, he too was badly burnt and became another of McIndoe's Guinea Pigs. As a result, Mounsdon sold the car on. As the car passed him in the Torquay street, Page noticed that its new owner also had a face marked by burns. This was such an ill-starred vehicle that he shuddered to think what would happen to the next owner.

When he drove back up to London in his own car a friend from Cranwell who had also been convalescing in Torquay helped him. Geoffrey steered with his wrists while the friend changed the gears. The friend was struck by how Geoffrey refused to let his endless medical procedures get him down and that he was as cheerful and amusing as he had been back at Cranwell.

In May 1941 Page celebrated his twenty-first birthday. His second summer in hospital was an equally unsettling time for Geoffrey Page as what had been left of summer 1940 following his crash. He would lie with his fellow patients outside in the sun on a mattress. Why am I trapped on this bloody mattress, he thought, when I could be up there in the cockpit of a fighter plane? Page sensed that his homespun technique of squeezing a squash ball for hours every day was doing the job, slowly improving the strength in his clawed hands. Perhaps one day there would be enough power in at least one hand to control a fighter aircraft?

Nonetheless, a year after he was shot down the RAF Medical Board visited him in hospital for an assessment. They reported that although his general condition was good 'the right eye cannot be completely closed...there is a keloid scar at the right eye and another on the neck and the left side of the face...movement of fingers still very limited. Extensive scarring of both hands.'

The reverence in which Archie McIndoe was held by Geoffrey and his fellow patients deepened as they sensed their own slow improvement. McIndoe's nicknames were 'The Boss 'or 'The Maestro' and the Australian patients called him 'The Supremo'. In contrast, McIndoe was unpopular with some surgeons from other medical disciplines. They were jealous of his talent and resentful of his occasional bursts of publicity. Just as he would never sugar-coat a message to his patients, he was blunt and sometimes bad tempered in front of various hospital committees. Inevitably, complaints by the Welfare Committee about the bad language and drunkenness of his patients were rudely rejected by McIndoe.

Archie McIndoe's spectacular work attracted press coverage which meant that the Queen Victoria Hospital rapidly became well-known nationwide. By the end of the war celebrities, including Clark Gable and Vera Lynn, had visited East Grinstead. Several prosperous families lived nearby in Sussex and were swiftly seduced by Archie's charm and his growing fame. He used his contacts among the local gentry to widen the social interactions of his patients by wangling them invitations to tea at Sussex country houses. Among the generous hosts were Elaine Blond, part of the Marks family who founded Marks and Spencer, and her husband Neville, and Kathleen Dewar of the whisky dynasty.

McIndoe was supported by Welfare Officer Edward Blacksell who had been a pre-war schoolmaster in Devon, and by a happy accident of military bureaucracy had been sent as a Physical Training Instructor to almost the only hospital unit in the country where the need for PT classes did not exist. His wise counsel made Blacksell an invaluable Welfare Officer for McIndoe, and the two men became good friends.

When Archie was puzzled that the take up for tea in Sussex country houses was slow, it was Blacksell who explained the problem, 'what happens after they have had a couple of cups of tea or a few beers, 'he said, 'They want to get rid of it and they're shy. With their injured hands they can't do it themselves. And they can hardly say to some respectable dowager, "Please, Missus, will you come into the lavatory with me and undo my flies?" What we need is something easier to undo than those damned buttons.' McIndoe and Blacksell were problem solvers. Blacksell had read about an invention in the USA called zip-fasteners. Immediately, McIndoe implored all his American friends at the Mayo Clinic to help. Soon after, the post in East Grinstead was awash with enough zips to fit all the trousers at the hospital.

Blacksell realised that he was of more value as a welfare officer than teaching physical training. He was often in the front line when patients suffered from despair, 'I know of no way of minimising that terrible despair that comes when a patient say, at three o'clock in the morning, when nothing has gone right and his graft has sloughed off, when he feels he has no more skin left to be grafted, when his girlfriend has left him, when he's made a hash of something and he sees no future in front of him and he's alone in bed, other than by just happening to be around. I remember saying to one Guinea Pig if he wanted to end it all, if he really wanted to do that, then I'd not stop him. He's still alive today.'[87]

Archie McIndoe's policy of speaking plainly to his 'boys' did not waiver as the war progressed. Flight Sergeant Alan Morgan had severely frost-bitten hands after passing out at altitude and wearing no gloves. After weeks spent trying to repair his 'little sticks of black' McIndoe sat on his bed and said, '"Right Alan. We'll have to take them off. You're due for the chop." He said it in a joking manner, but I knew he was serious. And I also knew he would do something good for me…I knew he'd make the best of a bad job, which he did.' McIndoe removed all Morgan's fingers but by rescuing his thumbs McIndoe ensured that Morgan could still have some grip.

Not every patient and their family were in awe of McIndoe's God-like status. Before he arrived at East Grinstead, Terry Hunt acted as a personal nurse to her husband of just nine weeks. The day after his first operation under McIndoe, 'I rang the hospital and found they had bandaged his eyes. This was the fourth time he had been blinded with bandages, the fifth time he had been blind. It was getting beyond a joke! I took down some daffodils from the garden for him to have and feel and gave him lunch; and in the afternoon a kind lady came and sang, and the sun poured in through the open doors.'

On her way-out Terry Hunt bumped into 'McIndoe's right-hand woman', Sister Jill Mullins, 'she told me that it had been a beautiful operation; they had put a Wolfe graft from his mastoid on his nose, and taken the scars from his neck, and trimmed his eyelids. The bandages were there to stop the bleeding. She said they had noticed that pilots bled far more profusely than other people.'

To Terry, McIndoe was just another doctor. She did not accept 'doubtful' statements about pilots bleeding more. She was cautious

87    Peter Williams and Ted Harrison, *McIndoe's Army*, London, Pelham 1979

about McIndoe and his 'creations' and turned her back on the jollity of Ward Three. She retreated into her marriage but in some ways regretted that, 'I realised now that David and I had kept ourselves to ourselves and it was too late to do much about it.'

Graft by graft, procedure by procedure, Pilot Officer Geoffrey Page's face was taking on a new look. Bill Simpson in the next-door bed saw that Geoffrey Page was making progress, 'Geoffrey had been given a new eyebrow- a crescent shaped deep graft of skin and hair having been removed from the side of his head and sewn neatly into place to form an eyebrow, that already realistic, would eventually settle down so it was indistinguishable from normal.' Simpson also noticed that Page's hands were improving and that his fingers, which had been curled up into his palm, were beginning to straighten.

In 1942 the outside world invaded the cloistered club of the Queen Victoria Hospital. The life of burned Battle of Britain pilots attracted enormous public attention when Richard Hillary's famous memoir *The Last Enemy* was published. Glowing reviews poured in, as did donations to McIndoe's unit at East Grinstead. Richard Hillary was now a literary celebrity, but if he thought that would soften the attitude of the men in Ward Three, he was wrong. Geoffrey Page read the book in hospital and privately thought it was a brilliant story that deserved its success. But in Page's view, Hillary was already too arrogant to be given further encouragement. He wrote to the author, 'I think it is beautifully written, Richard. In fact I'm surprised that a supercilious bastard like you could produce something like this... However, there's one thing I don't quite understand...You write of being an irresponsible undergraduate before the war, then, as a result, you change, and, presto, here you are a different person...In my opinion, you are still as bloody conceited as ever.'[88] It was only after the

---

88    Sebastian Faulks, *The Fatal Englishman*, Hutchinson, London,2006

war that Page expressed his true feelings about Hillary's book 'He was streets ahead of us putting words down on paper. It was the best book that came out of the war.'

Chapter Thirteen

# Wives and Girlfriends

The biggest challenge for the golden boys of the RAF was how to navigate relationships with the opposite sex. Confidence with women had been as shattered as their hands and faces. One day they were handsome heroes of the RAF, the next they were swollen mounds of burned flesh, looking totally different in the eyes of their wife or prospective girlfriend. Edward Blacksell saw this anxiety up close, 'How were they going to cope? How were they going to work? To eat? How were they going to attract a pretty girl? How were they going to manage courtship, making love?'[89]

These anxieties were personal and private. One Guinea Pig wrote of his deep longing for real love but could not see how this desire could ever be fulfilled. For all their bravado many Guinea Pigs were nervous anywhere near a young woman and fraught with sexual anxieties. These emotional concerns were heightened by the frequency of rejection by wives and girlfriends. Edward Blacksell noted that, 'Women were apt to make awkward visitors to the ward. Some took one look and screamed...a few of them are married but often the wives can't take it and fiancées have a habit of fading away.'

One day the attractive young wife of the Guinea Pig in the bed next to Geoffrey Page came to visit. Page immediately noticed an expression of horror flash across her face as she saw the pulped mess

---

89  Peter Williams and Ted Harrison, *McIndoe's Army*, London, Pelham, 1979

of her husband. She literally could not look at him and averted her eyes away. On the bedside table Geoffrey Page noticed a photograph of the handsome man his fellow patient once had been. Now he was almost unrecognisable. 'That was it', remembered Geoffrey Page,' His wife had just taken one look at him and said I can't live with you the way you look. That is a devastating thing for a badly mutilated man to hear.' He added, 'She just couldn't take it. They were divorced. You couldn't blame her really. He was a different man from the one she had married. But it took him a long time to get over it.' WAAF Igraine Hamilton was nursing a patient who had lost a leg, 'His wife came in and said, 'You won't be able to dance again'. He said, 'No, I won't.' She said, 'Well, I'm not going to be married to somebody who can't dance, and she left. And that was the last he saw of her.'[90]

Before their crashes both Geoffrey Page and Richard Hillary were handsome and intelligent young men who had no difficulty attracting women. Now Richard Hillary was a ghoulish sight. When his parents visited, 'His arms and legs were wrapped in bandages, and the clawed hands were propped in front of his face. His eyes had been painted with gentian violet, while the rest of his face and his hands were coated with black tannic acid. To conceal the horror of the burns they had covered his face with white gauze, in which was cut a narrow slit for the lips. The handsome boy with his big eyes, his black hair and his mocking, slightly cruel smile now looked like a corpse awaiting burial.'[91]

Although some women abandoned the men they were married or engaged to, others accepted the dramatic changes in the man they loved and carried on. Terry Hunt described seeing her new husband David, a classic case of Hurricane Burns, in hospital for the first time, 'David was lying on the bed. The newness of his accident was the sen-

---

90    *Imperial War Museum Sound Archive*, London, 30 March 1995
91    Sebastian Faulks, *The Fatal Englishman*, Hutchinson, London,1996

sation in the room. He himself was something brand new, and very real. I saw him just for a moment, his face and arms purple with fresh dye and swollen. I thought he had no eyes; and I thought they had not told me that but had left me to find out quietly for myself; and, curiously, how wise they were. Behind all this was David. I saw then, as I cannot see now, how we should manage his blindness.'[92] Some other wives and girlfriends were equally understanding. When Tom Gleave's wife saw him for the first time after his terrible injuries she just said, 'I don't know! Playing with matches again.'

There was a small band of women who were used to crooked hands and pulped faces, the nurses in the Burns Unit. They dressed the wounds of these men, hoisted them onto bedpans and wiped their bottoms. More than anyone they saw the character of the men beneath their burns. Bill Foxley had no hands, just black stumps and he was almost blind because of a scorched cornea. In 1947 he married Catherine Arkell, who worked at the hospital. Nurses were able to set the looks of a future husband to one side. Joy Jones was a well-respected theatre nurse who also married a Guinea Pig, 'Faces were just horrible - even the man I would later marry. The injuries were horrific. By the time he called a halt to the treatment and said enough was enough, he had new eyelids, a new nose, and new lips... he had sixty operations.'[93]

Some Guinea Pigs were desperately anxious about sex, but by no means all of them. The young pilots were mainly in their early twenties, with all that meant in terms of sexual appetite. The precariousness of wartime lives lowered barriers. The man you had just met might not be here tomorrow so why delay sex, or marriage? Geoffrey Page was disturbed in the middle of one night by a strange banging

---

92    Esther Terry Wright, *Pilot Wife's Tale,* London, Bodley Head,1942
93    Ann Standen quoted in Norman Gelb, *Scramble,* Harcourt Brace Jovanovich,
      USA, 1985

noise. When he got up to investigate, he saw a theatre trolley in a cubicle. On the trolley lay a nurse and a patient entwined together. As they made love the trolley was crashing rhythmically from wall to wall in the cubicle, the banging against the side becoming ever more violent as the tempo increased. Apart from Page the rest of the ward slept angelically through the noise.

On occasion towards the end of the war, one of McIndoe's private patients would share space with the Guinea Pigs. One such patient was a well-known Swedish film starlet who was having work done on her legs. One night the nurse arrived at the beautiful young woman's private room on her rounds. To her horror the starlet was making love with a badly burned French airman. The nurse ran out of the room in embarrassment. Next day, McIndoe demanded an explanation from the Frenchman but was ultimately more upset by the result of their love making than questions of morality. The couple's nocturnal coupling had pulled all the stiches from the legs of the Swedish starlet, and they had to be resown.

Did Archie McIndoe go too far in his expectations of his nurses? McIndoe certainly hired pretty nurses, but they also needed to be sympathetic and hard working. Liz Byrski was brought up in East Grinstead and now teaches at Curtin University in Perth, Australia. She reflected on the pressures some of the young women felt. One 17-year-old called Joyce told Birski, 'I don't have happy memories of East Grinstead. I was so ignorant it would scare me…I'd not had any experience with men…You were being pushed into putting up with things you wouldn't out up with from anybody else, and they were really embarrassing and…well…not nice …it ought to be a choice, not expected and then you got made to feel stupid if you don't want to fool around.'[94]

---

94    Liz Byrski, *Love and War*, Fremantle Press, Western Australia, 2015

Looking back, Joyce realised that she was very young, and ignorant about basic sex education. Perhaps, she reflected, McIndoe had a point that fraternisation with attractive nurses was good for the wellbeing of the brave pilots in his care? She also noted that some female staff enjoyed themselves with the Guinea Pigs, 'there was quite a lot of sex went on - and it was always in the air.'

Another nurse, Bridget Warner, was older at twenty-one and even in her eighties remembers the concern of some of the young girls, 'I loved those boys. Some of the younger girls used to get a bit upset. But they were only boys after all, and they'd been through something terrible…they were always flirting, I'll admit to a few rendezvous in the linen cupboard myself, but it was only fun, and you went along with it. Things were different; we were all out for the war and for getting these boys better. I don't know why people make so much of it. You did your bit and then a bit more.'

Most of the young Guinea Pigs proudly declared that the VAD acronym for voluntary nurses stood for Virgins Absolutely Desperate or Voluntary After Dark. Controlling the sexual behaviour of the young men in the hospital was not easy, particularly as McIndoe himself expected so much of his nursing staff. He told Matron Hall, 'These men have had to put up with a hell of a lot, so surely you and your staff can put up with a little bit of their nonsense.' As Margaret Chadd, the Lady Almoner, pointed out 'it depended how you would interpret little and nonsense.'

Dr Emily Mayhew's grandmother Beryl Daintry was a married VAD nurse and older than some of the young recruits. Having worked in an amputee hospital in Sussex, Beryl was more capable of dealing with any 'nonsense' than some of the junior nurses. She was close to Richard Hillary, and liked Geoffrey Page. Talented nurses in McIndoe's unit were rapidly promoted and working at East Grinstead was an amazing experience, 'Every nurse I spoke said it was the greatest experience of her life.'[95] Other nurses just saw the best in McIndoe's young heroes, 'They were wonderful chaps. They had a great sense of humour. I loved them...they were all England's best, the Battle of Britain people.' Even in this boisterous crowd Geoffrey Page stood out for his 'enormous sense of humour.'[96]

Liz Byrski also met a nurse called Gladys who explained how easy it was for the lines of behaviour to become blurred at East Grinstead, 'if there wasn't another man around, you'd have to go to the gentlemen's lavatory and undo his buttons and you might have to...well hold it for him. Now, you can do very personal intimate things for them every day because it is part of your job. But if you cross the line and go out with them on a date then these things might seem like something different'.

Above all this presided the immense figure of Archie McIndoe. He was an intimidating man for a young nurse to encounter. He was so determined that the whole staff did everything possible to heal the confidence as well as the bodies of his young heroes that his manner could become overbearing. Gladys summed it up well, 'Boundaries. He - Mr McIndoe - dissolved them all, that was the problem, and so some women were coerced into things they didn't want to do. But it was probably what saved those young men's lives, made them want to live. It's an interesting moral dilemma, isn't it?'

Gladys was right. Not only had the war blurred boundaries of behaviour, but everything had been speeded up. One day boys were opening the batting for the school cricket team and the next they were flying a Spitfire. Death, sex, and marriage all happened much faster in wartime. Even the shyest patient realised over time that many women saw behind the mask of skin grafts and pedicles. McIndoe's daughter Vanora thought that looks were less important for women because

95    Dr Emily Mayhew. Author interview,26 January 2023
96    Helen McAlpine, *Imperial War Museum Sound Archive 30261*, London, 2007-9

'they were not worried about the wrapping but what was inside the box.' Even with burned face and hands like the Guinea Pigs 'you can laugh a woman into bed with no difficulty at all. And they did.' Some Guinea Pigs even thought that post-accident they were more intriguing to women than before. Australian Guinea Pig Freeman Strickland was amazed at his success, 'The ladies used to like us. I had a couple of pretty sizzling romances in East Grinstead, I'm proud to say.'

Archie McIndoe's believed that the obstacle for women was not the scarred faces of his 'boys'. The claws and stumps that passed for hands were a more significant deterrent to romance, 'Faces -women, bless them, don't seem to notice after a time. Mutilated hands - those are what you never stop noticing; when he lights a cigarette, when he tries to do up his flies, when he holds out his hand to be shaken.' One wife of a patient told welfare officer Edward Blacksell, 'I do love him, I'm sure I do, but there comes a moment when he touches me with those hands and I can't help it, I cringe.'

Hands were Geoffrey Page's problem. His oxygen mask had protected his face from the very worst burning and, although there was plenty of 'ploughed flesh' it was still possible to see the handsome features of the young man before his accident. Page's sister Daphne and her husband arranged a welcome out party for her brother. This was going to be a serious test of McIndoe's handiwork thus far, 'The dinner dance at Hatchetts in Piccadilly was a great success, despite my embarrassment at being stared at by other diners who considered I was some sort of freak masquerading in RAF uniform. On reflection they were probably right.' One of the other guests was a beautiful young girl who, to Geoffrey's surprise, ignored his ruined face, 'The preliminaries did not take long, and soon we were jumping into bed the way God made us.' However, anti-aircraft guns outside the girl's flat boomed and explosions burst as if the guns were in the next-door room. This was too much for Page, 'Such was my fright I could not raise an eyebrow let alone any other part of my anatomy. The girl tried her best to elevate my morale, but each time the gun went off my enthusiasm waned. She was not amused.'[97]

Despite this failure the enthusiasm of the girl gave him confidence. He soon took the next step forward. McIndoe's Theatre Sister Jill Mullins was a tall, elegant woman with a delightful sense of humour. McIndoe relied hugely on her skill, and operating without Jill was 'hell' for McIndoe, he said. She would make McIndoe's 'boys' hearts flutter if she stroked their hair before surgery. If his patients saw McIndoe as God, then Jill Mullins was clearly the leading angel. Half of Ward Three were crazy about Jill and Geoffrey Page was no exception. He found himself falling in love with the beautiful green-eyed Sister. To his surprise and delight his affection was reciprocated, despite his horrific injuries. Their two-year love affair was a crucial platform in Page's recovery but there is almost nothing in his autobiography or elsewhere on record about this relationship.

In his own book Page merely writes, 'we had two years of great happiness together until I departed to fly to North Africa after leaving hospital. Jill Mullins was an attractive tall woman with corn-coloured hair. Her hair, combined with large green eyes and infectious laugh, made her a great favourite with the aircrew patients.' His notes added, 'Much of the time was spent with Jill and Archie at his cosy cottage or she and I would seek the bright lights of London to dine and dance alone.' In 1942 Bill Simpson noted that 'Geoffrey Page was engaged' but Page himself makes no mention of this.

Love, marriage, and sex, not necessarily in that order, were uppermost in the minds of the men in Ward Three. After that, their main anxiety was fitting back into the world of work. Some thought they could fly again; others knew they never would. As Welfare Officer,

---

97    Geoffrey Page, *Tale of a Guinea Pig*, Pelham, London, 1981

Edward Blacksell had the tricky task of resettling the Guinea Pigs into work. He soon discovered that the world outside East Grinstead was unprepared for the appearance of McIndoe's boys. When Blacksell escorted a Guinea Pig to buy an engagement ring the shop assistant fainted as soon as she saw the man's hands. One firm generously offered several jobs as liftmen, but Blacksell foresaw a problem, 'How can you ask a Squadron Leader to become a liftman?' A famous London store expressed an interest in placing East Grinstead patients in proper employment, 'But once they'd met one of the Guinea Pigs, they contacted us and said, "We'd love to help. But could you arrange for the men to wear some kind of mask."'

Other well-meaning supporters offered places to work and live on a farm in Cornwall, as far away from society as possible. These good Samaritans believed they were helping 'disfigured ex-Servicemen, many of whom find it difficult to mix with their fellow men owing to their grave disfigurement.' This was the complete opposite to Archie McIndoe's philosophy, and he replied to the offer bluntly, 'These boys are not lepers. They do not suffer from contagious diseases. They are learning to live normally. You may be interested to know that some of my most badly injured are already married to the prettiest wives, and quite a few have offspring on the way.'

Nor were the traditional approaches to occupational therapy of much value to the high-spirited young men at East Grinstead. For a burned Spitfire pilot embroidery or basket-weaving held no appeal. McIndoe's willingness to innovate, allied to his powers of persuasion, were useful once more. A firm of aircraft manufacturers called Reid and Sigrist set up a small unit in the grounds of the hospital with a handful of their staff supervising the patients. The Guinea Pigs turned out to be well motivated and highly productive. It was, one patient noted, 'the real thing'. This was most probably the first time such a factory had been set up within a hospital.

This novel approach was in sharp contrast to attitudes after World War One. His mentor Harold Gillies had no doubt told McIndoe of the difficulties twenty years earlier 'former patients struggled to re-integrate into society and many became isolated due to their physical appearances. Many ended up in menial jobs, one even in a travelling circus, labelled *the elephant man*. Depression was very common and sometimes suicide.'[98]

That fate was not going to befall Archie McIndoe's patients. He drummed up jobs for them when they left the hospital, battled constantly with the encircling red tape of bureaucracy, and was determined that they should all receive their full pensions. He even threatened a wheelchair and crutches march on Whitehall if East Grinstead didn't get the medical equipment the hospital desperately needed.

McIndoe was especially angered by the ninety-day rule. This laid down that a man who did not return to RAF duty after ninety days would be invalided out of the service with a limited disability pension. Archie McIndoe knew that many of the pilots in his care, like Geoffrey Page, would take years to be repaired, let alone ninety days. Page was horrified by the prospect of being invalided out of the RAF before he could fly again. Archie McIndoe waged war on this flint-hearted rule. None of my Guinea Pigs deserve to live on pensions made up of crumbs, he thought. Eventually the ninety-day rule slid quietly into disuse.

This did not signal the end of McIndoe's jousts with the Ministry of Pensions. Their decisions on disability pensions for McIndoe's patients were often arbitrary, regularly ignoring medical advice, including McIndoe's own recommendations. Supported by Edward Blacksell and the anaesthetist Russell Davies, who doubled as a welfare officer, McIndoe did not leave a stone unturned, a string unpulled, in his

---

98    Macnamara and Metcalfe, *Sir Archibald McIndoe and the Guinea Pig Club,*
      Medical Biography, 2013

struggle for justice. If a decision was not fair, he appealed, and in the first thirty-two appeals, his patients won thirty-one of them.

This was all part of McIndoe contradictory character. He was interested in money, yet often gave his service free for those with no resources. He was kind and humane, working hard for Guinea Pig welfare, but faced with stupidity or sloth he could become very angry. The Guinea Pigs treated Archie as a god, but he was as flawed as the next man. At the time, Bill Simpson summed McIndoe up, 'He is no angel, far from it; but he's a man you continue to like and respect after you have learned his faults...only we ourselves know what he has done for us.'

McIndoe's patients understood that life beyond the safe cloistered world of the hospital would be troubling. They also understood the value of self-help. On a bright Sunday in July 1941 with the midday sun streaming through the hospital windows highlighting the bottles of sherry on the table, Geoffrey Page became a founder member of what was eventually called the Guinea Pig Club. Membership was open to all aircrew who had been through the hospital at East Grinstead and needed the skill of the maxillofacial surgeons working there. McIndoe himself was elected vice president and was eligible for membership as *Chief Scientist* or *The Maestro*. According to the first issue of the Guinea Pig magazine in 1944 a further membership category was the *'Society for the Prevention of Cruelty to Guinea Pigs'*, that is those who took *Great Interest in Guinea Pigs*.

The members were boiled, mashed, or fried; boiled being that you were very lightly burnt; mashed being gunshot or other wounds which required plastic surgery; fried being that you were badly burnt. Geoffrey Page and the rest of Ward Three were most definitely in the fried category. The name Guinea Pig was eventually chosen because McIndoe's patients knew that was exactly what they were. The wife of one patient, John Hughes, was an artist and she drew a guinea pig on her husband's chest before surgery as a reminder to McIndoe and his team of the experimental nature of their work.

*Guinea Pig Club early meeting. Geoffrey Page in wheelchair. Archibald McIndoe far right. Courtesy: West Sussex Record Office*

The first meeting was an excuse to drink the sherry, and its primary purpose was as a drinking or grogging club. In true Guinea Pig spirit, the first treasurer, Peter Weeks, was elected because he was confined to a wheelchair, so he could not run away with the funds. Club Secretary Bill Towers Perkins had no workable hands and so couldn't write the minutes. Subscriptions were two shillings a year. The original name, the Maxillonian Club, recognised the maxillofacial surgery they had all experienced. It was, said, one Guinea Pig, 'more exclusive than Boodles, Bucks, Whites, and the Royal Yacht squadron, rolled into one.' Geoffrey Page called it, 'the club nobody wants to join'. Page blamed the birth of this grogging club on 'some bright clot who hadn't the sense to see beyond the end of his nose; he couldn't anyhow because he had a rhinoplasty.' McIndoe himself later wrote that, 'It has been described as the most exclusive club in the world, but the entrance fee is something most men would not care to pay, and the conditions of membership are arduous in the extreme.'

Geoffrey Page was a prime mover in developing the Club's welfare ethos. At the Club's second meeting he suggested that it needed to be more than just a drinking club. If the world beyond the hospital gates was hostile, the Guinea Pig Club should be there to offer mutual support. So the Club started a welfare fund, the 'Fire Brigade' they called it, with a smile on their burnt faces. Eventually, the RAF Benevolent Fund also supported the Guinea Pigs financially. Grants were offered to help Guinea Pigs resettle in the civilian world or to soften the hardship that was inevitable for those whose injuries were too bad for them to work. To many Guinea Pigs acquiring an ordinary, even boring, job equalled success.

As Tom Gleave, another founding member of the Guinea Pig Club, put it, 'No Guinea Pig shall ever be selling matches from a tray on the street corner. We would move heaven and earth if we ever found it happening. In fact, the biggest single achievement of the Guinea Pig Club is to have helped every member to save his face. His *other* face, that is, in a psychological sense, so that he could securely take his place once more in society.'

Despite this emphasis on welfare the Guinea Pig Club kept its formidable sense of irreverence. In their magazine Guinea Pigs were described as 'A rodent of the rat family that frequents beds and public houses. Once possessed a tail until a Hun got on it. These little rodents are widely kept as pets and are useful to medical science for vivisection. They also have a high rate of reproduction which makes them valuable in the study of heredity.' A 1946 feature on Edward Blacksell was headlined *Saving our Bacon: Blackie tells what happens to Cured Pig*. Housing was a major post-war challenge for McIndoe's patients and the July 1947 edition of the magazine noted, 'We have no means of making the Government put up more houses, but we have been able to encourage the local authorities to smile with favour upon Pigs in dire need of Sties.'

Bill Simpson described the early Guinea Pig reunions, 'One saw new eyebrows and ears; jaws and chins; lips and cheeks; legs that had been restored by graft, and hands that had recovered their usefulness. Each one a miracle himself was surrounded by similar miracles of surgical skill.'

The Guinea Pigs composed an anthem which was belted out enthusiastically at reunions. The first verse, sung to the tune of *Church's One Foundation*, goes: -

> *We are McIndoe's Army*
> *We are his Guinea Pigs*
> *With dermatomes and pedicles,*
> *Glass eyes, false teeth, and wigs*
> *And when we get our discharge*
> *We'll shout with all our might:*
> *'Per ardua ad astra'*
> *We'd rather drink than fight.*

Chapter Fourteen

# Return to Flying

After his eleventh operation, Geoffrey Page plucked up the courage to ask Archie McIndoe the crucial question that had been bothering him ever since he had been shot down, 'How long do you think it will be before I can return to flying?' McIndoe was typically straightforward in reply, 'You can forget about flying. You've done your stuff, now the other silly sods can get on with it.' Page understood how deeply McIndoe was affected by the death and injuries sustained by the young pilots, but he was not taking a negative answer, even from a man he respected as much as Archie. To Page, flying was like a highly addictive drug he could never be free from, 'There was nothing heroic about it. This was not about king and country. I just loved flying so much I couldn't see a future without it. I never thought of doing anything else. I just had to go on.'[99]

In April 1942 he chewed the situation over with Richard Hillary who had just finished writing his classic book *The Last Enemy*. Hillary was equally determined to fly again, and the two men had an impassioned discussion about which aircraft was easiest to fly with ruined hands. They were both tough characters and could act as a mutual support team. Hillary and Page decided to jointly harass McIndoe into supporting their return to operational duty.

99   Geoffrey Page, Author interview, Henley-on-Thames, 1984

Archie McIndoe was clear to both his young pilots, 'You haven't a hope in hell of getting back…not only do I not approve it. The Air Force won't let it happen.' In his minute-book he wrote about Page, 'The bloody fool wants to fly again. He'll never be able to do it, of course, but fancy thinking of it after all he's been through.' A despairing Geoffrey Page sought consolation from Jill Mullins. Jill looked at him sympathetically and put her hand tenderly on his arm. She explained that Archie was not being obstructive; he just believed that these two badly burned men had already done their bit for Britain. It was someone else's turn now. This interpretation was more encouraging than McIndoe's blunt 'no 'and offered Page renewed hope that he might fly again after all. His campaign started again with fresh vigour and after several weeks McIndoe finally gave in to Page and Hillary. He threw his hands up in disgust and said, 'If you're determined to kill yourselves, go ahead. Only don't blame me.' Then he sat down and wrote out medical certificates for the two young men.

The four weeks from early April 1942 were a flurry of grafts and procedures, as McIndoe tried to get his patient in as good shape as possible before was discharged. His middle and ring fingers were straightened. A scar on his eyelid was excised by the insertion of a large graft of skin from his upper right arm. His hand received a graft from his right thigh and both his middle and little finger were also grafted. The pre-discharge medical notes illustrate the physical challenges Page still had to face.

Three weeks before he left Ward Three it was recorded that 'he had considerable pain' in his index finger which, 'after removal of scar tissue was found to be scarred right down to the bone.' and 'grafts were taken down and found to have failed…evidence of pus underneath the graft…' It wasn't just his hands that were agonising. On 13 April it was reported that he was suffering with, 'much pain in the right eye since coming round from the anaesthetic'. The following day he was 'still complaining of pain sometimes sharp, other times bruising, in the centre of the eye.' Just a few weeks later, on 23 May 1942, a week after his twenty-second birthday, Pilot Officer Page was discharged from East Grinstead. McIndoe wrote to the RAF Medical Board, 'He is now practically finished as far as I can fix things. I know he is very anxious to fly...' Despite Geoffrey's physical shortcomings, McIndoe added, 'Psychologically he seems 100% for this.'

Now Geoffrey faced a much more difficult obstacle than McIndoe's sympathetic reluctance. He was dispatched to the Central Medical Establishment on the second floor of a rather nondescript building at the Middlesex Hospital, tucked away behind Oxford Street in London. As he looked round the large waiting room bursting with young men in RAF uniform, Geoffrey Page thought how out of place they looked. All of them would have been more at home in a world of green grassy runways and wooden dispersal huts. He eventually found himself sitting across the table from an adjutant, 'Third-degree burns, hands, face, and legs; gunshot wound left leg. You should get your bowler hat without any trouble.' Page replied firmly, 'I've come here to fly, not to be invalided out.' The unsympathetic adjutant was unimpressed, 'You haven't got a chance.' To Page, this was the RAF machine at its worst, a self-serving bureaucracy safeguarding themselves rather than helping their pilots or the war effort.

Geoffrey Page's heart was now firmly in his boots. He next endured several routine medical examinations, before being told to return after lunch. In a next-door pub, the pitying glances of the two barmaids were an unhappy reminder of what he now looked like. In East Grinstead the locals had long ago stopped staring at Guinea Pigs, but Page realised he looked grotesque to the rest of the pub's customers. He swiftly escaped, leaving his lunchtime sandwich virtually untouched.

Back at the Middlesex he was finally ushered into the President of the Medical Board's office. This man was more sympathetic, 'Apart from your injuries, you seem fit enough Page. What would you like us to do; invalid you out or give you a limited category, fit for ground duties in the UK only?' Page's heart sank once more. Ground duties? He steeled himself and turned to the Air Commodore across the desk. Emphatically he told the man that he wanted to fly, and even lied about having recent flying experience in a friend's plane.

The Air Commodore knew that Flying Officer Page was not telling the truth but, appreciating his determination, he asked Page to grip his hands. Fortunately, the hard work endlessly squeezing a rubber squash ball paid off. As he gripped the older man's hand, Geoffrey summoned up an almost superhuman strength, 'More strength in those hands than I could imagine possible'. There was a silence, interrupted only by the scratching of his fountain pen as he wrote. Finally, he broke the silence, 'I am passing you fit for non-operational single engine aircraft only. At the end of three months, and, if you've coped all right, we'll give you an operational category.'

As the words, 'Good luck, don't let me down', echoed in his ears, Geoff Page waltzed down the street with tears of joy cascading down his damaged face. He saw two elderly women staring at him with pity. One of them said, 'Poor boy. He must have heard some bad news - so young too!'

To add to his joy Geoffrey was given a week's leave. McIndoe never dwelt further on his view that his young protégé should not fly again and several jolly evenings with Archie, John Hunter, Bill Gardiner from the Whitehall and, of course, Jill Mullins, followed. While Jill and Geoffrey were away for a night on the town in London, McIndoe was disturbed at home after a long day in surgery by six young men in cycling gear who asked for a glass of water. Typical of McIndoe, he ascertained that the men were hungry and cooked them all eggs and bacon washed down with beer. It was obvious that the young cyclists had mistaken him for a household servant, not one of the most famous surgeons in the country. He was amused that when the men eventually left, he discovered a generous tip for the 'manservant' under a plate.

Page's initial posting was to an Anti-Aircraft Co-operation Unit housed at a grass airfield on the outskirts of Cardiff. By now it was 12 June 1942, almost two years since he had been so badly burned. To Page the AACU was a dull place, where pilots spent their time flying Lysanders and Masters along pre-arranged routes to train anti-aircraft personnel. It was as different from the dramas of the Battle of Britain as was possible in the RAF. The atmosphere in the Unit was one of discontentment, infected both by boredom and the self-importance of the Station Commander who had little interest in flying. The next three months might be dull, but Geoffrey Page was fully focused on taking these baby steps. He was delighted to be out of hospital after two long years and hopefully on the pathway back to combat flying, but inside he was deeply anxious. He asked himself a simple question; after so long, and with so many crippling injuries, will I be able to fly again?

His second day in Cardiff brought the crucial test both physically and psychologically; Page's first flight since that horrific crash. He was to go up in a dual control Master with another pilot as his instructor, before being allowed to fly solo. He slept poorly, dreaming intermittently of aircraft turning into fireballs. He could not face breakfast and nervously checked his parachute several times. His hands were shaking as he struggled into specially made gloves with long zippers down the side which enabled his bent fingers to work into place.

His co-pilot, Flying Officer Constant, offered genial words of reassurance. Any mention of orders from the Station Commander was met with words of derision, 'That bastard couldn't order a one-course lunch,' said the jovial instructor. Page's brain was too scrambled, his nerves too shredded, to take all this in. Beneath his oxygen mask Page was bathed in sweat. He could sense a note of anxiety in his co-pilot's voice. Could he call the flight off now? What would his excuse be? He could see the ground crew watching with interest. As he started to prime the engine, working the pump nine times, he was in significant pain, feeling faint, and still sweating profusely. Yet, settled in the cockpit, his confidence magically returned. Robotically he pushed the throttle forward. By nothing other than instinct he moved his hands and feet in the correct manner. He belted up the runway and lifted the little yellow gull-winged plane gently into the air. The wheels retracted neatly, and the ground below slipped away.

For a moment he relaxed but as he looked down his mind drifted back to his crash. He saw himself bailing out, the flames burning his flesh before he crashed into the ground, a charred corpse. At that moment the instructor's voice cut sharply through his grisly memories. The fear had not evaporated but at least it was under control. After three circuits his instructor cheerfully told him it was time to fly solo.

The next three months were filled with days of unexciting exercises but at least he was back flying. Like other Guinea Pigs, Geoffrey carried a special card with him inscribed 'In case of further trouble, deliver the bits to Ward Three, East Grinstead.' On 13 August 1942, exactly two years and one day since his terrible crash the Commanding Officer in Cardiff reported that he had flown 'about 50 hours without any trouble...has shown himself to be a very capable pilot.' The RAF Medical Board confirmed that a delighted Pilot Officer Geoffrey Page was granted an operational flying category. He asked to return to a fighter squadron but, before going anywhere, Geoffrey Page returned to East Grinstead for more surgical procedures. McIndoe gave him further grafts on his left hand with skin taken from his abdomen and excised a keloid scar on the right side of his face. Archie also inserted a new right eyebrow by grafting skin and hair from one side of his head in the shape of a crescent.

After a month in the hospital in East Grinstead, Page was posted to 132(Bombay) Squadron at Martlesham Heath in Suffolk on 12 October 1942 as a supernumerary flight lieutenant. He was thrilled to discover he would be flying Spitfires once again, 'the beautiful little fighter'. RAF Martlesham Heath had been a Battle of Britain station in 1940 but was now a centre for routine convoy patrols. This was un-exciting compared to the summer of 1940, but Geoffrey Page was just thrilled to finally be back in the cockpit of a fighter aircraft. Through the autumn of 1942 Page flew his Spitfire on a daily round of East Coast convoy patrols interspersed with gun or formation practice.

Even the routine was dangerous in the grey days of an English winter, especially if there was any hint of cockpit rustiness. Although plans for a German invasion had passed, the RAF still needed to en-sure that Britain's back door stayed firmly locked. The creeks and small harbours of Norfolk and Suffolk were attractive landing areas for any Germans on a recce. On one patrol he flew low at 500 feet over the North Sea, 'Grey sea and grey sky merged to form a canvas on which no horizon or ships appeared. Then the germ of fear began to grow and grow. Was I climbing or was I diving, in a turn, or flying straight?....I could feel the perspiration trickling down my neck from under the oxygen mask. More and more wildly I began a desperate rhythm firstly checking my instruments, then looking out at the bleak seascape, and then back to the instruments. I trusted neither my vi-sion nor the reliable facts the rows of little dials were telling me. I was bewildered and terrified. Knowing that my life expectancy was limit-ed to mere seconds if I didn't get a grip on myself, I forced my mind to stay glued on the faithful instruments until the period of stark panic had passed. Without doubt if I had relied on my senses, I would have crashed into the sea a few feet below.'

Despite this close shave, he was reassured that flying Spitfires was as delightful as before. But Geoffrey Page ached for more. He needed to prove to himself and everyone else that he could still be the combat fighter pilot he had been in 1940. He thought jealously of the pilots based further south, the men flying from Manston and Hawkinge, Tangmere, and Biggin Hill. Inside he felt his hate-filled revenge bubbling relentlessly away. Geoffrey wanted the Germans to pay the full price for his pain, one would be killed for every visit to the slab.

Page conjured up plans to lead an attack on a German army camp just over the channel. To his surprise the squadron commander agreed. The plan on 26 November was for three Spitfires to fly at low altitude and to hit the camp at breakfast time when the enemy was busy eating their German sausages. Their tactics were to fly over the coast and then head inland so that the camp would be hit from the direction they least expected.

As the Spitfires sped just above the waves in tight formation, Geoffrey Page knew that if he was hit by the formidable German flak batteries, he would have no chance. He was flying so low there would be no possibility of survival on the end of a parachute this time. The sweat of fear trickled down his face. His anxiety was not helped by his failure to see any of the landmarks or contours he had endlessly studied on the map and special photographs. As the sea disappeared behind him Page knew that he had missed his landfall.

To his dismay, there was no sign of an army encampment, but he spotted a barge puffing away on a canal. Barges were approved targets and so Page flicked his gun into the firing position and his 20mm cannon shells ricocheted into the vessel's wooden hull. His two fellow Spitfire pilots followed their leader northwards up the canal until they spotted several more barges loading up with grain. They swooped into action and the three aircraft blew holes in the sides of the vessels. They followed the railway line north and smashed the boiler of a railway engine. On the edge of a town, they saw a station and fired their ammunition into a second railway engine.

Geoffrey Page now had his bearings. This was Dunkirk, the same Dunkirk he had flown over back in 1940. Dunkirk was a town to be avoided because it was defended by a necklace of anti-aircraft guns. Page nervously gave his machine maximum power and headed low over the harbour wall towards safety. His concern was not imaginary. The sky was swiftly lit up by shells from the shore guns, as the three Spitfires danced their way through the danger. Mercifully, they were soon out of range of the enemy guns, and Geoffrey was safe. He was trembling but elated. He had completely failed to find the target of the army camp, but he had made a minor dent in the German transportation system. Two weeks later he discovered why he had completely missed the intended target. The long stiletto knife he carried in his boot possessed high magnetic qualities and had affected the aircraft compass. The result was that Page had crossed the coast south of Dunkirk rather than several miles to the north.

The heady excitement of his day trip to Dunkirk was still not satisfying enough for Geoffrey Page. Soon after, he applied for a posting to North Africa where he hoped to have more opportunity to strike back at the enemy. In February 1943 he was appointed as Commanding Officer at the Gibraltar Defence Flight. His departure to North Africa also signalled the end of his long love affair with Jill Mullins. Once again, in his autobiography he says almost nothing about the details of the break-up, 'Jill Mullins and I admitted to each other that the spark had gone out of our romance, and we agreed to remain firm friends, which we did until the last time I saw her.' He added in his unpublished notes, 'The breaking-up of a love affair is

not the happiest of things and I was shy of starting anything new because of the state of my hands and face.'

It was not as simple as that. Archie McIndoe had to use all his
empathy to nurse Jill through the break-up of what was clearly a
significant relationship. Nor did Geoffrey's anxiety about his appearance last long during his final leave before heading for Africa, 'To
my incredible surprise I found that female opposition to my wounds
was not what I thought it would be. Instead, my week's leave was
spent in sleepless nights in the happiest sense. My morale was at an
all-time high.'

Geoffrey's sea journey from Scotland to Gibraltar started inaus-
piciously. In the early hours of the morning, he heard a tremendous
crash. His mind inevitably slipped back to the summer of 1940. Page
and the rest of the RAF pilots on board were quick to put on their
life jackets and find a place of safety. Was this a torpedo attack? They
were half amused and half relieved to learn that even before their ship
had left Greenock near Glasgow she had collided with another vessel
in the convoy.

His posting to Gibraltar as Officer Commanding, Gibraltar
Defence Flight, was not the switch into active combat that he hun-
gered for. In February and March 1943, he flew patrols across the
water in North Africa, but action was limited. In addition, Geoffrey
had not reckoned with the burning African sun. The searing heat gave
him huge pain on his newly grafted skin and his scars were agony. On
2 April 1943 a specialist reported that 'this officer should be boarded
home. These grafted hands, with their skin, become very sensitive in
hot weather.'

Two days later the Medical Board in Gibraltar concurred, 'With
the advent of hot weather he has experienced a burning pain over
grafted areas of his hands and, to a lesser extent, in scars on the face…
these symptoms are becoming more aggravated as the weather be-

comes warmer...this officer is unsuitable for further service in hot climates.' This torture by sun gave him a jaundiced view of North Africa. The pyramids, he noted witheringly, 'stank of piss'. After three months he reluctantly requested a posting back to Britain which was granted on medical grounds. Page was pleased to be heading home and away from the sun, but disappointed by the recommendation of the Medical Board back in London that 'he was not fit for operational flying but is fit for non-operational flying in a temperate climate. His case to be reviewed in six months' time.'

Chapter Fifteen

# Mustang

Geoffrey Page was deflated by his miserable experience in North Africa and on returning to England was posted to a non-operational role in the Air Fighting Development Unit at Wittering in Sussex. His role was to assess all types of fighter aircraft, including captured enemy machines. Although he was pleased to at last escape the brutal North African sun, Page was unhappy with a non-operational flying role. As a result, he formed an alliance with another pilot who was equally desperate for action. Squadron Leader James MacLachlan's left arm had been shot off in the Battle of Malta. At least Page still had both hands, although they were painful, and one of them was ineffective. The two pilots laughed that between them they only had one hand that functioned fully.

Cheshire-born James MacLachlan had experienced an extraordinary war even before he met Geoffrey Page. As a twenty-year-old he flew a Fairey Battle with 88 Squadron over France in 1940. The Battle was no match for the modern German aircraft and Mac lost several colleagues in quick succession. He wrote, 'I want to have a crack at the Germans instead of sitting in a Battle and being shot to pieces.' Despite his obsolete aircraft, Mac damaged two enemy planes in France and was awarded the Distinguished Flying Cross (DFC). He went on to fly several sorties in the Battle of Britain and he is recorded as 'probably' having shot down a Heinkel 111 on 7 October 1940.

Malta was a vitally important strategic island for the war in the Mediterranean and North Africa. While Geoffrey Page was still in hospital being treated for his terrible burns, Mac was posted with a squadron of Hurricanes and two Skuas to reinforce Malta. They immediately found themselves in the middle of a self-inflicted disaster. The pilots took off from HMS *Argus* for Malta, but ten Hurricanes ran out of fuel and crashed into the sea like birds hit by stones. A Skua also crash landed having been hit by German flak. As many pilots had been killed in just one morning as some squadrons had lost in the entire Battle of Britain. The most likely explanation for this catastrophe was that there had been serious miscalculation by the Navy of the amount of fuel needed to reach Malta in strong headwinds.

MacLachlan was one of just three lucky pilots who made it to safety. He landed with just four gallons of fuel to spare. In the following months Mac was at the centre of the intense fight for Malta and served with courage and distinction. He was awarded a bar to his DFC on 11 February 1941 having destroyed two enemy aircraft in one day. The citation in the London Gazette praised his 'courage, initiative, and leadership'.

Just five days after this award, on 16 February 1941, Mac was in combat with Messerschmitt 109s over Malta. An off-duty pilot, Sergeant Jim Pickering was on the balcony of his flat in Valetta when he saw a Hurricane being chased over the city by an Me109. The German was only about fifty yards behind Mac when Sgt Pickering saw him shoot. Cannon fire smashed into Mac's cockpit and engine.

Mac described this shooting in his diary, 'Suddenly there was a crash in my cockpit - bits and pieces seemed to fly everywhere... my left arm was dripping with blood and when I tried to raise it only the top part moved, the rest hung limply by my side...I remember opening my hood. Disconnecting my oxygen and R/T connections and standing up in the cockpit. The next thing I saw was my kite diving away from me, the roar of its engine gently fading as it plunged earthwards....my arm was beginning to hurt pretty badly so I decided to pull my chute straightaway in case I fainted from loss of blood.'[100]

Mac could not find the ripcord and presumed that his parachute had been pulled off in his hurried exit from his Hurricane. He reconciled himself to a quick death. At least then my arm will stop hurting, he reasoned. Then he thought of his mother reading a telegram announcing her son's death. He made one more attempt to see if the parachute was intact. To his amazement it was, and he pulled the ripcord, 'There was a sickening lurch as my chute opened and my harness tightened around me so that I could hardly breathe. I felt horribly ill and faint. Blood from my arm came streaming back into my face, in spite of the fact that I was holding it as tightly as I could. I could only breathe with difficulty and my arm hurt like hell...I hit the ground with a terrific thud, rolled over once or twice, and then lay back intending to die quietly.'

Mac was carried by army stretcher bearers for half-a-mile across the fields to an ambulance. Then he was driven to a local field-dressing station where his arm was put in a splint, he was injected with morphia, and given a large swig of whisky. It was quickly clear to the doctors that Mac's arm could not be saved but he was so determined to fly again it was three days before Mac admitted the doctors were right, 'I began to realise there was no hope of saving my arm. The blood circulation was all right, but my finger movement was scarcely visible, and I could hardly feel anything in my hand. My whole arm began to smell positively revolting...I was terrified that without it, I should never be able to fly again.' Soon after, the young pilot finally relented, and his arm was amputated below the elbow.

---

100   Brian Cull and Roland Symons, *One-Armed Mac*, London, Grub Street, 2003

Mac persuaded Queen Mary's Hospital in Roehampton to design an artificial limb that might make it possible for him to fly a fighter aircraft again. After hours of careful calculation, they produced a metal arm with four spring-loaded pins like fingers which enabled him to work the controls on one side of the plane. His left arm was then clamped to the throttle and other levers. He said at the time, 'And now they're building me a special flying hand. When I get that, I shall feel like a kid with his first pair of long pants.'

By the summer 1942, not long after his twenty-third birthday, Mac had become an expert at night intruder operations. These dangerous missions required him to hover in the darkness near enemy airfields and pounce on German bombers as soon as they entered their landing pattern. Mac reaped havoc on the enemy, but he eventually needed respite from the intense risks of night flying and was posted to Wittering. When Mac and Geoffrey met in the mess, they looked a very strange couple. The Flight Lieutenant, medium height and trim with a scarred face and gnarled, damaged hands like bird's claws, and the Squadron Leader, over six-foot tall, blonde, slender, with a sharply pointed nose and what one colleague called 'an obstinate expression' topped off by his specially designed metal arm.

Mac was already an RAF legend and Page was on his way to becoming one. They discovered much in common; an utter determination to be back in action as soon as possible and a risk-taking spirit. He also shared with Geoffrey a deep hatred of the Germans. Andre Jubelin was in 1 Squadron, RAF, 'I am not surprised at Mac's hatred of them. It dated from the time when his arm had been smashed by the enemy's fire. He was the gentlest of men. But he had an account to settle. It was the price of his lost arm.'

A non-operational unit did not offer much excitement to a man like Mac, a feeling that Geoffrey Page instantly reciprocated. Spirits lifted when one of the fighters down to test at Wittering was a North

American P-51 Mustang, equipped with the latest Allison V-1710 engines and armed with two 20mm cannon in each wing. The Mustang was believed to be the fastest low-level fighter in existence, although Page thought it was probably too heavy.

The irrepressible MacLachlan cooked up a plan for low-flying solo raids on enemy airfields in France. He practised low-flying diligently and had his Mustang camouflaged to blend in with the green fields of France. But his initial solo operation had to be aborted when he was spotted by German fighters as he crossed the French coast. Hearing the story, Page approached MacLachlan and they decided that next time they would try together, one Mustang protecting the other.

However, Page was doubtful that they could persuade the authorities to let two injured men try a risky low-level raid on enemy territory. He described his Commanding Officer as 'an efficient officer and able pilot, the C.O. lacked a spark of adventure in his soul and, worse still, poor man, had been deprived of a sense of humour since birth. He would without doubt view the latest project as a crackpot idea dreamt up by two mentally deficient cripples.'

Mac was more confident. He was a well-respected Squadron Leader, and he was not going to bother with an unimaginative C.O. and went direct to Fighter Command. Before Page knew it, a second Mustang arrived and was swiftly tested and camouflaged. Their targets would be the Luftwaffe night-fighter bases south of Paris. The plan was to fly at tree-top height and hit the unsuspecting night fighters while they were testing their aircraft in daylight. The month was June 1943.

The two men were labelled by some as crazy adventurers. How were they going to bring off this daunting task with so few workable hands between them? Page knew they were 'a fine bloody pair'. The flyers were risk takers, but they understood that even good pilots needed practice, especially for flying so low,' Hours of practice flying had to be devoted to split-second teamwork at zero feet. A standard had to be reached that each of us would know automatically how the other would react under different circumstances...after weeks of training and planning we had at last felt we were ready to undertake our unique task. It now remained for the right weather conditions to prevail over our route.'

Page and MacLachlan moved from Wittering to Lympne on the Kent coast to wait for the optimal moment to launch their attack. A full cloud layer at about three thousand feet but with otherwise good visibility with little wind would be perfect. Scudding over the tops of French trees was dangerous enough without flying into a gale. When the weather forecast looked ideal for the following day, Geoffrey Page tried to catch some rest. But he was too restless to sleep, too busy rehearsing for his daring role the next day, 29 June 1943. When he finally did drift to sleep, he was woken by vivid images of burning aircraft. He was inside his Hurricane being roasted alive.

As he waited for his Mustang to be prepared, Page drowned in fear. Could two such badly crippled pilots survive this mad escapade? Why had he been so keen on this suicide mission? What if he crashed in a burning wreck again? MacLachlan's cheerfulness and confidence helped dampen the fear temporarily. The two pilots - one with burned hands, the other with only one arm - must have been a bizarre sight as they clambered into their freshly camouflaged green Mustangs on the grass airstrip on the Kent coast.

The Mustangs, painted with RAF markings but no squadron identification, were accompanied by an escort of Typhoon fighter-bombers and Page's fear evaporated as he mechanically went through his preparatory routine before he finally eased his heavily laden plane into the air at the end of the small airfield. Then the two pilots dived down to just twenty feet above the tops of the waves. The Typhoon escort sat slightly above and alongside them. Once in the air, Page's old fears returned, 'If my aircraft got hit, would it burst into flames the same way my Hurricane had on that previous occasion? Fire! This time I would not be at fifteen thousand feet and with the opportunity to bail out. I would be roasted alive at this low altitude before I could ever crash land the burning plane. My imagination even recalled the smell of my own burning flesh after such a long passage of time.'

Flocks of seagulls forced him to forget his old fears and concentrate on his low flying. Page knew that a bird strike would be fatal. As they reached the enemy coast, Page was conscious of a dryness in his mouth and stickiness inside his shirt. He inwardly chided himself for being so fearful before he had even fired a bullet. He was reassured by the presence of MacLachlan alongside him, 'a magnificent man'. He only had one arm, but he was a superb pilot who skilfully threaded his way across the green fields and red rooftops of France. Mac flew with his artificial metal arm clamped onto the throttle. As a result, he did not have a spare hand for the radio and so communication was impossible. Mac had a map casually lying on his lap as if he was sitting in a car going for a spin in the Home Counties. He had to fly the Mustang at a very low level and turn the pages of the map with his one hand at the same time. The two RAF pilots calculated that the Luftwaffe would never imagine that the RAF had the range to attack so far south and that by flying so low they would avoid detection from enemy radar.

On they flew, scudding just above the rooftops of Beauvais and over the Seine. Despite Geoffrey Page's fears, all was quiet in the French skies. Flying underneath high-tension electric cables was the height of their excitement, but also an indication of how low the two men were flying their Mustangs. Then ahead and just above them they spotted three German aircraft. Page steeled himself, automatically going through the routine he knew so well from 1940.

The three slow-moving bombers were unprotected and a relatively easy prey, but the two pilots needed to attack fast before the skies were full of Luftwaffe fighters defending their brothers. Mac smashed through the silence with rapid gunfire. Page watched in fascination as one German aircraft burst into a mass of flames and steel before wheeling down gently to its grave in the woods below. After swiftly shooting down the two other enemy planes, the men headed happily home. Almost immediately they caught sight of another German aircraft. Mac fired his four cannons which arrowed into the target and Page dived with pleasure to finish it off before it splattered on the ground in a wide arc.

Their day's work was not over yet. At Bretigny what Page called his 'blood lust' had a further chance to be satiated. Two Luftwaffe aircraft were coming into land. They were totally unaware that two Mustangs were close behind them until Mac ripped into one of them. Page finished the enemy off as the Junkers 88 smashed into the ground. The second aircraft had failed to notice the funeral pyre now blazing and continued unaware with his prearranged landing.

Mac attacked again, transforming the second plane into a ball of fire. The two RAF pilots were now subjected to a hail of defensive flak over the airfield which Page understatedly described as 'a little unattractive'. The two pilots dodged and weaved their way through the stream of lights and flashes and headed home to safety. The two men with only one good hand between them had shot down six enemy aircraft in a few minutes. The Germans had been taken completely by surprise. The bold but dangerous plan had paid off handsomely. Page and Mac slipped safely home under the benign cover of a rainstorm and headed straight for two well deserved pints of beer.

Geoffrey Page was thrilled by their unlikely success. He later wrote, with characteristic honesty, 'I felt my blood boiling with the exaltation of our recent killings. I gloated in my mind over the hideous scenes of violent death we had meted out. Vengeance was mine, and I was enjoying every moment of it. I felt my years in the hospital had not been in vain. This lust for killing was to grow and grow within me until the end of the war causing me to inflict hurt on others than the official enemy. Youthful innocence had died alongside Luftwaffe aircrews that eventful morning over northern France.'[101] In private unpublished notes, Page added that he was 'exulting in the blood bath Mac and I had indulged in at the expense of the Luftwaffe. Like a dog that has killed his first sheep so had I changed on this flight from enthusiastic amateur into a dedicated killer.'

The raid was so daring and successful that the Air Ministry's publicity machine shifted into gear. Photographs of one of the attacks were published in the *News Chronicle*. Mac told the paper modestly, 'We had the luck to see Ju's going into land. One actually had its wheels down as we both went in to attack. I hit it. Page finished it off. Then I looked after the second Ju88. He went down too.' Mac and Page were instant heroes. Archibald Sinclair, Secretary of State for Air, sent a message to MacLachlan, 'Congratulations to you and to Flt/Lt Page on your brilliant exploit yesterday.'

Page and One-Armed Mac, as he was inevitably called, were so exhilarated by their success that they planned a second hit and run raid. Escorted again by the Typhoons, they set out for another attack on the enemy in northern France on 18 July. As the two pilots left their escort behind and crossed the coast there was a burst of machine gun fire. Page realised Mac had been hit. Geoffrey Page saw his friend's Mustang head upwards from the treetops and at one thousand feet his

---

101  Geoffrey Page, *Tale of a Guinea Pig*, London, Pelham, 1981

parachute canopy opened. Mac must have thought about bailing out and then changed his mind. The aircraft glided towards a field, but Mac's landing speed was too fast, and the Mustang ploughed into the earth with its wheels still retracted. The aircraft smashed into an orchard, shedding its wings on the way, before ending up in a wrecked heap. Page hovered above like a bird, circling hopelessly around the wrecked plane for signs of life. He even thought about landing to search on the ground but that was not possible. He could see nothing, so he swooped down one last time to photograph the battered wreck. Then fearing the worst, he turned solemnly for home.

A gung-ho broadcast on NBC radio by a friend of Mac called Robert St John, created a sense of hopefulness, 'He got revenge for the way they shot off his arm. But now, well there's always hope that Mac got to earth safely. He may be in a prison camp or…it's more likely…that he may be in hiding, somewhere around Paris, waiting for the day when Allied troops will storm the French capital and he can take part in the battle. That is the saga of one-armed Mac, hero of the Royal Air Force.'

Geoffrey Page probably shared some of this hope but, having had a ringside seat at the crash, was realistic enough to fear the worst. The Operations Record Book recorded, 'No enemy aircraft were observed, so the accident may have been due to small arms fire or to technical failure.' Small arms fire was believed to be the more likely reason. It was not until years later that Page discovered MacLachlan had survived the crash and was captured but died in a French hospital weeks later. Rumours that he had escaped the smashed aircraft, joined the resistance, and been shot by the Gestapo were untrue.

The official version is that the crash resulted in serious head injuries, and that Mac was taken to Field Hospital 711 at Pont-L'Eveque. On 30 July 1943, in his absence, Mac was awarded a second bar to his DFC and Flt Lt Alan Geoffrey Page was awarded the DFC.

The citation in the *London Gazette* noted that MacLachlan and Page 'in the course of an operation over enemy territory, shot down six enemy aircraft, three of which were destroyed by Squadron Leader MacLachlan and two by Flight Lieutenant Page, while the other was destroyed jointly. The operation, which was planned by Squadron Leader MacLachlan, was brilliantly executed and the successes were worthily earned.'

On the following day, 31 July 1943, Squadron Leader James MacLachlan DSO, DFC died from his injuries and was buried at Pont-L'Eveque Communal Cemetery. He was still only twenty-four years old. French civilians covered his grave with flowers and two attended the funeral, which was conducted by a German priest.[102] On the tombstone it says:

> *In proud and loving memory of our dear Jay.*
> *Death is swallowed up in victory.*

---

102   Brian Cull/Roland Symons, *One- Armed Mac,* London, Grub Street, 2003

## Chapter Sixteen

# Hunting for Doodlebugs

There are no notes or logbook entries that illustrate the impact of James MacLachlan's death on Geoffrey Page. His only comment was that Mac 'was a very brave man'. Although he would never have betrayed his emotions to his RAF colleagues, Page's son Jamie later recalled that 'he was pretty cut up'. Whatever Geoffrey said or did not say, it was clear that Squadron Leader James MacLachlan had been an inspiring friend and leader.

Between the shooting down of Mac and his friend's death three weeks later, Page's logbooks take on a positively jaunty tone. Perhaps he was trying to cover up his grief about what had happened in France? On 23 July he flew an Oxford from Wittering to Church Fenton in Yorkshire and added, 'Bloody good party too!' Six days later he refers to flying a Spitfire and writes enigmatically, 'Eggs are binding as well!' That same day he records flying a Mustang from Hornchurch to New Church and then 'Grand party with Dandy and Dumbo'. Mysteriously, this social event is then crossed out. In September he returned from Leuchars in Scotland to RAF Wittering in Sussex, 'back to civilisation' as he put it in his logbook. Three days later he flew in a Barracuda from Wittering to RAF Bircham Newton in North Norfolk with Lt.Cdr Kendall - *'never again!'*, he noted.

His time at Wittering had ended in tragedy with Mac's death, and Page, now promoted to Squadron Leader was given a new role at 122 Squadron based at Gravesend. He only had time for one fighter sweep above Amiens and Abbeville and one bomber escort patrol to Holland, before being switched to 132 Squadron where he had briefly been attached as a supernumerary Flight Lieutenant at Martlesham Heath back in October 1942.

Page replaced popular Squadron Leader Franz Colleredo-Mansfield DFC, who had been shot down over Boulogne and crashed to his death near Berck-sur-Mer. One eyewitness noted 'he just went down into the drink. His number two flew around to see if anyone bobbed up to the surface, but no one did.'

Geoffrey Page met up with his new charges at RAF Castletown near Thurso in Scotland on 19 January 1944. Now the Squadron was deployed defending the vital naval base at Scapa Flow and in convoy escort duties. In Scotland it was so wild and windy that on some days Page would have to taxi down the runway with a member of the ground crew sitting on each wing to stop his Spitfire from flipping over. Once Page opened the throttle the two men would hurriedly jump off their wings.

Squadron Leader Page had no time to bond with his pilots because he was immediately sent on an elite three-week course to Milfield, an attractive airfield a few miles inland from the Northumberland coast. The course at the Fighter Leader School was full of wing commanders and squadron leaders, the most talented leaders the RAF could muster It was clearly spelt out to everyone that these were preparations for D-Day.

For three weeks the wild beaches of the Northumbria stood in for Normandy. The pilots relentlessly practised dive bombing on tanks and military vehicles. They learned the most fruitful angle of attack, the best range to fire from, and the optimal height from which to drop bombs. Alongside them operated scientists who analysed the effectiveness of bombs with different weights or fuses. During this time the elite group of leaders lived every waking minute in preparation for the invasion of Europe. When the time came, the most effective way to destroy the enemy needed to be second nature.

These intense weeks were not without risk as the pilots developed their new skills in wintery weather. Page was flying number two on a wild winter's day. The runway, gleaming icily in the morning light, was flanked by large banks of snow. When the leading plane blew in the wind, wheels skidding on the ice, Page took evasive action to avoid a nasty crash. As a result, he was forced perilously close to the three-foot snowbank lining the runway. As Page lifted off there was a thud, and his Spitfire shook. Geoffrey knew he was in trouble. Perhaps, thought Page, my wheel hit the snowbank. With a five-hundred-pound bomb on board this was an acutely uncomfortable thought. He could see no reassuring green lights on the dashboard and to his horror Geoffrey Page realised the engine was rapidly over-heating. If the engine died, he would have to land on his belly in a snowy field which was far too dangerous with a bomb on board. The Spitfire was flying too low to bail out, and anyway that plan risked the plane spiralling on and hitting a house.

Page circled towards the sea, desperately trying to throttle back to control the temperature. As he inched towards the coastline the gauge was screaming danger. The moment Geoffrey was over the beach, he pressed the button. The bomb dropped neatly into the sea. His load was dramatically lightened, so Page regained height and limped back to the airfield where he landed the Spitfire on its belly skidding on the snow and grass. He called this his first introduction to skiing. His logbook recorded, 'Skidded on snowy runway on take-off and broke oleo leg. Wheels up landing. No blame attached.' A week later, to everyone's horror, a fellow pilot blew up in pieces in mid-air, a reminder of the ever-present danger of flying Spitfires with large bombs on board. Page's logbook recorded that on 9 March, 'French pilot blew up in mid-air with his own bomb.'

At the end of his course, and having used up another of his nine lives, Geoffrey Page was finally able to take up the daily command of 132(City of Bombay) Squadron. If his gnarled hands made flying more challenging, his burns did not appear to hinder Geoffrey's romantic life. Page had no problem attracting the opposite sex. A month after his arrival in Scotland a young woman wrote to him, 'Last night you were my whole world, everything about you, your smile, your eyes, your whole being filled me with a happiness hitherto unknown…nothing mattered in the past, present, or future sense when you held me in your arms…every minute was heaven.' The woman understood, as so often in wartime, this was not a long-term relationship because he would be flying away soon but added 'I will always carry a torch for you.'

She was right. Geoffrey had pressing responsibilities with 132 Squadron. New Zealander, Flight Sergeant John Caulton, gave his impressions of the new boss, 'January 1944, that's when Geoffrey joined us. He'd been with us before up at Martlesham when I had first joined up. But he did not get on with the CO there, of course, understandably, (the CO was) a gutless character…Geoffrey had only just come out of hospital after being badly burned and after having many operations. I liked him and got on all right with him, he was an officer, and I was still a Sergeant at that time. Then he went to North Africa and of course the sun out there played up with his burns a bit.'[103]

Caulton, and the other pilots, were astonished that Page was still flying. They were aware that he was regularly on the phone to Archie McIndoe, 'He had scars on his face and hands; his hands were bloody cruel, curled up like claws really. I said it's amazing how the Airforce had him back.' They appreciated Page's charm and humour as well as

---

103  *www.john-caulton-spitfire-pilot.com*

his courage, but John Caulton struggled to understand why he was still flying fighters, 'He didn't have to go back. He could have lived on a pension, but he was young and stupid like the rest of us...he had heated gloves with a zip on the side so he could get them on and off. He was in a bad way really, he should never have gone back to flying, but he did.'

Page was also popular with the ground crews. He recognised the invaluable contribution that an effective team on the ground made to every combat pilot. Fred Ollett, a farm boy from Durham, liked him immediately, 'The first day he got us ground crew together and gave us a talk about what he wanted. Here was a Squadron Leader we were going to like and work with, unlike some of the other officers.'[104] But the ground crews never saw Page's hands because he always wore gloves, and frequently they had to help him with his straps in the cockpit.

In March the Squadron left their windy corner of Scotland and headed back down south, initially to RAF Detling in Kent. Their role during these months was to fly their Spitfires as bomber escorts, attacking enemy infrastructure and military targets in Northern France. The squadron escorted Mitchell bombers to hit marshalling yards at St Ghislain and Monceau - 'good bombing', Page wrote. Attacking more marshalling yards soon after he noted 'hopeless bombing'. In late March the Squadron lost Flight Sergeant Clark when his Spitfire was shot down near Chartres. On the ground, social activity was an essential release from the intensity of the war. John Caulton recorded the Airfield Dance at RAF Detling, noting that 'the party went tremendously well' and 'the Squadron had a party at the George and Dragon in Ightham, a vast meal, and lots to drink.'

---

104 Fred Ollett, *letter to Pauline Page*, Co Durham, August 2000.

As a leader, Geoffrey Page was inspiring but impatient to jump into action, always searching for a chance to attack the enemy. On 18 April the Squadron moved to RAF Ford in Sussex as part of preparations for the D-Day invasion. Five days later the Squadron were returning from a sweep over France when they spotted an E-boat, a torpedo boat, in a French river. Page asked his CO for permission to attack. He was refused, but flew restlessly up and down a French beach waiting for the RAF to give in. When the authorities relented, the pilots flew low over the riverbank out of the sun and soon the boat was smoking and listing. Caught the crew napping,' Squadron Leader Page wrote in his logbook. The Squadron claimed a 'destroyed', although this time not a Messerschmitt or Dornier. The incident was captured on vivid gun camera footage which is now in the Imperial War Museum. Page and his squadron are seen peppering the enemy boat relentlessly.

Page's logbook paints a vivid picture of a squadron ceaselessly in action, led by a pilot high on action. One day his logbook would record dive bombing of a target 'good bombing - plenty of flak'. Next it would be a mission to Germany, 'monster searchlights and train' followed soon after by 'attacked train loaded with tanks and armoured cars. Plenty of high flak from the Seine valley!' and 'Attacked ammunition train with two coaches left blazing. Heavy flak from Caen.' When his squadron was moved for a few days out of the active frontline to support army exercises in preparation for D-Day, Geoffrey Page's frustration rang loud and clear, 'Patrol over landing barges. Another bloody army exercise.'

In April 1944 the Allies launched a raid on Berlin with 1000 American bombers with Fighter Command, including 132 Squadron, in support. Geoffrey Page asked for ninety-gallon auxiliary fuel tanks to be fitted onto their Spitfires so that 132 possessed the full range to reach the German target. This was to be the largest daylight bombing raid of the war so far with around two thousand tons of bombs dropped.' Page was photographed studiously looking at a map with other pilots by the *London Evening Standard* who reported on the front page that, 'Observers said that never before had so many aircraft crossed the coast.' One added 'even the ground trembled with the roar of their engines.'

In the spring of 1944, 132 Squadron undertook a series of particularly perilous flying missions. The Luftwaffe were developing a bomb called a V1. These early relatives of cruise missiles were nicknamed 'doodlebug 'or 'buzz' bombs. When they hit the UK they caused havoc in the British civilian population. John Brasier was delivering the Sunday papers in Stevenage when he got a close-up view of a doodlebug, 'I ran down the side of a house and pressed myself against the wall. Dogs were barking- I had no idea what it was. I had no idea that it was a pilotless vehicle with a bomb in it. It was a terrible cigar-shaped thing with a fin and a flame belching out of the back, and a terrible humming noise. To see it so low, literally a hundred feet up in the air - I'll never forget as long as I live.'

From the first V1 bomb dropped on London to the final attack in 1945 what the Germans called 'revenge weapons' were responsible for well over five thousand deaths in the UK. It was no wonder they terrified the civilians of London and elsewhere. In late 1943, Allied reconnaissance had spotted many mysterious looking ski huts and ramps hidden away in the Pas de Calais. It was 132 Squadron's job to put these V1 or 'Noball' sites out of action. That usually meant flying an extra sortie. On April 13th they escorted bombers attacking marshalling yards at Namur. John Caulton noted 'it was a long show, 2 hours 55minutes, and everyone was surprised to find another show waiting for them. This time the Squadron took off with five hundred bombs in place, to bomb a 'Noball' target(V1) site near Abbeville.'

It was a dangerous role requiring skilful precision flying. In advance Geoffrey Page obsessively studied maps and aerial photographs. Then the squadron would head out from RAF Ford at about twelve thousand feet with one five-hundred-pound bomb and two 250lb bombs tucked beneath their clipped-wing Spitfire 1XEs. Squadron Leader Page would guide his team to the site and then carefully assess the situation before the attack. The targets were tiny, a couple of buildings no larger than cottages and a hundred-yard-long launch ramp, which the pilots called the ski jump. When they were past the French coast and vertically over the target the pilots would roll over and swoop down together, before dropping their bombs at the optimal moment. This precision flying was made more dangerous by the ring of 40mm anti-aircraft guns that surrounded the V1 sites. As soon as the pilots swooped down an anti-aircraft barrage would start, leaving the Spitfires of 132 Squadron to run the gauntlet of orange-tracer flak. The perils were highlighted on 28 May when they lost Flight Sergeant T G Turner in his Spitfire on a V1 raid near Calais.

Geoffrey Page described the dangers of attacking a V1 ski ramp, 'As you dived down you were sitting over a 500lb bomb, and you had to go through all this anti-aircraft fire. You'd see puffs of grey smoke and as you went through you prayed to the Almighty that your bomb or aircraft was not going to be hit. By the time you were through, all that you'd climb away with a sigh of relief and then head back to England.'[105] When Page was suffering from a heavy cold on one of these vertical dive-bombing raids the pressure was so intense 'it was as if someone had shot a bullet into my ear.' He felt he was playing a game of Russian roulette.

When his Squadron were not bombing V1 sites or escorting bombers, Squadron Leader Page looked for what the pilots called

---

105   Geoffrey Page, *Imperial War Museum Sound Archive 11103*, London

Ranger missions. These freelance hit and run raids across the Channel involved shooting-up German fighters that were refuelling and rearming before they were airborne. On one such mission in late April Page claimed an enemy aircraft destroyed as it was touching down, and the squadron also damaged several gliders that were on the ground.

Three days later six Spitfires left Kent at lunchtime. They were soon skimming low over rooftops and telephone wires. New Zealander, Flying Officer John Caulton, was flying so close to the ground he saw a farmer quietly ploughing his field look up and wave. Then, out of the fog that was rolling across the Dutch countryside a lone enemy aircraft emerged mysteriously. The German was immediately in fierce combat with Caulton. As the two aircraft duelled over the rooftops, Caulton was horrified to notice a haze of fuel vapour coming from his auxiliary tank. His oil gauge showed he was in serious trouble. Caulton jettisoned the tank, hoping it would not crash onto one of the houses below. He told Squadron Leader Geoffrey Page that his only option was to turn for home. Page replied, 'I'm sorry, old man, I can't help you, start walking.'[106]

While Flying Officer John Caulton was left to his uncertain fate, Geoffrey Page and his number two, Pilot Officer 'Paddy' Pullin, chased the enemy aircraft relentlessly. To Page's horror, he spotted the well-defended German-held airfield at Deelen in Holland up ahead. Now 132 Squadron would have to contend with intense anti-aircraft fire as well as the Luftwaffe. Despite that, Page continued to chase the Messerschmitt as it headed towards the safety of the airfield. Page's own height was only fifty feet and he hit the German in the tail setting the aircraft alight. Despite this, the pilot still managed to put his wheels down at Deelen and land his fiery aeroplane. With his superior speed, Page roared over the top of the Me110. Anti-aircraft

---

106  *www.john-caulton-spitfire-pilot.com*

guns mounted on the top of hangars and buildings spat intense volleys before he wheeled safely for home through the heavy enemy fire.

It was only afterwards that Page recognised the skill of the enemy pilot, Major Hans-Joachim Jabs, 'I had to give the German pilot full marks for his courage. He calmly lowered his wheels and flaps and proceeded to land whilst I was just about two or three hundred yards behind him pumping cannon shells and bullets into him as fast as I could.' In his haste to escape, Page did not see the Me 110 burst into a fireball. Nor did he see Jabs and the rest of the three-man crew abandon their plane and roll dramatically into a ditch.

Geoffrey Page was right to fear the enemy's powerful anti-aircraft guns. His number two, Pilot Officer Pullin, was hit by the German defences, his Spitfire bursting into flames and smashing into the trees on the edge of the airfield. Flt/Sgt Armour's Spitfire was hit in the Perspex hood, cutting the pilot's head, and Flt/Sgt Trigg limped home with half his wing tip missing. With John Caulton not accounted for, the raid had resulted in two Spitfires being damaged and two lost.

As the rest of Page's squadron struggled home, John Caulton limped on for thirty miles before his damaged Spitfire finally gave up. He was forced to crash land and was captured. The New Zealander's kneecap was smashed, 'It was unpleasant, there were bits and pieces everywhere'. A lump had also been taken out of his head when he hit the gunsight. A couple of hours after his dramatic capture, John Caulton was visited by a German officer. The man did not give the Nazi salute and spoke reasonable English. He asked if Caulton was flying the Spitfire and when Caulton replied, 'Yes', he added that 'I was flying the other one.'

This was Major Hans-Joachim Jabs the German night-fighter ace from Lubeck, who just hours before had narrowly escaped death when hit at Deelen airfield by Geoffrey Page. The two men talked amiably for twenty minutes, and Caulton thought he was a decent man. A photograph was taken with Caulton, wounded head clearly visible, and Jabs's crew. Then Jabs signed a piece of paper and added in German, 'please let this prisoner keep this souvenir of Major Jabs.' Years later, when he discovered the identity of the German pilot, Squadron Leader Page wrote in unpublished notes about the incident, 'One of my pilots, a young New Zealander, promptly did a head-on attack on this Me110 and it almost goes without saying that having picked on a top scoring German night fighter ace, he was just as promptly, shot down.'

## Chapter Seventeen

# D-Day

There was relief for Squadron Leader Geoffrey Page and 132 Squadron when D-Day finally arrived six weeks later. All his training up in Northumberland had given Page a keen sense of anticipation. This was a pivotal moment in the war and after the desperate defence of the Battle of Britain it was encouraging now to be on the offensive. But Page knew it was still a huge task to land thousands of troops on the Normandy beaches and to push the Germans out of the countries they had occupied so ruthlessly for four years.

Page had already distinguished himself in a D-Day rehearsal. Pilots were dropped miles from base, to simulate being caught behind enemy lines. They were given twenty-four hours to find their way back. Page was too tired to walk. He spotted some American ambulances readying themselves. One still had the key dangling temptingly in the ignition. Page hopped in and drove away at Spitfire speed. An American guard fired a shot at this mysterious man who had stolen his ambulance. Arriving back at base hours before the other exhausted pilots who had walked all the way home, he was praised for his initiative.

The day before the invasion, Page and two other Squadron Leaders were summoned into a large conference room by Group Captain Jamie Rankin. They were given maps and large-scale documents containing their orders. Behind the senior officers sat ninety

RAF pilots. The three squadrons at RAF Ford in Sussex would be covering the American beaches of Omaha and Utah from first light on D-Day. As Jamie Rankin outlined to them the enormous size and infrastructure of the invasion, Page looked down at his gnarled hands. His mind drifted back to 1940. He noticed that his palms were wet with moisture.

Geoffrey Page found it difficult to sleep that night. He felt tired, but too restless to spend a full night in bed. He was weary with this war and burdened by responsibility. Overhead, British bombers broke the peace of the night sky. Page knew that they would soon be followed by hundreds of landing craft. He reflected, 'Asleep in their beds the people of England slumbered peacefully on…unaware that many of their fighting sons would find their rest beneath the rich soil of Normandy.'

His two flight commanders, 'Skipper' Vinden,[107] a Norwegian, and Mike Graham, were also awake early. They were full of boyish spirits, just as Page himself had been four years earlier in the Battle of Britain, 'I suddenly felt old and alone. Despite my twenty-four years it seemed to me that a chasm of time divided me from my two flight commanders…idly I wondered if Skipper or Mike would still be alive at the end of the day. The Norwegian, I felt, had a lesser chance of survival. His fanatical desire to kill anything German could easily lead to his own undoing. As for myself, I did not really care. Death would at least allow me to shed my mantle of tiredness. No more would there be that tight knot of fear gripping my insides every time a new operation was signalled through from group headquarters.'[108]

That night while Geoffrey Page was wrestling with his melancholy thoughts, the American 82nd Airborne Division of paratroop-

---

107 Page calls him Skipper Vinden in his autobiography, but correct name was Arnt Augestad Hvinden.
108 Geoffrey Page, *Tale of a Guinea Pig*, Pelham, London,1981

ers had already left for France, 'We flew in V of Vs, like a gigantic spearhead without a shaft...below us we could see the glints of yellow flame from the German anti-aircraft guns on the Channel Islands. We watched them curiously and without fear, as a high-flying duck may watch a hunter, knowing that we were too high and faraway for their fire to reach us...in the pale glow of the rising moon I could clearly see each field and farm below. And I remember thinking how peaceful the land looked...'[109]

In the hour before departure, Page gave his pilots a final briefing. Precision and discipline were essential. In exactly 47 minutes, the Squadron would rendezvous over Omaha Beach. He emphasised that no pilot should deflect from their beach patrols, even to shoot down an enemy aircraft. Then the men ran to their waiting Spitfires. As he went through his routine checks in the semi-darkness Page felt cold. He watched the clock anxiously; timing was critical today. At the appointed second he gave a thumbs-up to the ground crew and started his Merlin engine with a roar. The Spitfires were to fly in six pairs, and he watched as they burst into life. Then they headed down the runway and smoothly lifted off into the early morning light. Page turned to check that his pilots were all in formation. In a few minutes 132 Squadron would see the Normandy beaches below. More than four thousand Allied aircraft would be in operation on D-Day and beyond. Geoffrey Page's Squadron might be just a cog in a huge wheel, but he was determined they should play their part effectively.

Soon Page made out the shape of the Cherbourg Peninsular. When he looked down his spirits lifted as he spotted an invasion armada of an unimaginable scale 'I saw a sight that brought a flood of feeling into mind and body, both of which had felt little emotion, except resentment for so long. Hundreds of ships of all shapes and

---

109   General Matthew Ridgway, *Soldier,* Harper and Bros, New York,1956

sizes, from vast battleships to small barges, littered the surface of the sea.' At first light they were hovering over Omaha Beach. Page's mind flicked back to the desperation of Dunkirk and St Valery a few years before. This time 132 Squadron flew up and down giving the protection from the Luftwaffe to the Allied troops below that they had not been able to offer in 1940.

Sitting above the beaches at about a thousand feet Page had a dress circle view of the whole of the Normandy landings. He noticed the tremendous pounding taken by the small vessels from the rough sea and imagined the sea sickness being experienced down below, 'We felt sorry for the troops coming across in the landing craft, thousands of vessels from big battleships down to little landing craft… then to get out of a landing craft onto a beach and to be fired at, you had to be a brave man.'

He was right. The men in the invasion flotilla felt the full might of the recently reinforced German defences. They struggled out of their landing crafts waist deep through the water, heavily laden with cumbersome weapons and supplies, and still reeling from hours of vomiting on the rough sea. Many were cut down as soon as they reached the beach with more than two thousand casualties on Omaha beach that day. Page knew he was very lucky to be in the air and not on the beach. As he looked down on the brutal scene below, he realised his hatred of the Nazis was still very close to the surface.

After patrolling the beaches watchfully for an hour, the Spitfires were relieved of their duties. There had been little evidence of the Luftwaffe, and the Allies appeared to be in control of the skies above the beaches. The Squadron headed back to Sussex and gulped down some breakfast while their aircraft were refuelled, before they set out on another patrol. Geoffrey Page felt guilty that he and his squadron were safely tucking into their breakfast toast while soldiers were being killed out on the Normandy beaches. Geoffrey Page was one of the few pilots, perhaps the only one, who had seen both the retreat from Northern France and D-Day from on high. He marvelled at the contrast: the first desperate and defensive, the second aggressive and planned.

As they sat enjoying the peaceful interlude between sorties over Normandy, Page and his two flight commanders heard a strange noise overhead. It was a big Sterling bomber that was towing a glider crammed with troops. The bomber was struggling to pull such a heavy load and one of its four engines had stopped. The pilot knew he would never make it to France with one engine short and released the glider from the towrope. The glider touched down successfully on the grass. Immediately troops holding guns poured out of the glider's hull. They were ready for action and happy to shoot anyone in their way. Fortunately, the pilot shouted at them just in time and the confused soldiers lowered their weapons, as they realised they were not in Normandy but rural Sussex. As Page laconically noted, 'The tea wagon pulled up to complete their embarrassment!'

There was a clear pattern to Page's flying for the next five days. Regular hour-long flights over the beaches in his Spitfire before the squadron was relieved and flew home to Sussex for breakfast. Once pilots and planes were refuelled, they headed straight out again on another protective beach patrol above Omaha and Utah. In his ringside seat over the Normandy beaches Page scarcely saw the Luftwaffe, to the disappointment of his pilots. The average flying time in the D-Day phase of the war was six or more hours each day and the final aircraft would land back in Sussex after 11 p.m. at night.

If anyone expected the war to be easy after the Allies had landed on the Normandy beaches, they were wrong. In a succession of bloody battles of attrition on the ground many more Allied troops died in the subsequent battles than on D-Day itself. 132 Squadron's role now was to destroy and disrupt the German supply lines in the

Battle of Normandy. This involved almost non-stop flying behind enemy lines to shoot up any military vehicles on the roads.

On 18 June, Page shared a damaged FW190 east of Evreux with another pilot. This followed a long tail chase before firing off so much cannon that Page ran out of ammunition. A few days later Page destroyed another FW190 near the strategically vital communications centre of Caen. His combat report concluded, 'The aircraft was seen to crash land in such a manner that must have rendered it a complete write off. I have since returned to view the a/c and the engine and half the fuselage have burnt out.' The attacks on the enemy supply lines were relentless, 'dive bombing concentration of troops in a wood south of Caen,' was followed by '1 truck flamer, 2 badly damaged and I armoured car damaged'. Almost every day, Page and his squadron were hitting ammunition dumps and destroying enemy vehicles. But there was also danger all around, and on 18 June Flight Lieutenant Day was shot down and killed.

A week later Geoffrey Page returned from a London nightclub as first light gently broke over the airfield. He was surprised to see the station buzzing with activity at such an unearthly hour. He was told, 'We are off to bloody France, we are not coming back.' 132 Squadron was being moved from Sussex to a mud airstrip in Normandy. They had been given just an hour's notice to leave. Page crammed his paltry belongings into his Spitfire, using a long-range tank that had been fitted to his aircraft for an eventuality such as this. Two hours after arriving back from a night club visit he was now regretting, a sleepy Page and the Spitfires of 132 Squadron landed in Normandy. A wheat field had recently been bulldozed to create a single landing strip. The fine dust from the wheat found its way unerringly into clothes and food. That was annoying but not as dangerous as dust choking the mechanisms of machine guns and cannons.

Accommodation was in tents in the adjoining orchard and although showers were swiftly rigged up, a Normandy wheat field was a far cry from the home comforts of the Officers' Mess at RAF Ford. The men's initial delight in being on French soil after four years of German occupation was tempered by the lack of facilities. The parked Spitfires were carefully spread out through the orchards and fields to reduce the potential damage from any German bombing raid. Geoffrey Page was underwhelmed by his new, unglamourous, accommodation. 'Fed up, f****d, and far from home', he wrote in his logbook on 25 June.

Dwight Eisenhower, the American overall commander, understood the importance of destroying the enemy's supply lines used for weapons and food. German lorries, armoured cars, and motorcycles were relatively easy targets for the RAF. Spitfires, armed with cannons and machine guns, were well equipped to break up the German logistical supply lines. On 29 June alone, 132 Squadron destroyed or damaged seven trucks, an ammunition dump, five armed cars and an anti-tank gun amongst other successes. Only the tanks, plated with heavy armour, were not vulnerable to attacks from Page and his colleagues. The fighter-bomber Typhoons took care of those.

The German 17SS Panzer Division directly experienced these RAF attacks. One German soldier noted, 'Our motorized columns were coiling along the road towards the invasion beaches. Then something happened that left us in a daze. Spurts of fire flicked along the column and splashes of dust staccatoed the road. Everyone was piling out of the vehicles and scuttling for the neighbouring fields. Several vehicles were already in flames...the length of the road was strewn with splintered anti-tank guns (the pride of our division), flaming motors and charred implements of war.'[110]

---

110  Quoted in Milton Shulman, *Defeat in the West,* Secker and Warburg, London, 1947

The summary of the June flying hours, signed by Squadron Leader Page, indicated that 132 squadron had flown 772 sorties and covered 257,625 miles. Amongst all this intense activity there was still time to improve their humble living conditions. The Squadron was part of 125 Wing which comprised four squadrons. It was reported that the Wing had built a 600-seat theatre, 'the stage must be the best in Normandy - it is a really remarkable achievement. The Squadron Adjutant had some previous experience of dance bands and has taken the Wing Band in hand-we hope it will sound better in future - it would be a great help if they played in tune!'[111]

As a Squadron Leader, Geoffrey Page was too busy to watch a show in the new theatre, but he had time to reflect on his war. He had only just passed his twenty-fourth birthday, but he felt much older. Geoffrey Page was characteristically honest about his emotions, 'Skipper Vinden [ the Norwegian] and I each in our own way revelled in the daily blood bath, and time on the ground to us was a necessary evil...although I exulted at the sight of my cannon shells ripping into the lurching vehicles as they careered about the narrow Normandy lanes, my lust lay in the desire to destroy enemy aircraft.' What had happened to the carefree young man that Geoffrey Page had been a few short years before? He admitted to himself that the cheerful young student who had crashed his plane in Sussex when he tried to impress a girlfriend, had been transformed into a relentless killing machine.

Next, Page devised a plan which would allow him to destroy enemy aircraft as well as armoured cars and lorries. The dust from the wheat field where they were billeted was clogging the cannons on the Spitfires. Surely, asked Geoffrey Page to himself, we should test the cannons to find out if they are functioning properly? Of course,

111  www.wartimememoriesproject.com

his men understood that the true purpose of these tests was to shoot up Germans. Page's 'cannon tests' were the perfect camouflage for his ongoing killing campaign.

The 'tests' benefited from the element of surprise, but as they only involved a tiny number of British aircraft there was always the risk of being outnumbered. On a wildcard mission in July 1944, Page and two other Spitfires were flying at 1,000 feet miles behind enemy lines when they encountered thirty German fighters, odds of ten-to-one. In trying to escape such overwhelming numbers, Page was hit by cannon shell. Smoke filled his cockpit. His mind immediately turned back to his torching by fire in 1940. Blood was running down his left leg into his flying boot. He had taken a large cannon shell, or possibly a bullet, in the thigh but the adrenaline anaesthetised him from over-whelming pain. His Combat Report stated, '...hit by cannon shell which entered the cockpit on the starboard side, just behind my right foot. Splinters entered by left thigh and my leg went numb...dog fight continued for a few more minutes and I found myself being continually attacked.'[112]

The wounded Squadron Leader was being hunted down by the enemy. The attack turned into a duel; quite simply kill or be killed. Tracer flashed by him. Then he exploited the superior turning circle of the Spitfire. He pulled his aircraft into a tight climbing turn close to the ground, easing his Spitfire round towards the tail of the German. Only a few feet above the treeline, the hunter tried to shoot Page down, but he fired while on the edge of a stall. The enemy 109 turned over and smashed into the trees twenty feet below. Geoffrey Page circled slowly as smoke curled up from the woods. The smouldering wreckage could just as easily have been his Spitfire, he thought.

---

112  Geoffrey Page, *Personal Combat Report*, National Archives, Kew, London

Geoffrey Page had used up another of his lives, but it was a further German 'kill' to add to his list.

*Photographed by the RAF taking off from Longues-sur-Mer July 1944 (Imperial War Museum).*

Page spent two weeks in a field hospital with his leg injury before he was able to re-join his squadron, and it was two further weeks before he could fly again. His frustration at being unfit for combat was reflected in his logbook entry for the day he was wounded, 'Teach me not to stick my bloody neck out.' On that same day, July 7 1944, the Squadron received news that Page had been promoted to Wing Commander. The Operations Record Book recorded, 'S/L Page is to be made W/C flying, an appointment which gave a great deal of pleasure to everybody.' As Wing Commander he was now the leader of four squadrons with a pool of eighty aircraft and one hundred and twenty pilots to draw on. Alcohol-fuelled celebrations followed that evening in the nearby town of Bayeux.

A letter to his father a few weeks after his enforced injury break highlighted their uneasy relationship. Page could have been a public schoolboy writing home with results from a house cricket match, rather than the youngest Wing Commander in the RAF[113], and highly decorated, 'My Dear Daddy, I was delighted to hear from you again, and the only reason I have not written before is pure and simple laziness. Quite a few things have happened since we last met. I was wounded again in the thigh and had a short sojourn in a field hospital with a month off flying but fortunately I am back on the job now. I rose to the exalted rank of Wing Commander two months ago and I have now got four squadrons instead of two...'

On 14 July the Squadron lost Warrant Officer J H Reeves who was shot down and killed by the friendly fire of an American Mustang. Later that same day Geoffrey flew his first sortie as a Wing Commander, and he was able to chalk off another German. A violent tank battle was raging on the east side of the River Orne. Page could see smoke curling upwards from burning tanks. The Spitfires spotted a group of thirty Focke Wolfe 190s flying along steadily. Somehow, they had failed to notice a dozen RAF Spitfires closing behind them. Page fired at the rear German plane from three hundred yards and saw his strike hit the enemy's fuselage followed by a white flash. Brown smoke poured out of the enemy aircraft. Page closed in tighter. A hundred yards away he fired again. He could see pieces of metal blowing off the Focke Wolfe as his bullets thudded into the plane which was now diving gently down to the ground. Page assumed the pilot was dead and was astonished when the German straightened the plane out and performed a brilliant landing right in the middle of the tank battle. This was no time for admiring flying skills. Page and a second

---

113   Brendan 'Paddy' Finucane was made a Wing Commander aged 21 in June 1942 but died in action three weeks later.

Spitfire flown by Sergeant Ford closed in and raked the fighter with cannon fire, peppering it full of holes.

Page was so determined to chalk up another 'kill' that, after Group refused to count this victory as confirmed, an angry Geoffrey Page drove a vehicle to the site of the crash. The area was so heavily mined he had to thread his way along the tank tracks from the battle with great precision. It was a risky enterprise, but Page navigated the dangers successfully. When he returned to the airstrip brandishing a rudder and a swastika-covered fin from the wrecked 190 his success was moved up from 'probable' to 'confirmed'. This was his fourteenth aircraft destroyed. Page had endured fifteen operations. There was one more to go.

One evening, Page and some colleagues headed into the local town of Douai for a night out. They found an abandoned German Opel staff car and clambered into it. In Douai they enjoyed themselves flirting with the beautiful daughter of the local innkeeper. Her father was very pro-British and soon liqueurs and wine were on the house. It was a happy but unsteady band of pilots who made their way hazily back to the airfield.

There are differing accounts of what happened next. In one, the men found a dark country lane blocked by a fallen tree. In another, the merry men from the RAF were stuck at a closed railway level crossing in a small blacked-out village. Whatever the location of their stop what happened next was the same in both accounts. Figures appeared menacingly out of the shadows. Geoffrey Page suddenly felt a gun being rudely shoved into his stomach. It was the local French resistance, who were armed with sub-machine guns.

RAF wings on a dark country road could easily be mistaken for German eagles. The German car they had borrowed, and flying boots that looked like jackboots to the French resistance, further fuelled suspicions. Page finally recalled enough halting schoolboy French to say, *'Il faut pas tirer sur nous, nous sommes les anglais.'* An Australian pilot added to the confusion by proclaiming that his colleagues were Pommies, like the apples so famous in Normandy. The sub-machine gun was prodded deeper into Page's stomach. He was now feeling frightened. The resistance fighters prepared to shoot these 'Germans' on the spot.

At that moment more tough-looking resistance men arrived and fortunately one of them spoke a few words of English. Geoffrey said they were English pilots. With the guns still trained on them, the pilots were taken to the local police station where after two hours of interrogation they finally convinced their captors that they were friends not foe. Page was relieved. After so many close escapes from death it would have been galling to have been shot by the French while liberating them from the Nazis. When the resistance finally realised their mistake, further drinking of brandy in the local bistro followed. Page heard one still puzzled policeman, say at the end, *'C'est Pommies de l'air, pas pommes de terre.'*

In the middle of all this action Wing Commander Page had to return to the Medical Board for a check-up to ensure he was still in the appropriate flying category. On 6 July 1944 they noted that he had flown 180 hours in Spitfires without difficulty but that his hands 'will probably be a permanent deformity...he has ascended to 30,000 feet and has had no trouble with the grafted areas on his face and hands.' Page's status as an operational pilot was confirmed.

Back in Normandy, Page was on full alert when he was informed that Feldmarschall Erwin Rommel, the legendary 'Desert Fox' and commander of German forces in Normandy, was in the area. Rommel was rumoured to be launching a German counterattack against the Allied forces. To Wing Commander Page, killing Rommel was an intriguing challenge. His old squadron,132, was part of Page's 125th Wing and they soon spotted a German convoy. Could the Feldmarschall himself be in one of the vehicles? The Spitfires swooped down to attack at a low level, but this was certainly not the sitting duck they imagined. The sides of the German lorries were lowered revealing a fearsome array of armoury which immediately blasted shells and bullets at the low flying Spitfires.

Whether this convoy was a decoy for the transport Rommel was travelling in or was just an unpleasant coincidence is not clear. In any event, the Allies did not have to wait long before their hunt for Rommel bore fruit. Just after 5 p.m. on 17 July a German staff car was spotted breaking out of the Falaise Gap. The Allied Forces were alerted, although no one could be certain it was Rommel travelling in the German car, especially as it was odd that the Desert Fox was not in an armoured vehicle but an open topped car without even basic camouflage.

The Allies' luck was in. Feldmarschall Rommel was being driven back to the front line after an urgent meeting at his Panzer tank headquarters. On the Liverot-Vermoutiers road Rommel's vehicle was attacked by Spitfires. Several 20mm shells raked the car, severely wounding the driver in his left arm and causing him to lose control. The vehicle crashed into a tree and spun off the road. Rommel was thrown out of the car, fracturing his skull in three places, and severely injuring his face. Germany's Normandy commander had been surgically removed from the battlefield.

Decades later it is still not agreed whose Spitfire was responsible. Squadron Leader Johannes Jacobus Le Roux of 602(City of Glasgow) Squadron, part of Wing Commander Page's 125th Wing (83rd Group), is credited by the RAF. Amongst a range of other claimants, some commentators credit Canadian Charley Fox of 412 squadron RCAF (Royal Canadian Air Force), who strafed a staff car that evening.[114] That allows the likelihood that a pilot nicknamed the 'Flying

---

114   Reginald Byron, *Who Shot Rommel?* Tangmere Military Aviation Museum,2016

Fox' put the 'Desert Fox' out of the war. The identity of the pilot who seriously injured Rommel has never been definitively established.

There were yet more twists to come in this strange story. Three days later, on 20 July 1944, there was an attack on Hitler, and Rommel was suspected of supporting the assassination attempt even though evidence that he wanted to kill Hitler was lacking. Rommel was sacked from his post and his brilliant military career was terminated. A willingness to tell Hitler the ugly truth about the war and Rommel's wish for a change of leadership were enough to seal his fate. He was given an ultimatum. Either commit suicide and the German public would be told Rommel died honourably from his injuries, or the legendary military leader would be charged and executed as a traitor. On 14 October, three months after the attack on his staff car, Rommel committed suicide by poison. A German General took him into a car and gave him a cyanide pill to self-administer. Four days later he was given a grand State funeral.

This bizarre death of one of Germany's greatest wartime military leaders was in the future. For now, 125 Wing was interested in improving living conditions. The accommodation for the Wing in Normandy was very basic and Geoffrey Page and the other leaders did what they could to provide home comforts. So, 125 Wing built their own pub. A British newspaper headline read, 'RAF have their own bar in Normandy'. Apparently The Get Some Inn proudly displayed a proper inn sign. The report added, 'Wing Co Page, DFC and bar, performed the launching ceremony by cracking a bottle of Scotch over the sign.' The Squadron was relieved to learn that the bottle was empty and not a drop of precious liquid had been wasted.

Geoffrey Page was a popular leader always looking for ways of cheering up his men. In Normandy, not content with opening a bar, he boosted morale by flying back to England and filling up his reserve tank with good British beer for his thirsty pilots and ground crews in France. His mechanic, Fred Ollett, also jokingly asked his boss to bring back a white loaf as the airmen were all fed up with hard biscuits. On his safe return to the Squadron Page pointed to the machine gun panels, 'I opened them up and there were lovely white loaves of bread. He had taken out the machine gun bullets to put in the bread.' Then he said 'if you get your drinking mug you will get some beer out of the jettison tanks.'[115]

This was typical of Geoffrey's leadership. On another occasion he found that Fred Ollett's steak and kidney pie he was eating for his evening meal was 'off', so sour that his trusty mechanic could not eat it. Page, wrote Fred, 'After sweeping away the flies, tasted it and spat it out. He then took me down to the cookhouse and made them give me a fresh dinner.'

When Page was promoted to Wing Commander, the leadership of 132 Squadron fell to Squadron Leader Ken Charney. Page and Charney, accompanied by Skipper Vinden (or Hvinden), set out in late July for another so-called cannon test. They were shocked to see around sixty enemy aircraft in formation. The numbers gave the three Spitfires odds of twenty to one. Page gave a sharp intake of breath but remained undeterred. As the Spitfires attacked the unsuspecting enemy Focke Wolfe 190s all hell broke loose. The Germans had seen the Spitfires. Now cannon fire was spraying in all directions as the enemy broke their formation. Page could see that Skipper had been hit but he managed to isolate one Luftwaffe machine. From a hundred yards he pressed his gun button and saw bits of metal fly off the FW190 as his bullets hit home. Page was transfixed by the German aircraft as it turned onto its back and plunged into the earth below and exploded into a fireball. It was time to escape the chaos of so many enemy aircraft, spinning around like crazed ants.

---

115  Fred Ollett, *letter to Pauline Page,* August 2000

The Falaise Pocket, or Falaise Gap, in the Calvados area of Normandy was almost the only way out for around 100,000 German troops trapped in Normandy. The Allies threw everything at closing this escape route, and the Germans were equally desperate to keep the Falaise Gap open. Spitfires, Mustangs, and Thunderbolts were all in action. Artillery fire was relentless. A failure to tighten the noose around Falaise quickly enough enabled thousands of experienced German soldiers to escape from the Pocket and fight another day. Estimates vary but about the same number were taken prisoner with more than 10,000 Germans dead. Almost nothing else was left standing. When the Falaise Pocket was finally closed, General Dwight Eisenhower described the 'killing fields' where 'it was literally possible to walk for hundreds of yards at a time, stepping on nothing but dead and decaying flesh.'[116]

British Army officer Zbigniew Mieczkowski from Poland described a similar scene in his self-published autobiography, 'The massacre among German units was enormous. Masses of men killed and horses and heaps of destroyed vehicles everywhere. The whole scene was enveloped in the sweet odour of dead bodies which haunted us for weeks to come.' From just two hundred feet above the enemy Geoffrey Page could clearly see the burning vehicles described by Mieczkowski. Red Crosses were tied across lifeless German tanks. Page spotted arrogant-looking German soldiers idly playing cards while their truck was in flames. He gave them a strafing of bullets for good measure. During July, 132 Squadron destroyed or damaged twenty-five enemy aircraft and destroyed almost a hundred enemy transport plus ninety more damaged.

Until now the human beings Page had shot had been inside their machine which made killing impersonal. Then, on a solo 'can-

116  Dwight Eisenhower, *Crusade in Europe*, Doubleday, New York, 1948

non test' sortie, he spotted a lone military dispatch rider stopped on a little S-bend on the road below; a legitimate military target, quietly studying his map. Lining up the rider in his sights, Page caught the final glance of the man as he looked up and saw the danger above him. As the bullets ripped into him, the German threw his left arm up as if to shield his face. Page hated himself as bullets tore into the man and his bike. This simple, almost helpless gesture, haunted Page long afterwards, 'I shall always remember that and not be proud of it.'

American fighter pilot, Quentin Aanenson experienced similar feelings in Northern France when he shot at a group of Germans on an open road, 'I remember the impact it had on me when I could see my bullets just tearing into them. We had so much firepower that the bodies would just fly some yards…this was my job. This is what I was trained to do…but when I landed, I felt sick. I had to think about what I had done.'[117]

Geoffrey Page found it hard to forget the defensive arm gesture of the unprotected dispatch rider as he brutally extinguished the German's life in a hail of bullets. To Geoffrey Page this was a reckoning. His hatred was no longer directed towards the Germans, but himself. His long hate-fuelled battle with his inner-self had been so all-consuming that it threatened to destroy Geoffrey just as effectively as any German with a gun, 'I found myself not liking myself. I was full of hate, and it was damaging me. I felt myself drained of energy. Mind you, I was exhausted by my operational flying, but how long can you carry on a vendetta?'

Strafing the defenceless German dispatch rider finally brought his long, self-destructive, journey to an end, 'Although only twenty-four years old I felt like an old, old man. It all seemed so purposeless now. I had left hospital with a seething desire to destroy;

---

117   Ken Burns/Lynn Novick, *The War*, Public Broadcasting Service, Alexandria, Virginia,2 October 2007

this ambition seemed shallow and puerile. Nevertheless, the deed was now done and where did I go from here? I was tired, dead tired, both physically and mentally. The girlfriends I'd had since leaving East Grinstead hospital I'd treated as doormats. Hate had filled my heart. Now hate was spent, leaving a void.'[118]

Back with the squadron, he couldn't talk about this incident for days. But Geoffrey Page never forgot the defenceless man raising his arm. It was this vivid image that haunted him for decades after the war. His son, Jamie wrote, 'My father had a recurring dream after the war. He would wake up in horror. He was that close to the German dispatch rider cowering on the ground that he could see his arms up defending himself from the bullets of my father's Spitfire. Of course, the man was shot to bits. My father carried this image with him for the rest of his life.'[119]

118  Geoffrey Page, *Tale of a Guinea Pig*, Pelham, London, 1981
119  Jamie Page, Unpublished notes, Cornwall, 2013

Chapter Eighteen

# Arnhem

In August 1944 Wing Commander Geoffrey Page swept over Paris in his Spitfire, but stories of the city's liberation proved to be premature. Page noted in his logbook, 'Flew over the Arc de Triomphe at 10,000 feet. Heavy flak encountered - liberation of Paris - balls!!' A few days later the anti-aircraft guns of the enemy finally fell silent, and Paris was French again. Geoffrey Page and a handful of his pilots headed off from Normandy in their RAF jeep to explore the newly liberated city. Their reception from the locals was overwhelming. Wine flowed as freely as the Seine for the next two days, before the pilots returned to their base.

From Northern France Geoffrey Page and 125 Wing moved up to Antwerp, which had also been freed from the Nazis. Antwerp had been a vital supply port for the enemy and the Germans desperately needed to reoccupy Antwerp. The war in Belgium was still far from over. A canal ran alongside the airfield and on the other side of the water sat entrenched German positions. As RAF planes came into land the enemy would aim their shells at the runway. Page was staying in a tent, but the continuous enemy shelling made sleep impossible. The Wing Commander was relieved when the local Mayor, grateful for the city's liberation, offered him a suite in a swanky city centre hotel. No German shelling and a hot bath were a heavenly combination. By day, the 125th Wing was very busy with fighter sweeps, but at night Antwerp proved a fine city to party in. This included an inadvertent visit to a high-class brothel where Geoffrey and a senior colleague spent their spare cash on alcohol rather than sex.

Although the war in Europe had entered its final chapter the Luftwaffe had made a good recovery from their defeat in Northern France. They had re-equipped rapidly, with their factories turning out a record number of single-engine fighters. As British troops attempted to establish a bridgehead in Holland by securing river crossings over the Neder Rijn, the Waal, and the Maas, Geoffrey Page knew that the enemy was far from beaten. Operation Market Garden, as it was called, relied on taking the bridges in sequence, with the final frontier being the bridge at Arnhem.

John Wray, who was destined to take over Page's Spitfire Wing, immediately saw the vulnerability of thousands of British Para troops transported by gliders, 'I saw this enormous glider train full of Para troops coming towards us. There must have been two hundred of them. It was like a great flock of birds travelling at no speed at all... there was no way I could see that they could cross that coast without getting slaughtered.' [120]

Preparations for the Battle of Arnhem started badly. The First Airborne Division were dropped too far from their objective and were badly hit. Liaison with the ground was poor and little attention seems to have been paid to the requirements of close support from the RAF. A temporary airstrip was bulldozed on what looked like a turnip field for the Spitfires to use. On his first day in the area Page saw large fires burning around Arnhem. His anger at the plight of the British troops on the ground was deepened by foggy flying conditions. The silence of the flat countryside was only broken by the sounds of the bloody battle for Arnhem, but the fog made Page's Wing impotent. By the time the weather had cleared the paratroopers had been decimated.

---

120   John Wray, *Imperial War Museum Sound Archive* 12371, London

Page was devastated by his inability to help, 'Poor bloody sods, I thought. For a moment pity filled my heart as I surveyed the murderous battlefield thousands of feet below...for days now the Red Devils had been fighting a losing battle against the onslaught of the Wermacht. Tragically foul flying conditions had prevented close air support during the critical days, and the massacre of the paratroopers had proceeded uninterrupted.'[121]

Not that the RAF were safe themselves. The new air strip for 125 Wing was vulnerable to enemy attack, and Page's adjutant and a cook were killed in an enemy raid. On the ground, paratroopers continued to die in large numbers. The few that managed to swim across the wide river told terrible tales of the battle. These chilling stories from the men who arrived shivering from their watery escape drove the RAF pilots on even harder.

On 25 September Page's Wing lost two pilots from his former squadron, 132, and two days later two more Spitfires were lost near Arnhem, although this time their pilots survived. On the day between these two losses, Page's Spitfire XIV's found themselves under a surprise attack from eight Messerschmitt 109s. Above the bridges a dog fight broke out, Spitfires versus Me109s, just like the Battle of Britain. Page used all his experience to seek height advantage as he chased an isolated enemy plane. Page placed himself directly behind and slightly below the 109. It was a blind spot. From 150 yards he pressed the firing button and saw black smoke pour from the Messerschmitt. His number two, Flying Officer Derraugh, watched the enemy aircraft spinning helplessly down before crashing into the ground. Page was a Wing Commander now and this 'kill' left him unsettled. He had now shot down fifteen enemy aircraft, one for each operation on his

---

121   Geoffrey Page, *Tale of a Guinea Pig,* Pelham, London 1981

hands and face. He did not want to kill another German pilot and find himself in a strange, unhappy, credit.[122]

On 27 September the Daily Sketch reported under the headline '**Some of the Few In Arnhem Battle**' that 'Wing Commander Geoffrey Page was in the thick of it yesterday when Spitfires from the RCAF (Royal Canadian Air Force) Wing shot down eight without loss.' But the Allies were not having their own way. The autumn leaves had not yet dropped and the thickly wooded areas near Arnhem provided excellent cover for German anti-aircraft guns.

On a sunny day, Geoffrey Page was in the aerial frontline once again attacking German positions close to the bridgehead. This was his final flight at Arnhem before returning to the UK on the expiration of his tour of duty. Feeling relaxed and safe, he came into land at Grave (or B-82) airfield southwest of Nijmegen in the hazy sunshine, using the curved approach that experienced Spitfire pilots favoured. Suddenly, Page's Spitfire flipped to the right, smashed into the ground, and cartwheeled across the airfield, breaking in half. To anyone who had flown with Geoffrey Page it was impossible that he could have made such a beginner's mistake, but it looked to the naked eye that he had stalled his Spitfire.

Geoffrey Page quickly switched off the ignition and relief that he had not been engulfed in flames a second time swept over him. His aircraft had smashed into pieces as if it was made of Lego. Page was in pieces too. His back was broken, and his much-repaired face was pulped, with blood pouring down his cheek. With his left cheek he had broken a quarter inch steel plate that supported the gunsight. Geoffrey Page had survived the Battle of France, the Battle of Britain,

---

122  Page's autobiography implies this was his sixteenth kill, but reliable sources have his total as fifteen. Shared and damaged aircraft left room for differing claims in the fog of war.

D Day, and the Battle of Normandy, but Arnhem had finally brought his war to an end.

The first man on the scene was Fred Ollett, Page's loyal air crew for three years. He was repairing a Spitfire a hundred yards away when his Wing Commander smashed into the ground. It was Fred who instantly instructed the injured pilot to switch his engine off to avoid fire. Then he just quietly talked to Geoffrey to keep him conscious until more help arrived.

Page was dimly aware of Fred Ollett and other airmen running anxiously towards him and then hands lifting him out of the tiny cockpit of his Spitfire. He was gently carried on a stretcher and placed in the back of an ambulance. John Wray was another eyewitness, 'The Spitfire just flicked over and cartwheeled across the airfield. It looked as if it had stalled and one of the worst sights is to see an aircraft cartwheel. Fortunately, it didn't catch fire and we dashed over; got old Geoff out - he'd bashed his already battered face on the gunsight. The doc gave him a check and he was all right though he had concussion, so I took him back to our farmhouse. He was slightly delirious all night and kept on about how he could have been so stupid as to stall on an approach.'

That night, John Wray, who was taking over command of Page's Spitfire Wing the next day, slept alongside the injured Wing Commander on their two camp beds in the farmhouse kitchen. A delirious Geoffrey Page repeatedly calling himself an idiot for stalling his aircraft and making such a ridiculous mistake. Page was such an experienced pilot that John Wray could not believe that Geoffrey had made such an elementary error.

The next morning Wray inspected the smashed aircraft and worked out what had happened, 'He'd been hit by a bullet which had gone through one of his aileron wires. The additional tension as he landed snapped it and caused him to flick over. He was very lucky to survive.'[123] Page was relieved to know that the crash had not been his fault. He carried a flask with him that was a replica of the one he lost in the sea when he had been shot down in the Battle of Britain. He wryly remarked later, 'After many weeks of fighting, the flask and I crashed back at our airfield in Holland.'

After his troubled night in the farmhouse, Page was moved to an RAF casualty clearing station based in a convent. Before the war no male had crossed this threshold since the fourteenth century. The young Wing Commander was superbly looked after by the nuns. The Mother Superior made a deep impression on him with her grace and kindness. He was less impressed with the padre from the Church of England who prayed robotically at the foot of his bed.

He was sorry to leave the Mother Superior and the other nuns behind, but the medical officer saw his new patient as an easy ticket to a few days at home. He accompanied the smashed-up pilot back to England on a transport aircraft. Geoffrey Page's war as a combat pilot had come to an end. Before he left Holland, Geoffrey said a warm farewell to his men. His long standing-mechanic, Fred Ollett, wrote, 'He thanked us for helping after his crash, and so ended three years of excitement with one of the great fighter pilots of the RAF.' To add to his Distinguished Flying Cross and Bar, in December 1944 Wing Commander Page was awarded the Distinguished Service Order. The citation stated:

> *On two occasions in July 1944 while on cannon test, he encoun-*
> *tered upwards of thirty enemy aircraft. Each time, he attacked*
> *without hesitation and shot down one of the enemy. On the second*
> *occasion he was wounded by cannon shell but flew safely to base.*
> *Later in October 1944 he sustained severe injuries when his air-*
> *craft crashed after being damaged by anti-aircraft fire. Apart from*

---

123  Norman Franks, *Scramble to Victory*, William Kimber, London,1987

*his individual exploits, Wing Commander Page has infused the entire wing with his own fine fighting spirit. Under his command sixty enemy aircraft have been destroyed together with a large number of transport vehicles and tanks. This splendid achievement has been largely due to the brilliant leadership of Wing Commander Page.*

Page felt relieved when his taxi turned into the drive of the Queen Victoria Hospital in East Grinstead once again. It had been nearly three years since he had been driven past the same neat green lawns. Geoffrey Page was home again.

Chapter Nineteen

# Guinea Pig Take Two

Wing Commander Geoffrey Page was one of only two McIndoe patients to be so badly damaged they became a Guinea Pig for the second time. As Page was wheeled into the small casualty room, he heard Archie McIndoe say, 'The trouble with you is that you're just plain clumsy.' Sister Hall was equally welcoming. 'My goodness, not you again', she said.

Once again Geoffrey Page found himself in a bed in the legendary Ward Three. McIndoe no longer needed to convince the medical establishment that the holistic care of burns patients was right. The Guinea Pig treatment, complete with beer barrels and pub visits, was now accepted as the best way to heal active young men psychologically as well as physically. Page was older now, and a Wing Commander, and he immediately noticed changes. Other surgeons had emerged alongside McIndoe to deal with increased patient numbers. Prominent amongst them was Ross Tilley, an innovative Canadian plastic surgeon who shared McIndoe's views on all-round patient care, and Percy Jayes who had been a young assistant in 1940 and was now an accomplished surgeon in his own right.

The other change Geoffrey Page noted was the absence of familiar faces. Page missed the comradeship of his old friends in the beds around him. Looking around at the young patients he felt like a mature student in a lecture room full of nineteen-year-old undergraduates. Some senior nurses were still in post, but many had moved on.

Geoffrey's favourite haunts had changed too. The cinema at the much-loved Whitehall had been hit directly by a bomb on a Friday afternoon in 1943. It was an afternoon screening of the cowboy film *Hopalong Cassidy* and so children and their mothers were amongst the one hundred and eight dead. The small hospital at East Grinstead was overwhelmed with the casualties, and many of the dead and injured lay in the corridors before space in a mortuary or a hospital ward could be found. The Ward Three nurses and doctors, led by Percy Jayes, worked round the clock on more than two hundred injured patients. Archie McIndoe himself was in hospital following a hand operation for Dupuytren's contracture which was causing the surgeon's fingers to bend inwards. Jill Mullins quickly telephoned him in his hospital bed at the London Clinic. McIndoe knew his fingers were not yet good enough for the operating theatre, but he dashed down from London to supervise the work and, like all the hospital staff, toiled through the night.

On his return, Page was surprised to find himself missing Richard Hillary. He remembered throwing eggs at him in a temper three years before. Perhaps the stains were still on the wall? But Richard Hillary would not be coming back because he had been killed in a training accident in Scotland in January 1943.He was twenty-three years old. During a night flight in poor winter weather conditions his Bristol Blenheim crashed, lighting up the Scottish night sky. Both Hillary and his Observer/Radio Officer, 37-year-old Sergeant Wilfrid Fison, died.

Geoffrey understood Hillary well because they shared the same courageous spirit. When claims were made that Hillary had committed suicide by deliberately crashing his aircraft, Page was angry. He had seen at close quarters Hillary's will to live, as well as his courage and integrity. He was certain that this was not a man who would ever have taken the life of the radio operator/observer who shared his Blenheim with him.

The probable reason for Hillary's death was that he was simply not fit enough to fly. Neither the strength in his hands, nor his eyesight, were good enough for night flying. Just before his accident Richard Hillary visited Archie McIndoe. Archie respected Hillary's bravery, 'Fame and literary recognition were his in generous measure…instead he chose to go back and fight again.' Hillary told the surgeon that unless he stopped night flying, he would be killed. McIndoe warned the Medical Officer at Hillary's RAF station in Scotland that the damaged left eye of the young writer was not standing up to night flying. He urged that Hillary be sent back to East Grinstead for further repair work and asked the medical officer that if he could 'restrain him from night flying, it might save him from a very serious accident.' He was in no doubt that if Hillary continued to fly 'it can only end one way'.

McIndoe's warning letter marked Private sat unopened on the Medical Officer's desk for two weeks because the doctor was on leave. By the time McIndoe had received an evasive reply it was too late, Richard Hillary was already dead. Hillary had insisted that McIndoe wrote privately to the Medical Officer because, as a newly famous author, he did not want his wish to stop flying to become public. That bleak night Richard Hillary looked weary when he clambered into his Blenheim and his observer, Wilfrid Fison, although able, didn't have the night-flying experience to get the pair out of trouble if necessary. Hillary's unfitness to fly at night, especially in bad winter weather, made McIndoe's prediction that it can only end one way' come tragically true. McIndoe wrote, 'I often think of him in that last moment - his crippled hands fighting for control of his spinning plane - the cold sweat pouring from his body, the screaming crescendo of the engines, his patchwork face frozen in that mocking twisted smile...'[124] Archie McIndoe also noted sympathetically that, although his arrogance was too much for many of his ward mates in East Grinstead, as time passed Hillary's feelings for his fellow patients grew 'more kindly and were touched with a deeper understanding of human frailty.'

In the months between July and October 1940, 544 pilots died in the Battle of Britain. Hillary was just one of nearly 800 Battle of Britain pilots who survived the Battle of Britain but went on be killed later in the war. That meant that of the nearly 3000 men who flew in defence of Britain in the summer of 1940 the chances of being killed by the end of the war was close to one in two.

On his return to Archie McIndoe's care, Geoffrey Page again endured grafting procedures on his hands and face. But the bullets he had taken in the leg in Normandy were also causing him great pain. McIndoe did his best to alleviate the problem but inside Page knew that with his leg, his smashed back, his gnarled hands, and his twice-damaged face, his days of flying in combat were finally over. There was a part of him that was very sad to see that phase of his life pass by, but another part was relieved. He was still only twenty-four.

This time his stay in East Grinstead was measured in weeks not years. The RAF medical board concluded that after leaving the Queen Victoria Hospital three months on the ground would aid both his physical and mental recovery. His next overseas adventure would unexpectedly change his life as profoundly as the Battle of Britain or Arnhem.

---

124  Archibald McIndoe, *Valiant for Truth*, Guinea Pig Magazine,1943

Chapter Twenty

# America

Archie McIndoe watched out for his damaged flock after they left hospital as conscientiously as when they were directly in his care. He found them jobs, fought for their pensions, and assisted their social lives. It was McIndoe who wangled Geoffrey Page a trip to America. Page was invited to foster Anglo-American understanding by sailing to the USA on the Queen Elizabeth to give a series of goodwill lectures across America about his remarkable wartime experiences.

When his ship docked, Page was stunned by the brightness of New York. In the Big Apple there was no blackout and the twinkling lights contrasted vividly with the drabness of wartime England. In January 1945 he set off on his first assignment to the twin cities of Minneapolis and St Paul. His first lecture was to a class of five hundred agricultural students. They were all women. He was nervous but all went well until he described waking up some villagers in France for refreshments as 'knocking up'. Five hundred young female students gasped and tried to suppress their laughter, before the lecture ended with wild catcalls and whistles. The smiling college Principal explained to a mystified Page that 'knocked up' meant pregnant in the USA.

At Menlo Park in California, Geoffrey gave a talk at the Dibble General Hospital which had been activated by the US Army in 1943 as a unit for burns. Both the similarities to and differences from the

Queen Victoria Hospital would have struck Page. Nurse Betty Bayse Hutchinson described the patients as if they were in Ward Three in East Grinstead, 'Blind young men. Eyes gone; legs gone. Parts of the face. Burns - you'd land with a firebomb and be up in flames. It was a burn-and-blind centre...he didn't have eyebrows, a complete white mass of scars. The pedicle was hanging off his neck. He had no ears - they had been burnt off.'[125]

However, in America's equivalent of the Queen Victoria Hospital, nurses were banned from relationships with anyone except officers and even then, dating was not encouraged. There were no barrels of beer or pianos in the wards. When patients were later moved to Pasadena, letters were written to the local paper complaining about how the men looked and suggesting it would be better for the patients if they were kept off the streets. This was certainly not East Grinstead, The Town That Didn't Stare.

After his talks, Geoffrey Page was widely praised. 1st Lt Paul Lilly at Dibble General Hospital wrote that the patients 'enjoyed his visit and were impressed by his modesty'. The British Ambassador had furnished Page with letters of introduction to British celebrities in Los Angeles. Using this introduction, when Page arrived in the City of Angels he called the home of the British actor Nigel Bruce and his wife Bunny. Bruce was famous for playing Doctor Watson to Basil Rathbone's Sherlock Holmes. They were delighted to hear from him and invited him to lunch. The occasion must have been a roaring success because Bunny and Nigel invited Geoffrey to stay with them rather than be stuck on his own in an anonymous hotel. There was plenty of room, they said, as one of their daughters was now married to Jay Gould III of the famous railway family, and the other was serving with the Royal Canadian Air Force.

---

125   Studs Terkel, *The Good War*, Pantheon Books, New York,1984

There followed a wild social whirl, almost as tiring as endless sorties in a Spitfire. Nightclubs and parties, dinners and studio visits, filled his days and nights. He was British, an RAF pilot, and a decorated war hero, so Geoffrey was feted everywhere he went. Joan Fontaine and Dorothy Lamour both featured on his busy social calendar and British expatriate actors like Aubrey Smith, Ronald Colman, and Richard Greene warmly greeted the young pilot. His scarred face and clawed hands appeared to go unnoticed, and he was a centre of female interest, including a close attachment to actress Barbara Sears.[126] One night his hostess, Bunny Bruce, was amused to find Geoffrey creeping into the house, his scarred face smothered in lipstick. It was with sadness that Geoffrey finally said goodbye to his new circle of friends and the glamourous social whirl of a city bathed in eternal sunshine.

Back in England, the end of the war in Europe heralded the euphoria of victory followed by the complex challenge of picking up the threads of pre-war life. The young boys who their mothers and sisters, girlfriends and fiancées, had seen off to war had come back as men. Terry Hunt, whose husband David was one of McIndoe's Guinea Pigs, sensed the change, 'It was four o'clock in the morning on VE Day in Cardiganshire. The victory beacons were going out. I thought of those who weren't there to share that moment and then I realised that the golden years had gone. They had dried out with the fire.'[127] Geoffrey Page too sensed that 'the golden years' had ended. His burns notwithstanding, the war had given him a clear-cut purpose in life.

The future for Geoffrey and thousands of other members of the armed forces was uncertain. Nothing was ever going to be as exciting as flying Hurricanes or Spitfires. In their early twenties the fighter pilots

---

126 Sears was married but estranged. She divorced in 1947. The following year she married into the very wealthy Rockefeller family.

127 Interview with author, 1981

had reached the pinnacle of their lives. Was the rest just going to be a downhill anti-climax? Terry Hunt observed of her husband, 'David said he'd rather do war again - including the burning up - than be an edge-tool worker in a ghastly place like Wolverhampton.' Geoffrey Page carried the physical scars of combat, and like so many others, emotional wounds too. Page recognised that his life had reached a peak of excitement as a twenty-year-old, but other battles still had to be fought and won. How would he integrate back into society? Could he ever replace the drama and comradeship of his wartime life? Was he capable of bringing up a family, clothing, feeding, and housing them, especially with his ruined hands? All these challenges had to be met and he also knew he would face further operations and grafts over the following decades.

On VE Day, 8 May 1945, Geoffrey Page was a Wing-Commander but still just twenty-four. His twenty-fifth birthday was a week away. He was a fighter pilot to his gnarled fingertips. Flying fast aircraft was as central to his life as breathing. Page's first instinct was to join the war against the Japanese in the Far East, which was still in full fury. However, the cannon shell that had been lodged in his leg for years urgently needed to come out first, so he was sent back to the Queen Victoria Hospital for another month to have both the cannon shell and his tonsils removed. While he was in hospital, he received a surprising letter from Nigel Bruce in Hollywood. It contained a photograph of a beautiful young woman. It was the Bruce's daughter, Pauline, who was serving with the Royal Canadian Air Force. This was, Nigel Bruce asserted, a photograph of the woman Page was going to marry.

While he recovered from the operation on his leg, Geoffrey Page fired off a letter to Pauline telling her about her father's intentions and saying that she should consider herself 'to be engaged'. He also warned her not to misbehave with all those Canadian airmen. He didn't think much more about the jokey correspondence. Nor did Pauline Bruce but she quietly admitted to herself 'I liked the idea every woman liked the idea of going out with a Battle of Britain hero.' Once the shell in his leg was removed, Wing Commander Page turned his attention back to fighting in the Far East. Once again, Archie McIndoe rescued the young man who had been like a son to him. The surgeon bluntly told Geoffrey that flying in the steamy Far East was a stupid idea.

Archie McIndoe took Geoffrey to Scotland for a spot of shooting and fishing. That lifted Page's spirits hugely, but his uncertain mood surfaced in the hotel register. He gave his address as 'RAF home for broken down airmen' complete with a drawing of a guinea pig with the caption 'What no gloves!'. McIndoe's register entry including the observation 'squirrel pie first class'.

Soon after, Flying Officer John Caulton of 132 Squadron bumped into Geoffrey who was having dinner with his sister in Bournemouth to celebrate his birthday. Caulton had been captured in 1944 when Geoffrey Page had led a raid on the German-held airfield at Deelen. Caulton had just been repatriated from his prisoner-of-war camp in Germany and the two men were delighted to see each other.

Wing Commander Page was about to take some leave and suggested that the two former pilots from 132 Squadron took a tour around the pubs of Southern England in his sports car. One night they finished up in East Grinstead and inevitably gravitated towards the Queen Victoria Hospital. Page knew the nurses so well that the two pilots spent a few nights sleeping in the hospital as if it was an hotel. McIndoe entertained them to dinner one evening.

Through the RAF network, Page learned that the major aircraft manufacturer Vickers Armstrongs had a vacancy for a test pilot because one of their team had been killed in an accident and another pilot had fractured his skull. Presumably with Archie McIndoe's help,

Geoffrey Page managed to remain in the air force but be seconded to Vickers as a test pilot in June 1945. His contentment increased when he received a light-hearted reply to his letter from Pauline Bruce in Canada. Geoffrey was happy as a test pilot for the next six months, and at the same time his application for a permanent commission in the RAF was accepted. He was also awarded a place at the Empire Test Pilots School which was so prestigious every course attracted hundreds of applicants.

To his disappointment Geoffrey's plans had to be put on hold when his test pilot course was postponed. The RAF decided that as a regular he needed to sharpen his administrative skills and sent him on an admin course which was much less interesting than flying for Vickers Armstrongs. While he waited for a new Test Pilots course, Page was given a job as Personal Assistant to the senior RAF officer on the Military Staff Commission at the newly-formed United Nations in New York. For an action man like Page, an office job at the UN proved to be deadly dull. He spent his time making paper airplanes and throwing them forlornly out of the window. His work for Air Chief Marshal Sir Guy Garrod seemed largely to consist of putting out place names for dinner parties, but at least he was back in the USA which he had grown to like very much, and he was halfway to California.

After a few months he finally made his way west once more. He was looking forward to all the fun in Los Angeles and renewing both his friendships with the community of British actors and his relationship with Barbara Sears. He had not thought about Pauline Bruce in any serious way, but he was without a girlfriend and was intrigued by her. She looked lovely in her photograph but that didn't mean much. Page was invited to stay once again with Nigel and Bunny Bruce by their other daughter, Jennifer. Soon after his arrival he saw a beautiful dark-haired young woman pass the window in her tennis outfit. They were briefly introduced by Jennifer. Geoffrey Page was transfixed. This introduction to the tall, elegant, woman in white with her grey eyes and a sparkling personality was to change his life every bit as much as his horrific crash in the Battle of Britain.

Chapter Twenty-One

# After the War

Young men and women wasted no time in love, sex, and marriage after the war. Years had been lost while the men were fighting, and all too often husbands and boyfriends were no longer there. The time for long, gentle, courtships was over. The war had changed relationships between the sexes, and romance moved faster now. Thinking about Pauline Bruce before he met her for the first time, Geoffrey was secretly struck with terror. He had placed himself in an absurd situation where he had corresponded with a young woman about getting married, but he had never sat eyes on her.

Pauline Bruce did not share this fear. She had only known Geoffrey Page for three days when she proposed to him, 'It was love at first sight…I'd been out playing tennis and saw this dashing man standing there. We both looked at one another and that was it. It was instant… He has such charisma, I knew without doubt that I could be very happy with this man, even though he was a stranger.' [128]

To Geoffrey Page it was extraordinary that this beautiful woman wanted to spend the rest of her life married to a man with burned hands and face. After all, Pauline apparently had half the Royal Canadian Air Force chasing her, so she was not short of suitors. Somehow in the surprise and confusion Geoffrey contrived to say, 'no but I'll think about it' and mumbled something about 'being married

---

128 *Woman's Weekly,* London,2001

to his aeroplane'. His indecisiveness was probably not helped by the strange location of this proposal. Pauline and Geoffrey were attending a circus party given by the famous radio pioneer A. Atwater Kent, and she proposed on top of an elephant. Nonetheless, Pauline was not giving up. Two days later she tried again, and a calmer Geoffrey said yes. Guests at their engagement party included some of Hollywood's biggest names like Douglas Fairbanks and Ronald Colman.

No doubt in 1945 a marriage proposal from a woman was unusual, but Pauline's initiative showed that the traditional rules of courtship had disappeared in the jumble of war. Pauline never doubted her decision, 'When I saw him that first time, I was impressed by how good looking he still was. I had seen other burns cases in the RCAF in Canada, so it never bothered me with Geoffrey at all. But when I told a former boyfriend I was engaged to Geoffrey he said, "But how can you marry a man with hands like that?" '[129]

What is impossible to verify was Pauline's revelation years later to Tony Edwards, a Trustee of the Battle of Britain Memorial, that Pauline was engaged to another man at the time she met Geoffrey. Geoffrey's rival in love was reportedly Donald Douglas Jr, heir to his father's huge Douglas aircraft empire and American Olympic sportsman. Whether the couple were formally engaged, or just thinking about it, was not clear but Pauline chose Geoffrey and never regretted it.

The wedding nearly never happened because of Geoffrey's remarkable capacity for near misses. His best man was John Mitchell who was Churchill's navigator during the war. What could be more appropriate than two distinguished wartime airmen flying themselves to California? The two men cheerfully set off west from New York in a little plane, an Avro Anson. As the flight progressed, they grew concerned they could see no landmarks below. Europe was peppered

---

129 *Daily Mail,* London,2000

with railway lines and villages, church spires and rivers, but middle America was just a vast emptiness. As they flew on for hours into nothingness the fuel gauge displayed ominously close to empty. As they headed over the wide-open spaces of Indiana the little plane was completely out of fuel. It was as embarrassing as it was risky, but their only option was to crash land.

To their relief Geoffrey made a safe emergency landing at Greenfield. Geoffrey Page had come full circle from his crash in Sussex as a nineteen-year-old student years before. Once more the local press missed the full story, just reporting that 'the left engine suddenly quit' as the British aviators emergency landed to refuel at Greenfield and that 'the only damage to the plane was a broken propellor and damaged flaps'. If they had worked out the full story the press would have had a field day. 'Battle of Britain Hero and Churchill's Navigator get lost flying over the USA' would have been an eye-catching headline, thought Geoffrey Page.

The two embarrassed airmen made it just in time for the wedding. On 31 August Geoffrey Page enjoyed a bachelor luncheon where the Special was Top Sirloin, New York, or Filet Mignon steak for $2.50. The next day, one year after the end of the war, Geoffrey Page and Pauline Bruce were married in Santa Barbara, California. Many of the British Hollywood film community were guests at the service and at the reception afterwards at *El Mirasol*. Nigel Bruce wrote to Geoffrey that he was 'damnably happy to have you as a son in law...although I am her father, I can honestly say you are getting for a wife one of the sweetest and finest girls.'[130]

It was on their California honeymoon that Pauline Page first confronted the reality of marriage to a man who had been so badly burnt. She had quickly grown to love her new husband's sense of

---

130   Nigel Bruce letter, Los Angeles, 25 August 1946

humour and his empathy towards others, and she accepted his physical limitations. For the rest of his life, she did up the top button of his shirt. But the honeymoon was the first of many occasions when, 'Sometimes in the middle of the night, Geoffrey would wake up in a black fit of depression and would say to me, "Sorry, I can't talk to you darling, go away".' The first time this happened Pauline sat at the top of the stairs and wept, 'He was remembering what had happened to him and afterwards he was apologetic. He couldn't help it.'

*Geoffrey and Pauline Page wedding September 1946, California*

In those days PTSD (post-traumatic stress disorder) was not a recognised condition. Many pilots returning from the war were damaged mentally as well as physically. There was little or no help and they just had to get on with life. Given the burns and injuries Page endured it was no wonder that nightmares surfaced regularly. For the rest of his life, Geoffrey would often wake up in the middle of the night dreaming that he was trapped in a burning aircraft. Or sometimes the nightmare would simply be the relentless, never-ending ringing of a telephone as if he was still in dispersal waiting to be scrambled. Even his son Jamie regularly had childhood nightmares about a strange man entering the house and setting fire to his fingers with matches.

It was impossible for returning pilots like Geoffrey Page to remain unchanged from the excited teenagers who joined up in 1939. American fighter pilot Quentin Aanenson spoke for all wartime airmen when he warned his fiancée how much he had changed, 'I live in a world of death. I watch my friends die in a variety of ways. Sometimes it's just an engine failure on take-off, resulting in a violent explosion and there's not enough of him left to bury. Other times it is deadly flak that tears into a plane. If the pilot is lucky, the flak kills him but usually he isn't, and he burns to death…fire is the worst. One of my good friends crashed on the edge of our field. As he was pulled from the burning plane the skin came off his arms. His face was almost burned away. He was still conscious and trying to talk. You could not imagine the horror…I have lived for my dreams for the future but, like everything else around me, my dreams are dying too…I am not the same person you said goodbye to. No one could go through this war and not change. We are all casualties.[131]

---

131  Ken Burns/Lynn Novick, *The War*, Public Broadcasting System, Alexandria, Virginia, 2007

Like so many others, Page had no option but to hide the trauma of wartime and adjust to his new peacetime reality. Geoffrey Page returned to England with his new wife to take command of 64 Squadron flying Hornets at Linton-on-Ouse near York on 10 July 1947, but not before another operation on his right hand at East Grinstead. After the tedium of his job at the UN in New York, it was good to be back flying. But the drabness of post-war England proved a difficult adjustment for Pauline after the brightness of California. She had lived in America since the age of ten, and her view of England was romanticised. When she became pregnant, Pauline developed a craving for avocados. In a country that had scarcely seen an orange for years such an exotic fruit was impossible to buy. Nonetheless, Geoffrey miraculously conjured an avocado up from somewhere but by the time it arrived in Yorkshire the avocado was black and inedible.

To add to her unease, Pauline was frightened whenever her husband flew. One day she heard a huge explosion on the base and feared the worst. When Geoffrey walked through the door soon after, the look of relief on her face was transparent. For the first time Geoffrey started to question his future as a pilot. The Hornet had significant teething problems and four young pilots were killed in Yorkshire. Would, feared Pauline, her husband be next? She knew he was an excellent pilot, but he had had so many miraculous escapes she feared his luck would not hold out forever.

She was probably right. Geoffrey Page was tasked with flying a group of very senior Army officers up to Stockholm. His co-pilot was Mike Graham[132], who had flown with him on D-Day. On their return journey both experienced pilots nodded off in the cockpit due to some excessive late nights in Sweden. They hadn't fully levelled off the aircraft and when Page woke up, he discovered the plane was in

---

132   Graham later founded the famous hotel Il Pellicano in Porto Ercole, Italy

a gradual descent. He was so close to the water that he could see the white caps of the waves just below. He eased on the power and the aircraft headed safely upwards. Afterwards the Army top brass innocently congratulated Page and Graham on a wonderfully smooth flight.

In September 1947 Wilhelmina, Queen of the Netherlands, made Geoffrey Page an Officer of the Order of Orange-Nassau, a major decoration in Holland, to mark his contribution at Arnhem. But that did not stop the cold, biting wind of a North Yorkshire winter being particularly painful for Page's repaired face and hands. To compound the difficulties, Page and the officer commanding RAF Linton-on-Ouse never got on. The Station Commander had never even flown the Hornets that made up Page's squadron. To complete the frustration, the Hornets were without long-distance fuel tanks or gunsights. What are these aircraft for, wondered Geoffrey Page.

Geoffrey and Pauline talked animatedly about what to do next. They even canvassed the views of Archie McIndoe because the circulation in Page's hands was growing worse as the bitter Yorkshire winter deepened. The discussions culminated in Geoffrey Page formally leaving the service to which he had given so much in 1948. As he ruefully observed, 'The RAF was reducing its size and they had plenty of pilots with two eyes.' His final RAF Medical Board noted that 'in cold weather both hands become blue and ache violently' and that, although he could fly, there was stiffness and deformity in his hands. They accepted the advice of Sir Archibald McIndoe, and he was invalided out of the RAF.

As a final act Geoffrey and Pauline attended an investiture at Buckingham Palace where Page received his DSO and DFC (he was also awarded a bar to his DFC) from the King on 24 March 1948. Pauline and Geoffrey decided to return to the blue skies of California where the eternal sunshine would be better for his hands, and they had a ready-made circle of friends and family. Before that, however, there was the small matter of Pauline's pregnancy. They rented a tiny cottage in Sussex and soon after Shelley, the first of their three children, was born.

Pauline and Geoffrey were very happy together, 'He was such a modest man, and our house was full of fun and laughter.' Pauline was pleased to be back in Los Angeles with her new child, close to her parents, and away from the austerity of an England still recovering from six grim years of war. Settling in the USA was more difficult for her husband. The locals did not call him Geoffrey but Al, because his registered first name was Alan. This unwanted new name added to the loss of his identity. Until recently he had been defined by his status as a senior RAF leader and wartime pilot. Now he no longer knew who he was.

Welcome though he was amongst the expats in California, a job was hard to find for a foreigner given how many American servicemen had returned from the war. The Chairman of the giant American aviation company Lockheed wanted to give a post to such a remarkable pilot but could not justify employing an overseas citizen. With the door to the aviation industry shut in his face Page was forced to take a night job at Kodak where he pushed trolleys of film around. He was especially conscious of his still-gnarled hands, as he trundled the film around in the semi-lit night-time corridors of the laboratory. For an RAF hero and Wing Commander this was a demeaning time in his life, 'I loathed every minute of it…with a family to keep I just couldn't afford to be without a job, but I hadn't cheated death twice and recovered from those horrible injuries to end up as a manual labourer.'

Geoffrey and Pauline's close friends in California were fellow Battle of Britain pilot Tony Bartley, and his famous actress wife, Deborah Kerr, who later became godmother to one of Page's sons. Despite the support of friendship, it was not a surprise when the unsettled couple moved back once again to England where Page's experience and status in the RAF still had a value. Once again, it was Archie McIndoe who rode to the rescue. On a visit to California, he was disturbed by how miserable one of his very favourite Guinea Pigs now was. A month later Page received a letter from McIndoe inviting him to come back to England to make his mind up about the future. Archie also enclosed an air ticket.

With McIndoe's support, Geoffrey Page found a proper job in September 1953 selling aircraft throughout Europe for Vickers-Armstrongs (part of the British Aircraft Corporation from 1960), manufacturers of the Wellington, stalwart RAF bomber of World War Two. Page was happy in his new role based at Weybridge in Surrey, on an annual salary of £1200 and he became a successful aircraft salesman throughout Europe. It was a relief not to be pushing trolleys of film cans around a dimly-lit film laboratory. In April 1954 the Guinea Pig magazine noted his return to England with typical irreverence, 'We gather he will be a sort of travelling salesman, so if a Pig arrives at your front door to ask if he can interest you in a supersonic fighter or ram-jet bomber, please don't slam the door in his face.'

Page was happy selling aircraft but, once again, his war wounds intervened. The dampness of British winters made his gnarled hands ache with pain. So he moved to Geneva where the winters were dry, and for three years he ran a successful sales agency for the British Aircraft Corporation. But when the Anglo-French Concorde arrived it was clear that a French speaker was essential for running an agency in Switzerland, and Page had to look for another job. Once again, he found himself out of place.

Geoffrey's wartime life had been so extraordinary his peacetime existence was never going to match up. The most exciting moments of his life had all happened between the ages of twenty and twenty-four. As his son Jamie summed up, 'Despite the horrendous injuries and suffering that he had undergone, he was what might be called today an adrenaline junkie. He simply loved flying planes. It was as simple as that. Peacetime was dull for him. A lot of pilots suffered from the same thing and my father and his other RAF colleagues all drank like fish, probably to alleviate the tedium.'[133]

His sister Shelley recognised the same phenomenon, 'Like so many young men in the war, the highlight of his life happened in his early twenties, and, in some ways, it was downhill after that.'[134] She also understood that heavy drinking by her father and his friends was their way of navigating through the dullness of peace. Depression and nightmares were also never far away. 'Mummy had to put up with some real black dogs,' she recalls. Page himself was honest and not regretful about his life,' Perhaps we passed the peak of our lives at twenty, but I would do it all again. I wouldn't change a line of it.' Then he would add with a twinkle in his eye, 'Although, I could do without the being burned bit.'

Geoffrey Page was a man of contradictions. His virtually non-existent relationship with his father and his total rejection by his famous uncle added to the complexity. On one hand Page was an intelligent and kind man with a friendly demeanour and twinkly humour. On the other, toughness was hard-wired into him and when he was angry, he would turn white with fury. He kept a bamboo cane in a cupboard, largely as a deterrent, that he would use very occasionally. Parental discipline was mainly asserted by the scary tone of his voice. His daughter Shelley observed, 'There was a very hard side to Daddy. Obviously, there had to be. Otherwise, you don't survive all that. He never had any problems with killing Germans at all, except one, a motorbike rider. He was close enough to look into the man's eyes, and it haunted him for the rest of his life.'

---

133  Jamie Page notes, Devon,2013
134  Author interview, London,2022

He was a very good and loving father, as his children recognised. He was also a caring and kind uncle to his niece Ann. Geoffrey was his daughter Shelley's hero, but he was not easy to grow up with because his expectations were so high, 'I suppose I've spent most of my life trying to make him proud of me.' The father-daughter relationship was good but, as she grew into a precocious teenager, the two would sometimes go for weeks without speaking to each other, 'I absolutely worshipped him but at times I wanted to kill him. I can put him on a pedestal, but I know all the stuff underneath too. I respected him hugely.'

Shelley wished her father had never left the safety of the RAF, 'My father should never have left the RAF. It was where he belonged. I think that after he retired from the air force as a young man, and before the idea of the Battle of Britain Memorial, were years in the wilderness for him. The RAF was really home for Geoffrey.'[135]

Money was an eternal peacetime struggle. When Geoffrey Page gave up the British Aircraft Corporation after more than a decade, the family moved to a village near Lake Geneva where he set up as an independent businessman. The devaluation of the pound against the Swiss franc and his desire to provide the best for his children did not help the family economics. Despite Geoffrey's uncertain finances, his three offspring were all sent to expensive private schools. The dreadful school reports regularly carried home by his son Nigel made Geoffrey cross about the school fees he could ill afford.

Geoffrey was constantly turning wheels to maintain the lifestyle he wanted for his family. Through his Hollywood connections he enjoyed many contacts in the world of film and books, and there were several attempts to add to his income by writing. Stage plays, films, and books were all gleams in his eye. He wrote optimistically

135  Shelley Gubelmann, *Memorial Service for Geoffrey Page,* London, October 2000

to his sister Daphne in 1952 from a hotel in Los Angeles, 'I am happy to be able to tell you that I sold my first story last week; it is to be made into a film for a television show...if I can become established as an author in the film world there is no limit to the amount of money that can be made.'

This American project was never produced. On his own, or working with a producer or writer, several stories were written in outline form, but none reached the screen. The only outlet for his literary efforts appeared to be the Guinea Pig Club magazine which published two of his stories, although he did act as an advisor on the 1981 ITV drama series *A Perfect Hero* starring Nigel Havers which was very loosely based on Richard Hillary's story. Writing a successful film or television drama was more difficult than Geoffrey imagined or had been led to believe. The response from Mark Bonham Carter at the publisher Collins on 16 November 1954 to a fictionalised version of his life was probably typical, 'The form you have chosen is the wrong one...the only chance with this book is to write it as an autobiography.' Page's attempts at fiction continued, but eventually he listened to advice and after over thirty years of work, *Tale of a Guinea Pig* was a welcome autobiographical success.

Even in peacetime Switzerland it was difficult to escape the war. He once caught a group of former German officers singing Nazi songs in his local auberge. He shouted at them angrily to stop, which they did. This was not before he had tipped cigarette ash over their table. In the same auberge or the local café he would run the gauntlet of war bores. One neighbour regaled with him with a story of when in the Swiss Army he bravely faced the danger of seeing German troops on the opposite bank of the Rhine. Wing Commander Page, DSO, DFC, and bar who had experienced an altogether more confrontational war just listened patiently and smiled inwardly to himself.

Even when he stopped flying, Geoffrey's risk-taking spirit remained undimmed. On the Geneva-Lausanne motorway he smashed through water at a high speed in his Mini. The car aquaplaned, somersaulted three times, and crashed into the barriers at the side of the road. Miraculously Geoffrey was unhurt, but the Mini was a complete, and very expensive, write-off. This was not the last car crash. He organised a huge annual air show at Bex near Montreux. After the event he was driving down a steep mountain road with endless hairpin bends when the brakes on his BMW failed. His pilot's training sprang into action, and he calmly slowed the car down with the gears before running it off the road into a tree. His wife was shaking with fear, but Geoffrey was more upset at writing off another expensive car than the near-death crash that he and Pauline had just survived.

Pauline summed up her husband's astonishing capacity for near misses in a poem entitled *Crashing Through the Years*:

> *Aircraft crash, number one*
> *Showing off and having fun!*
> *Number two was far, far worse.*
> *Fried, and just escaped the hearse,*
> *Number three bashed face and neck*
> *Aircraft was a total wreck.*
> *Number four, your leg was shattered,*
> *You survived, that's all that mattered,*
> *Arnhem Bridge was number five,*
> *Your back was broken, you survived.*
> *Number six, a small black car*
> *It was gone, but not dear Pa.*
> *Your favourite car was number seven.*
> *We survived but it's in heaven.*
> *Life's had its share of wrecks and crashes*

*But you've outlasted all these smashes.*
*The years roll on and time goes by*
*We're still together you and I.*
*With fondest love my darling boy*
*You'll always be my life and joy.*

Pauline's bitter-sweet poem did not bring an end to the family's share of 'wrecks and crashes'. In England Pauline was hit by another car as she backed out of the driveway of *Manston Elms*, the aptly-named Surrey house Page had designed himself. Geoffrey was unmoved by the threat of injury or harm. His son Jamie recalled, 'I remember banging my head against the windscreen and being quite shaken up by it. When we got back inside the house, I remember there was not much sympathy from my father, actually no sympathy at all, he just got angry with my mother for having crashed the car. I don't think it was because he could be unsympathetic. It was more that he was always short of money.'

That might have been why he flirted with the world of MI6. He certainly had several connections in the espionage universe and his international aircraft sales work left him well placed to feed information to the intelligence services. His sales circuit took him to Hungary, Bulgaria, and Yugoslavia where he met with representatives of their national airlines and wined and dined with military attachés in various embassies. It might have provided helpful additional income. Joining the dots together, his family think that providing intelligence information was likely. His daughter Shelley says, 'There is no evidence, no back up, but he knew people in that business. There was a connection but not a formal one. I don't think he was an actual spy but occasionally passed on pieces of information.' It is a story that is impossible to corroborate.

Given his horrific wartime injuries and much decorated RAF career, Geoffrey long-running fight for a fair disability pension must have been hurtful. After the war he was awarded a lowly 50% disability pension by the Department of Health and Social Security (DHSS). Archie McIndoe, however, was determined to win a fair deal for one of his 'boys'. The Medical Officer for the Guinea Pig Club wrote to the DHSS on 10 November 1948, 'I am writing to protest against the disablement assessment of 50% in respect of the above-named…I have been asked by the Consultant in Plastic Surgery to the RAF, Sir Archibald McIndoe, to place before you, his opinion.' Archie's opinion won the day, and on 26 November Squadron Leader Geoffrey Page, D.S.O, D.F.C and Bar, was awarded an interim disability pension of 80% and his diagnosis was extended to include his cannon shot wounds in the leg and his broken back.

Geoffrey Page's battle against the benefits system continued for the rest of his life. In 1956, sixteen years after his accident, a medical examination recorded that his scarring included, 'The cheeks, eyelids, top of nose, and forehead are affected. Part of the scar is graft, and this is dead white and conspicuous…cannot extend fingers or thumbs fully, cannot make a fist. Grip is poor.' Despite this, Page's pension level was reassessed every two years and both the 'interim' status and 80% level of his disability pension continued from 1948 to 1980.

It must have been humiliating for a very proud war hero to be endlessly examined by disability appeals panels and medical boards. As Geoffrey grew older the pain from the spinal injuries suffered at Arnhem was almost unbearable, but he never complained. In 1980, the consultant examining his back concluded that 'it was impossible from the information at my disposal to come to any view as to the relationship between his lumbar degeneration and the injury suffered in World War Two.' It was not until 1981, at the age of sixty-one, that Geoffrey Page's disability payment was increased to 90% pension.

Fortunately, the Royal Air Force Benevolent Fund recognised the immense contribution Page had made to the war effort. The Fund was sympathetic and generous, and a significant supporter of all Guinea Pigs. Page received grants towards the education of his sons totalling £2411 on 22 October 1977. When Geoffrey struggled with the rent and repairs to his cottage in Oxfordshire the RAF Benevolent Fund again helped with loans and grants. It must have been hard for a man of such achievement to ask for charitable support to maintain the roof over his family's head. But Geoffrey Page would be the first to say that his wonderful family and amazing flying experiences made him rich beyond money.

After the war it was not just the DHSS who were an adversary for Page. Children were now the enemy rather than the Nazis. They would point at him and ask their mothers about his face. It was these unwittingly cruel comments and the occasional looks of pity, or even of disgust, that he found most difficult to cope with. His memories of his crash in 1940 never dimmed. Decades after he could still vividly remember the smell of burning cordite and would add with laconic humour, 'and the smell of burning flesh - my own'.

In this uncertain post-war world, the Page family and the McIndoe's grew increasingly intertwined. McIndoe was godfather to Geoffrey's daughter, Shelley, who called him Uncle Mac. His daughter Vanora became Shelley's godmother. McIndoe's wife, Connie, was godmother to one of Geoffrey's sons, and Pauline Page was godmother to McIndoe's granddaughter. McIndoe was always willing to help Geoffrey with a job or a pension or the pain in his hands. His wartime fame and brilliance provided the perfect platform for a remarkable post-war career. He developed his lucrative Harley Street practice and was so skilled at refashioning noses, debutantes would say, 'I'm saving up for an Archie.' Among his patients were the Hollywood star Ava Gardner, dancer Margot Fonteyn, and the Duchess of Windsor.

However, Archie McIndoe always made certain he spent enough time in East Grinstead. There were always faces and hands to be repaired, Guinea Pigs who needed further operations. He was a regular at their reunions and always available for medical examinations. In 1947 McIndoe was knighted, and his elevation was celebrated in an even wilder Guinea Pig reunion than usual. One Guinea Pig fell from the roof and McIndoe spent much of the dinner stitching up the man's leg.

At the Guinea Pig Reunion in 1948 Geoffrey Page's father-in-law, Nigel Bruce, flew over from Hollywood to speak at the Annual Dinner. Many of those present, including Geoffrey, had still more operations and procedures to endure. There was a powerful sense of comradeship and common purpose amongst the two hundred or more Guinea Pigs in the room. McIndoe told those present, 'The Club stands secure and four-square to all winds that may blow…tonight within these walls sit men who have with each other more than two thousand operations. They have lost and regained enough skin to paper these walls and have donated enough pedicles to hang Hitler.'

On 31 January 1948 the doors of the legendary Ward Three closed. The beer barrel was empty, the saline bath dry, and the piano taken away. Any remaining patients were moved to the 49-bedded Canadian Wing which had been built with the generosity of the Canadian government and its people. A party was held to mark the closure. In the *Maestro's Message* in the Guinea Pig magazine McIndoe described Ward Three as, 'the physical and spiritual home of so many extraordinary men in the short life of seven years…they will recall that sense of brotherhood, the disappointment and excitements, the temporary setbacks and eventual triumphs.' McIndoe went on to recount the vital role played by Ward Three following Dunkirk and during the Battle of Britain and the Blitz when Ward Three 'sat more or less on the frontline'. He concluded that 'this is a story to be told before the name that was Ward Three sinks into oblivion. It is a great tale and worthy of the telling.'

The three central figures at East Grinstead were called *The Immortal Trio* by their patients. Ironically, Archie McIndoe, Jill Mullins and John Hunter were outlived by almost all the Guinea Pigs whose faces, hands, and lives they had saved. On 9 August 1953, John Hunter died. The large, ebullient character full of humour and bonhomie was a brilliant doctor, 'I've seen no one to touch him as an anaesthetist,' observed McIndoe. On Hunter's fiftieth birthday in 1948, Geoffrey Page, on behalf of the Guinea Pigs, gave him a cigarette case inscribed to *John the Giant Killer*. John Hunter was visibly moved by Page's short speech in tribute. In the 1950s the Hunter and McIndoe grew apart because of professional differences and at the same time Hunter's overwork and chronic diabetes took a severe toll on his health. The spray of carnations at his funeral carried a card reading, *'In loving memory of and with great regret for Our John of the enormous heart, from Guinea Pigs all over the world.'*

Archie's wife Adonia and the children finally returned from America in 1943, following a volley of anonymous letters accusing her husband of having affairs. Archie and Adonia had been apart for three years and their relationship was difficult to rekindle after so long. Adonia thought her husband had changed and she was unprepared for his newfound semi-celebrity status as Britain's best-known surgeon.

Jill Mullins worked with McIndoe for over twenty years until 1957. He was quick to acknowledge that he could not have been so successful without her skill. Following the end of her two-year affair with Geoffrey Page, the relationship between Archie and Jill stretched beyond the professional. At social gatherings from 1940 onwards Jill had often been by McIndoe's side. That did not change after Adonia's return. When McIndoe's strained marriage came to an end, Mullins and McIndoe became as inseparable off duty as they were at work. After Archie and Adonia formally separated in 1946, McIndoe and Jill Mullins grew even closer. For a time, they lived together in his house and later McIndoe bought her a cottage near East Grinstead. Jill hosted parties for Archie, grew close to McIndoe's daughters and went on holiday with him. They spent long happy periods together. When he heard about the two of them, Geoffrey Page was not surprised, 'They had been working together closely for so many years I don't know why it hadn't happened before.'

However, when McIndoe's divorce finally came through a few years later and McIndoe announced his engagement, it was not to Jill Mullins but to Mrs Constance Belchem. Connie had been married to a British General and her marriage was faltering as clearly as Archie's. How much Jill Mullins knew about McIndoe's intentions is unknown. It seems that Jill told friends that she expected to marry McIndoe. That was certainly something Archie's daughters would have welcomed. Perhaps Jill instinctively knew that much as McIndoe adored her both as a woman and as a colleague, he was never in love with her enough to marry her? Or maybe his engagement to another woman was a total surprise? The answers are unclear.

Despite this obvious rupture the pair continued to work together, and Mullins built a mutually respectful relationship with the new wife of the Maestro, but both their working and social lives were inevitably never as warm as before. In 1957 Jill Mullins finally stopped working with McIndoe and married a businessman called Stanley Denton in South Africa. When she returned to Britain in 1959, McIndoe, Connie, and the Guinea Pigs made her very welcome but in October 1959 on the boat back to South Africa she suffered a stroke. McIndoe was contacted and plans were made to fly Mullins urgently back to London but before she could be evacuated from the ship, she died from a second stroke. McIndoe telephoned Geoffrey Page within minutes. He was upset because Jill had been such a vital part of his life at an important crossroads. She was forty-nine.

Archie McIndoe reflected on their twenty-two years together, 'I think those wonderful gentle hands of hers were concerned in almost every operation I carried out on a Guinea Pig. There can be few of them who will not remember her green turban and Titian hair, with the reassuring smile on her attractive face…no one will ever equal her as a surgical assistant. Her hands were magic. They were long and strong and infinitely gentle and steady. She used them with grace and easy facility…she worked with me for twenty-two years and in that time thousands of patients passed through her care. She made countless friends who will always remember her with affection. It is sad to reflect that just at the time when she could have enjoyed to the full a happy life, she should have been cut down…we can be glad that she lived when she did. She was a real woman, and we will not see her like again.'[136]

Sir Archibald McIndoe himself had worked exceptionally hard during the war, performing 2,300 operations as well perpetually fighting for his 'boys'. He had already lost two-thirds of *The Immortal Trio*, and on 12 April 1960 McIndoe died of a heart attack in the early hours of the morning. He was aged just fifty-nine. He is the only civilian buried in the RAF church, St Clement Danes. One of his Guinea Pigs, Sergeant Paul Hart, remarked on hearing of his death, 'he gave up everything. For us, he was as close to God as a man can be. For us the pattern has been broken. There will never be another Archie Mac.' Another noted that they had lost 'the joystick of our ship'.

Losing Archie was a devastating blow for Geoffrey Page. 'He probably died of overwork,' he observed, 'he drove himself so hard.'

---

136  Sir Archibald McIndoe, *In Memoriam*

Page had lost his surgeon, his father figure, and the man who battled for him against the system. Archie had done so much for Geoffrey, not just in the war but in the fifteen years afterwards, 'He was devastated. They were very close. He was daddy's father, and daddy was like a son to McIndoe,' says his daughter Shelley, 'Whereas his own father, he couldn't care less about when he died. As far as I know he only ever saw him once as an adult, when we all went down to Devon.'

McIndoe died too young but left behind a remarkable legacy. It was not just the young men whose lives he had given back and who worshipped the surgeon who had restored their hands, faces, and their confidence. More than that, McIndoe's remarkable wartime crusade had embedded plastic and reconstructive surgery within the National Health Service. There were only four reconstructive surgeons at the start of the war but by the end scores of doctors trained by McIndoe were in practice, including fifty Americans he had trained at East Grinstead in advance of D-Day in 1944. Among them was Tom Rees, who went on to become one of America's best-known surgeons and co-founder of Flying Doctor Service of Africa, with Archbald McIndoe and Michael Wood.[137]

His innovative treatments for burns entered the mainstream and were still relevant for decades after his death. A 1996 study by Yvette Godwin, who had once been a Senior House Officer at the Queen Victoria Hospital, examined four of McIndoe's badly burned patients more than fifty years after their initial treatment. In a paper published in the British Journal of Plastic Surgery, Godwin concluded that many of McIndoe's techniques were still valid and that these were successful outcomes where the reconstructions had blended successfully with normal facial contours.

---

137 Now, the charity AMREF.

Generations of surgeons following behind McIndoe benefited from his willingness to experiment with fresh ideas. Ken Lavery, Medical Director at Queen Victoria Hospital (2007-16) acknowledged his contribution, 'McIndoe was never scared to be first, always pushing the envelope...he was a surgical pioneer. He dealt with patients no one else knew what to do with. He was always willing to walk into untracked territory and to have the vision to say, yes, this is the direction we should travel.'[138] Baljit Dheansa, Consultant Plastic Surgeon at the McIndoe Centre at the Queen Victoria Hospital agrees about the benefits of McIndoe's risk taking, 'He went out on a limb. Although it was experimental in some people's eyes, radical in other people' eyes, he put the patient at the centre of his thoughts. He was geared towards making their lot better.'[139]

Archie McIndoe's other significant legacy was the Guinea Pig Club which was a model self-help group. He understood better than anyone the emotional needs of burnt young pilots in their early twenties. The anaesthetist Russell Davies, who worked with McIndoe for nearly twenty years, had a close-up view of the Boss. In a lecture for the Royal College of Surgeons in 1976 he said, 'To the best of my knowledge there has been one characteristic of McIndoe's that has never been described. I believe that McIndoe's greatest quality was that of courage.' To Davies it was Archie's bravery to defy convention, to innovate, and to stand up for the whole patient both in hospital and afterwards that made him great.

With the help of his wealthy friends, Elaine and Neville Blond, the Blond McIndoe Research Foundation was born and is still a leading centre for research into burns treatment. A research institute in New Zealand is also named after McIndoe and his mentor and fellow Kiwi, Harold Gillies. The Queen Victoria Hospital houses the

---

138   Ken Lavery, *Hurricane Rash*, BBC Radio, London, 8 May 2012
139   Baljit Dheansa, *Hurricane Rash*, BBC Radio, London,8 May 2012

McIndoe Burns Unit. A sculpture of McIndoe adorns the High Street in East Grinstead, a town full of streets and buildings named after McIndoe and his Guinea Pigs. McIndoe, Mullins, and Hunter all died young but were never forgotten by the Guinea Pigs. At the annual Reunion photos of all three of *The Immortal Trio* adorned the walls for years and glasses were raised in a toast to all three of them.

One of the strange curiosities of the post-war years was the friendships between the best-known RAF pilots and their Luftwaffe counterparts. There was still an old-fashioned sense of chivalry amongst many of them, 'I've got one or two very good friends and I mean really good friends. A German pilot, apart from the language and a certain mental outlook, they are still pleasant people. We have a lot in common from flying fighter aircraft and there's no bitterness or acrimony.'[140] In 1979, Wing Commander Page was invited as a Guest of Honour by the Luftwaffe Fighter Pilots Association to a convocation in Munich for fighter pilots from all over the world, both friends and former enemies. Convocation was clearly a long word for beer festival.

Amongst the other guests was Lubeck-born Hans-Joachim Jabs, who was such a successful pilot he was awarded the highest military honour available in the German military, the Knight's Cross. On 29 April 1944 he had been unlucky enough to encounter Squadron Leader Geoffrey Page and his Spitfire squadron above his home base at Deelen in Holland. There followed a dramatic cat and mouse game with both sides taking hits, until Jabs wounded aircraft could fly no more and he was forced to make an emergency landing. Page strafed the Messerschmitt before he headed home through a barrage of anti-aircraft fire.

---

140  Author interview, Henley -on-Thames,1983

When Jabs finally met his lead attacker in Munich thirty-five later, he explained, probably over a German beer, what happened that day. For the first time Page learned that the Luftwaffe pilot had deliberately sought the sanctuary of the airfield and their impressive array of anti-aircraft guns. He was also surprised to discover that he had hit the aircraft flown by Jabs and it had burst into a fireball. 26-year-old Jabs and his crew rolled out and had taken shelter in a ditch.

Jabs laughed and explained that he had not been upset by nearly being killed, but by losing his plane which was stuffed full of bacon he was transporting as extra food. That day the bacon had been so well and truly smoked that the hungry German pilots were driven mad by the intoxicating smell of the rashers as they sizzled in the aircraft's wreckage. As a gesture of friendship and goodwill Geoffrey Page sent Jabs a kilo of British bacon and insisted that it was much tastier than anything Jabs would find in mainland Europe. Page reflected that the two men had much more in common than trying to kill each other in 1944, 'To illustrate the stupidity of war, we are now very good friends, and he has invited me, the New Zealand pilot [John Caulton], who fortunately survived, and all our wives to go and stay with him and his charming wife in Germany.'[141]

Although he was on good terms with the men who were once trying to kill him, Page was cautious too. 'He was not', says Air Chief Marshal Michael Graydon, 'dramatically pushy. There were one or two Battle of Britain veterans who were personalities par excellence and were always the centre of attention...Geoffrey was just a thoroughly nice person.'[142] Although it could be a useful source of funds, Page found some of the post-war pilot celebrity circuit distasteful, 'I can't name names but there are certain characters on both sides, the Luftwaffe and the Royal Air Force who have cashed in on their war-

---

141  Geoffrey Page, unpublished notes, Geneva, 1979
142  Author interview 2 August 2023

time exploits to earn a few pennies. I find this unattractive because so many other people got killed and so on. To exploit something which you should have been doing anyway which was part of your military duty, I find distasteful.'[143]

His own note entitled *Strange Encounter* gives a further insight. In Munich Page met Adolf Galland who was Germany's top-scoring fighter pilot with over one hundred 'kills'. Although Galland was a pleasant man, Page knew he had supported Hitler and had received some of his medals directly from the Fuhrer. After the war, the US Airforce warned the new German government about Galland's apparent Nazi sympathies, a claim Galland denied. His note of the event in Munich concludes, 'The other British element in Munich consisted of Douglas Bader and Bob Stanford-Tuck. Also present was Adolf Galland, the German fighter ace and the three of them go round the world raising money for charities etc and I have christened them the *Bader-Mein Gott Gang*.'[144]

Not all former Battle of Britain pilots were impressed by Galland. Squadron Leader Edward Donaldson whose 151 Squadron shared RAF North Weald with Geoffrey Page and 56 Squadron, was shot down in his Hurricane over the channel in late June 1940. He parachuted into the sea where the Germans continued to shoot at him, 'the shells started coming over even when my head was under water.' Donaldson met Galland after the war and concluded, 'I still didn't think much of his conduct that day, for he must have known that my Hurricane was dead as far as fighting again, but he never stopped shooting.'[145]

---

143  Geoffrey Page, author interview, East Grinstead,1982
144  A wordplay on the Bader- Meinhoff Gang who were terrorising German at the time
145  Sq Ldr Edward Donaldson, Daily Telegraph, London,1980.

It was Douglas Bader who Page reserved his strongest criticism for. He was a huge admirer of Bader's work for the limbless, 'His visits to the limbless in hospitals were a great morale booster. That side of him was fabulous.' As the years rolled on and Page grew to know Bader better, he saw the other man's interest in self-promotion increase, 'I find the publicity seeking side unattractive. Whenever there is a camera, Douglas pops up and he expects treatment now almost as if he was royalty. I would almost put it as egomania. The salt of life for him is publicity but you have to balance this against the tremendous example he gave. But I think he is a bullshit merchant.'[146]

In June 2023, when author Ben McIntyre called Bader 'racist, snobbish and brutally unpleasant to anybody he considered to be of a lower socio-economic order' he was caught in a volley of culture wars and accused of trashing a national hero. But, as Geoffrey Page pointed out, it is perfectly possible to be brave, do good things and be thoroughly self-absorbed and unpleasant at the same time.

Page's beloved Guinea Pig Club, of which he was a founder member, only saw him at their annual *Lost Weekend* reunion occasionally, 'I'm not an old comrades type of person, but that is up to each individual. I enjoy coming once every few years, but I certainly don't turn up every year because reminiscing about the good old days falls flat after a couple of years…my memories are both pleasant and unpleasant. You can't live in the past because it is a waste of time.' When he did attend, Page displayed his customary charm and good humour. When a fellow Guinea Pig, Sam Gallop, asked his wife Pauline to dance 'he smiled benevolently and said to her "Be gentle with him. He has tin legs".'[147]

At the 1949 weekend reunion when the members were still young, 225 Guinea Pigs drank 3000 bottles of beer, 125 bottles of

---

146  Battle of Britain Society of Utah, Salt Lake City, July 1982
147  Sam Gallop, email 21 April 2021

whiskey, and 72 bottles of sherry. The number of bottles of wine consumed remains unknown. It was no wonder that these annual reunions became known as The *Lost Weekend*, although a church service and a darts match also were included in the calendar. The following year was hailed in the Guinea Pig magazine headline. It read ***What a Weekend! Guinea Pigs Over Run East Grinstead, McIndoe's Army Lets Its Hair Down.***

The *Lost Weekend* dinner gave Archie McIndoe an annual chance to speak directly to his Guinea Pigs. He emphasised the self-help aims of the Club, 'we are the trustees of one another', and the confidence they should all share 'Misplaced sympathy from the public plays no part...the Club stands four square and flourishes in an unstable world.' Even at the pinnacle of booziness in September 1949 he announced that at the end of their first decade the Club was moving from *Operation Knife* into a different post-war era which he called *Operation Get Cracking*. He noted that already fifty-three Guinea Pigs were being financially supported in civilian life by the RAF Benevolent Fund. Although, as one member pointed out 'Pigs will continue to be stabbed and chopped at intervals', McIndoe's major surgical efforts for the RAF ended a few years after the war. Now it was as much about ensuring employment and fair disability pensions. He was clear, 'Every Guinea Pig is an individual with the dignity of his own rights and privileges that are inalienable.'

Geoffrey Page was a popular Guinea Pig, not just a founder member and a war hero but a regular, witty speaker at the early dinners. In the 1948 magazine he is described, 'Geoffrey looks the part. He is just what one would imagine a young Battle of Britain pilot to look like. And he is modest and sincere.' The writer added that Geoffrey did not want to discuss his medals, 'How very typical of Geoffrey Page.' In a speech at the Lost Weekend three years later in

September 1951 Page said, 'The Guinea Pig Club is a really happy family, one big happy family. Let's keep it like that - always.'

As the years wound forward and the Guinea Pigs grew older, The *Lost Weekend* was a more sober occasion. The list of members who had passed away in the preceding year was read out with a solemnity underlined by the endlessness of the roll call. The room was littered with the human wreckage of war but except for the scarred hands and faces it could pass for any reunion of old colleagues. One observer noted how good looking the women at the weekend were, despite their physically damaged husbands. At the dinner I attended, there was warm applause when three men badly injured in the Falklands war are introduced. One was blind and another had both his legs blown off.

The presence of the Falklands veterans highlighted the fundamental dilemma the Guinea Pig Club faced in the last decades of the twentieth century. The Club was literally dying out. Geoffrey Page was clear that the accumulated knowledge of the Guinea Pigs should not disappear with the last survivor. Page was keen to make the Club open for following generations, for burned civilians and servicemen alike, but the Club was resistant to change. Even McIndoe himself could not always persuade the Guinea Pigs to bend to his will. Back in 1945 he was heavily defeated when he wanted to elect Jill Mullins, and Sister Hall as female members. A later attempt by McIndoe to include wives and partners in the Club was also repelled.

Geoffrey Page's wish for the Guinea Pigs to be 'one big happy family...always' did not last. In the following decades his love affair with the Guinea Pigs cooled. He still valued the comradeship of what he called 'an extraordinary group of people' but he was concerned about the future. He wanted Guinea Pigs to look forward and open their arms, before it was too late. In March 1980 Page wrote openly to the Editor of the Guinea Pig magazine protesting that he had 'repeatedly' stated that the Club 'had much more to offer than its current activities' but noting that 'there are certain members who want to keep our Club as an elite group. However, I sincerely do not believe that the majority of Guinea Pigs are so selfish and narrow-minded that they do not want to help their fellow human beings…' Page also pointed out that he had 'never had the courtesy of having my suggestions recorded in the Minutes of the AGM'.

Against this view was ranged most of the Club who were happy to visit hospitals and charities as individuals but jealously guarded entry to their Club. They firmly believed that membership should be restricted to those from the RAF who had been treated at East Grinstead. As the Editor replied to Page, 'The Guinea Pig Club is an elite group and I for one wouldn't have it otherwise.'

This disagreement about the future direction of the Club Page had helped found grew increasingly bitter. His daughter Shelley was in no doubt about the intensity of her father's feeling, 'He felt strongly that the Club was also there to help other people who were burnt, but it wasn't. It was all about them. They never opened their arms and said come into the fold. It made him very angry. He visited burns patients in a personal capacity, but this was never the policy of the Club.'[148]

It is hard to imagine two braver men than Page and Chief Guinea Pig Tom Gleave, both founder members of the Club back in 1941. Yet, the correspondence between them was rancorous. In 1983 Page accused Gleave of behaving dictatorially in his running of the Guinea Pig Club asserting that the AGM 'was run in a manner I thought shame making and one which brought great discredit to the club.'[149] McIndoe's daughter Vanora weighed in and added in a

---

148   Author interview, London, August 2022
149   Geoffrey Page, letter to Tom Gleave, 3 November 1983

letter to Gleave that 'human dignity and democracy have come off second best'.

Peter Procter's hands, face, and body were terribly burned in a motor racing accident at Goodwood. He was helped by Guinea Pigs but was never eligible for membership. His views echoed those of Geoffrey Page, 'I'm firmly convinced that the Club has a lot to contribute. They've helped me, they've helped a lot of people. It would be a shame to let the Club die out. On the other hand, I can understand the feelings of many of them, that this is a special Club, a unique Club…because it is so special the Club almost has a duty to carry on. To go on spreading the word that it is possible to survive, to those who've been burned in a rather less glamorous way than in a crashing aircraft or an exploding fighter plane.'[150]

At the Club's annual meetings Page regularly sounded an alarm bell about the future of the Guinea Pig Club. He said, 'We are reaching the stage when, like the elderly reader of *The Times*, we turn to the Obituary columns every morning and, if our name's not in it, we decide to get up and shave, ready to face the new day…' He added the vivid image of the final annual meeting taking place between 'the last two survivors each in a bathchair?' As I write this, only two Guinea Pigs remain, and both are over a hundred and one. I don't know if they are in bathchairs. One of them, Sam Gallop, is Chairman of the Guinea Pig Club. The other centenarian survivor, Jan Stangryciuk, now called Jan Black, had all his war medals and cash stolen from his home in London in 2022 by thieves pretending to be water inspectors.

When these two surviving members[151] have passed away the Guinea Pig Club, a unique and brilliant association, will finally close. The Club's reunion weekends were wound up back 2007 when the Club had two hundred ageing members. The charity number has

---

150   Peter Williams and Ted Harrison, *McIndoe's Army*, London, Pelham Books,1979
151   Since writing this, sadly both Sam Gallop and Jan Black have died.

been handed back and any remaining funds have been transferred to the RAF Benevolent Fund to meet the needs of the fifty or so surviving Guinea Pig widows.

At its peak the Club had six hundred and forty-nine members, mainly British but also men from eighteen countries, including Canadians, Australians, New Zealanders, Poles, and Czechs. Thirty of the repaired Guinea Pigs, including Richard Hillary, who flew again were killed later in the war. Many Guinea Pigs married and had 'piglets', as their children were called. The Guinea Pig Club will continue to be remembered in the museum in East Grinstead, much of which is devoted to the story of McIndoe's 'boys', and on a memorial plaque in the Queen Victoria Hospital nearby. Bob Marchant, the last Club Secretary, and probably the final survivor of the men and women who worked with McIndoe, has toiled tirelessly to keep these important stories alive for future generations. But Bob knows that the Guinea Pig Club is dancing its last waltz now.

One Guinea Pig mystery remains: a Soviet fighter pilot called Vladimir Razumov, later known as the Red Guinea Pig, was shot down and severely burned. He was a popular patient and, with their customary skill, the staff at the Queen Victoria Hospital successfully rebuilt him. In July 1946, just before his treatment came to an end, the burns victim received two visitors from the Soviet Embassy. They took Vladimir Razumov for a walk in the park, and never returned. The Guinea Pigs believed 'that he had been snatched from the Maestro's knife and repatriated to the rear of the Iron Curtain... by the lumbering hairy boys of the NKVD.' [152] All subsequent attempts to find his whereabouts failed, the Red Guinea Pig became the Disappearing Guinea Pig.

152   East Grinstead Museum

For a man who was reserved about both reunions and celebrity fighter pilots, Geoffrey Page did more to preserve the memories of the Battle of Britain than anyone. He was astounded that there was no national memorial to The Few and resolved to do something about it. As Dilip Sarkar, the author of over fifty books about the Battle of Britain, put it, the lack of a Memorial was 'to one man in particular, inappropriate; his name was Wing Commander Geoffrey Page'. As a result, Geoffrey founded a new venture to build a permanent memorial, the Battle of Britain Memorial Trust.

When the £2.5 million appeal for funding was launched at London's Guildhall in May 1991, Air Chief Marshal Christopher Foxley-Norris echoed Page's feelings when he said, 'It is astounding and deplorable that the battle which undoubtedly determined the passage of World War Two and affected the history of our country is not commemorated at all. This monument will stand as a permanent tribute to those young men who died for their country in its hour of need.'

Geoffrey Page was elected as Chairman of the Trust at their first meeting on 22 September 1990, and it was his vision that brought to life the beautiful Battle of Britain Memorial on seven acres of land overlooking the sea near Folkestone. Many contributed to the success of the Memorial by giving generously of time or money, but the Trust's current Chairman, Richard Hunting, is clear where the founding credit should lie, 'Geoffrey had enormous charm and charisma. He was very engaging. He was the inspiration behind the memorial, the Founder. He led the charge.'

The Memorial sits proudly on the Kent coast not far from where Geoffrey Page was shot down in 1940. It was opened by the Queen Mother on 9 July 1993. The opening itself was yet another drama amongst the many in Geoffrey Page's life. Air Chief Marshal Sir Michael Graydon, an experienced fighter pilot himself, recalled, 'The weather was terrible. I flew a communications jet down to Manston and by God it was rough. The heavy jet was buffeted about in the wind. Can you imagine was it was like in a helicopter?'

This was July, but the wind was so fierce that guests could see the helicopter transporting the Queen Mother swaying from side to side. Both Air Chief Marshal Graydon and aerospace executive Tony Edwards were told that the weather was so appalling that the helicopter crew suggested that it would be sensible to turn back, but the Queen Mother was determined. 'My boys didn't turn back in 1940 and I am not going to now,' she replied, and the helicopter swayed on to its destination.

As Graydon and Edwards both acknowledge, the story may or may not be true, but the Queen Mother certainly persisted in apocalyptic weather. Despite the guests, their hats, and the tent they were housed in all threatening to blow away, the Memorial was successfully unveiled, and a great day was enjoyed by all. Once again, the Battle of Britain pilots had triumphed against the odds.

In the years that followed a new visitors' centre, a resource centre, replica fighter aircraft, and a library were all added. In 2005 a Memorial Wall was opened which bears the name of every Allied air crew confirmed as having taken part in the Battle of Britain. It also fittingly houses the Geoffrey Page Centre dedicated to education, and a precise replica of his Hurricane, number P2670, in which he was shot down and so badly burnt in August 1940 is on the site.

The centrepiece of the Memorial, which was generously bequeathed by Dover Council, is a sandstone statue designed by Harry Gray of a seated pilot staring out to sea, deep in reflective thought. Some close to the Memorial affectionately call it Geoffrey but the pilot is deliberately emblematic and anonymous, with no name, rank or nationality attached. The sandstone plinth bears the crests of all the squadrons who fought in the Battle of Britain. Back in 1940 the sky over this section of coast was so full of ferocious action it was dubbed Hellfire Corner. Looking out over the Channel, it is possible for visitors to imagine Page and hundreds of other young pilots heading into battle to defend their country. Coquelles, where the Eurotunnel Terminal now sits, was the base for many German pilots, just a five-minute flight away. This is a fitting Memorial to all Battle of Britain pilots, and to Geoffrey Page in particular.

Page viewed the Memorial through the same lens as the Guinea Pig Club. He wanted it to be alive, a way of offering enduring support to the men and women of the services who were suffering from hardship, 'A memorial is just bricks and mortar. I feel strongly that if money comes from visitors in years to come it should be passed onto Royal Air Force charities, as opposed to just being something to look at.'[153]

The long battle to fund a worthy Memorial was not without problems. Geoffrey's persuasiveness and energy were vital to fund raising but his vagueness with budgets caused alarm. At one point some Trustees resigned because they were worried about the finances and Geoffrey's relaxed approach to them. The financial generosity of Clive Hunting, the Chair at the time, enabled the Trust to escape from any immediate difficulties. As Tony Edwards, who joined as a Trustee soon after, thought, 'Geoffrey was a visionary leader. He just needed someone with their financial feet on the ground alongside him.'

Eventually John Beazley, an experienced accountant, was able to settle any financial nervousness. Shirley Slocock brought clarity to the project and made things happen. She admired Geoffrey who was 'warm, witty, and delightful to be with' but saw that he was sometimes too trusting when it came to money, 'He was a delightful young man who had never grown up. There was a naivety about him. The real world had somehow left him untarnished, untouched.' [154]

---

153   Meridian News,9 July 1993
154   Author interview,24 May 2023

Whatever the wobbles it was Geoffrey Page's inspiration and energy that brought the idea to life. As Richard Hunting said, 'Without him there would never have been a Memorial.'

The benefits of the Memorial worked in both directions. It gave Geoffrey Page a sense of purpose as well as some of the status that had been eroded in the post war years. The Memorial put his sharp mind to good use. His daughter Shelley says, 'I think it was very morale boosting. It suddenly gave his life an important purpose. Daddy was never one for trying to impress people, but he liked to be acknowledged. It made him feel better. I suspect that he spent a large part of his life thinking he hadn't done very well since the war.'[155]

Geoffrey Page was loyal to the Battle of Britain Memorial right to the end of his life. He tried not to miss any event however frail his health was. These final years were marked by his beloved Pauline's failing health, with growing signs of dementia. He was, remembered Shirley Slocock, 'very caring. He was completely devoted to Pauline. As she faded, he was very attentive. And she was devoted back.'

At his eightieth birthday lunch in 2000 he was as gracious and charming as ever. His own health was fading, and he had lost weight significantly, but he had sworn to live long enough to witness the sixtieth anniversary of the Battle of Britain. At the end of the lunch, he publicly thanked his daughter for helping him so much, and then sarcastically added, 'All she's got to do now is to take her husband's Swiss army knife and screw down the lid of my coffin.' Shelley Page was a huge support to her father and fully understood the context of this comment, 'I think he had had enough. He'd had more than forty operations. He was tired of all the pain, the operations and Mummy's health. In later years the pain was unbearable.'

---

155 Author interview, August 2022

With his life-long determination Geoffrey Page made it to the sixtieth anniversary of the Battle of Britain's opening day in July 1940. Despite Pauline's dementia and his own poor health, the indomitable spirit Page had shown in the war was still visible. He was now so thin that one guest said he was 'like a piece of thistledown held together by his suit'. Richard Hunting noted in his diary that when Geoffrey visited the Battle of Britain Memorial for the last time, 'he was very frail but fully on the ball and with a great sense of fun.' Among the other guests that day Geoffrey was delighted to reacquaint himself with one of the Margate lifeboat crew who had rescued him from the sea in August 1940.

Less than a month later, on 3 August 2000, Geoffrey died. Like so many Englishmen of his generation he buried his emotions. A few days before his death his daughter Shelley was sitting by his bedside helping him sip a drink. She plucked up the courage for the first time to tell her father that she loved him. 'The response was even more amazing…'I love you too', he said. 'And that was a first.'

Geoffrey Page had reached the age of eighty which was remarkable, given that Archie McIndoe had once told Page that his body had endured so much in wartime, he would be lucky to live beyond sixty. In his final days, his family asked if their father wanted to be buried or cremated. He told them that he wanted to be cremated, 'You might as well finish what the Germans started.' The cremation took place on 12 August, the exact date he had been shot down on sixty years earlier. It was a Saturday, and the crematorium was not open but, given the circumstances and the extraordinary coincidence of dates, the local council opened just for the Page family.

Appropriately his ashes were later spread from the air over the Battle of Britain Memorial near Folkestone. The day unfolded in a way that would have appealed to Geoffrey Page's sense of humour. In the dry language of the Civil Aviation Authority the licence issued for a flight that day read 'the articles to be dropped shall consist of ashes of no discernible weight'. A family friend called Robert Lamplugh flew a Mustang, an aircraft Page himself had operated with conspicuous success in tandem with One Armed Mac, over the Memorial. At the rehearsal, the pilot used ashes from his fireplace instead of the real thing but unfortunately they blew wildly back into the Mustang as the ashes were released. Lamplugh had wisely anticipated this disaster and had brought with him a pair of women's tights. He cut holes in the bottom and gently squeezed Geoffrey Page's ashes out of the tights above the Memorial, and then completed a victory roll towards France. Pauline was pleased that the ashes fell across the spot where Geoffrey probably used to look out towards the enemy. There was, recall the Page family, not a dry eye in the house.

There was a huge outpouring of respect for him in the formal obituaries. To his family, the informal observations from those who worked with him during the war were just as important. Pauline received a letter from Fred Ollett, who worked with Page for three happy years as a mechanic. Fred had been first on the scene when Geoffrey Page crashed at Arnhem and smashed his face and back. The letter to Pauline Page concluded, 'He was a remarkable man, and straight forward...I have told my grandchildren about this great fighter pilot I was lucky to have served with for three years.'

Among those who wrote to Shelley was his old adversary Hans-Joachim Jabs, 'I have always admired your father for his braveness and fairness.' A second mechanic praised 'his great humanity, his courtesy, his kindness and his sense of humour'. Others understood how deep his pain had been in recent years and noted that his wartime courage was 'the least of it...he was quite simply the bravest man I have ever known.'

It was Archie McIndoe's daughter Vanora who perceived that Geoffrey Page was also a man of the contradictions, 'Such a complex man. Plagued by unfulfilled dreams and disappointments and, of course, by constant pain for so many years but always uncomplaining, always valiant. For us life started slow, and simply got better but for him the peak came early and then slid slowly downhill. Through upbringing and a war, he learnt to conceal his emotions so successfully that sometimes I think he didn't know himself what he was really feeling…I suspect he has finally put out his hand and touched the face of God, which may come as something of a surprise to both of them.'[156]

Air Chief Marshal Sir Michael Graydon had enormous respect for what Geoffrey Page and his fellow Battle of Britain pilots achieved. He put their contribution in a wider historical perspective, 'The Battle was pivotal to the war and if we had lost - and it was a close-run thing - there was a very real prospect that Hitler would have invaded…they would have had supremacy in the air. This country would have been in very big trouble without those pilots.'[157]

At the packed Service of Thanksgiving for the life of Wing Commander Geoffrey Page at the Royal Air Force Church of St Clement Danes in London on 16 October 1980, Air Chief Marshal Sir Christopher Foxley-Norris said of Page 'even in the context of the Battle of Britain he was the bravest of the brave'. The next morning *The Times* printed this eye-catching observation above the masthead on the front page. The Battle of Britain inspired many extraordinary acts of bravery, but the Air Chief Marshal's assessment was a fair one. Page's son Jamie was fully aware of how remarkable his father was, 'Obviously there were many other very brave people in the war on all sides and fighting in all countries, but I think that what made my father special was that having been so badly burnt, having spent two years in hospital undergoing endless plastic surgery operations, was his will to go back to flying and to return to the battle…anybody who

---

156  Reference to the well-known poem *High Flight* by J McGee
157  Author interview 2 August 2023

has been so painfully injured, to have his hands nearly burnt down to the bone, and want to go back to operational flying must have been a very extraordinary person.'

Pauline Page died in December 2002, two years after her husband. She was described in her Guinea Pig magazine obituary as 'beautiful, funny and loving'. I met Pauline several times and she was gracious and intelligent, as well as funny and beautiful. Given Geoffrey's injuries and the inevitable struggles to adjust emotionally and financially to peacetime, Pauline was the family's rock. At Geoffrey's Service of Thanksgiving his daughter Shelley credited Pauline Page and Archie McIndoe as the two people who changed Geoffrey Page's life.

Forty-one years after he was shot down Wing Commander Geoffrey Page was finally in possession of a 90% pension. The doctor compiled a list of his injuries, which are worth repeating: -

### Precis of War Wounds to Wing Commander A.G Page, DSO, DFC (and bar) 1939-45

*1940: Shot down in flames during the Battle of Britain Wounds: Severe Third degree Burns of hands and face plus gunshot wounds to the left leg. Period in hospital-2 years*

*1944: Normandy Invasion: Gunshot wound to the left leg from aerial combat. Hospitalised in Field Hospital in Normandy Beachhead*

*1944; Battle of Arnhem: Crash landed as a result of enemy action. Wounds: Fracture of right antrum and lower spine, plus concussion. In Field Hospital in Arnhem, later transferred to East Grinstead Hospital, United Kingdom*

*Recipient of 90% Disability pension. Still current.*

The document concludes with a note that was so typical of both Geoffrey Page's humour, he could have added it himself,

*'Other Injuries: Spiral break of Fibia and Tibia of right leg in post -war skiing accident.*

His daughter Shelley's epitaph caught both sides of her father, 'He was a remarkable man, one of the kindest people you would ever meet. But there was a will of iron there too...he could inspire love and anger all in the same breath but my goodness I am glad he was my Daddy."

But who better to sum up Geoffrey Page than his wife Pauline. Her conclusion was simply, 'He was a gutsy man, my husband. A very gutsy man.'

# Acknowledgements
and Author's Note

In 1981 Geoffrey Page wrote his autobiography, *Tale of a Guinea Pig* (Pelham Books,1981). This was the result of more than thirty years of effort, stopping and starting, switching between non-fiction and fiction, and then back again. The result, which owed a good deal to his family's determination that Geoffrey should finally complete his story, was an exciting Boy's Own autobiography, full of vivid description, laced with humour and candour.

The book was a deserved success and was republished by Wingham Press in 1991, and more recently in an amended version as *Shot Down in Flames* (Grub Street,1999). Given the success of such a readable book why write a biography? That was the question I asked myself when I first discussed a book project with Geoffrey's son Jamie. He had read and very much liked my earlier book *Churchill's Few* (Mensch,2020) and wondered if I was interested in a new book about his father. On reading through Geoffrey's autobiography again and examining some unpublished material, I felt sure that the time was right for a biography, a reassessment, of one of the most remarkable and courageous pilots of the Battle of Britain and beyond.

For all its qualities Geoffrey's autobiography was now over forty years old. The two biographies of pioneering burns surgeon, Archibald McIndoe, who played such a significant role in Geoffrey Page's life and in *Fighter Boy* were even more ancient. Autobiography speaks with a personal voice; biography enables more context and perspective; the views of those who knew Geoffrey builds a rounded and more layered portrait than his autobiography.

Almost inevitably, given his natural modesty, Geoffrey Page's own book underplays his bravery and resilience. Now, with the help of family archives, many stored in a Dorset garage for years, I have been able to piece together the jigsaw-puzzle pieces of this astonishing man's life. In addition, a new book offers the chance to examine both the challenges and triumphs of his life after the war, which culminated in his inspiration for the beautiful Battle of Britain Memorial at Folkestone.

None of this would have been possible without the help of his surviving children, Shelley and Jamie. Their support was boundless, and their openness to my exploration of any less heroic moments in their father's life was admirable. I owe them both an enormous debt. Many thanks also to Geoffrey's niece Ann Handley Page who endured my visit with good humour and who safely kept a substantial treasure trove of Geoffrey's documents.

Outside the family, many thanks to Bob Marchant, Secretary of the Guinea Pig Club, who was unfailing helpful on several visits to the archives in East Grinstead. Gratitude also to everyone I spoke to about the Battle of Britain Memorial, including Richard Hunting, Patrick and Janet Tootal, Sir Michael Graydon, Tony Edwards, and Shirley Slocock. The RAF Museum in London diligently holds Geoffrey's Page's logbooks and other material. Emily Mayhew of Imperial College, London University was an insightful contributor. Thanks also to John Caulton, Julia Gregson, Peter Williams, and Squadron Leader Jillian Starling (56 Squadron) for their help.

As ever, my publisher Richard Charkin was a huge support. He commissioned this book quickly and edited the copy himself. Visiting the international HQ of Mensch in South West France was always a pleasure. Phillip Beresford has excelled himself again with a terrific cover design.

Thanks also to Jane Nairac, Peter Moore, and Andy Saunders for their research efforts for the original *Churchill's Few* Yorkshire Television documentary in which Geoffrey Page appeared.

This book would have been impossible to write without the encouragement of Janet Willis. Her support has been steadfast, and her patience unwavering. There is no one whose views on a manuscript I value more, and her thoughts and corrections were full of insight.

As I explained in *Churchill's Few*, I also owe a giant debt to my father, Ted Willis. In the 1930s he spoke out against Fascism so robustly that he was among the 2300 men and women put on Hitler's Black (or Special Search) list, the Gestapo's notorious *Sonderfahndungsliste GB*. If the Nazis invasion had been successful, no doubt he would have been one of the first to be rounded up and executed. So, without Geoffrey Page and everyone else who won the Battle of Britain, I would not have been born, let alone written this book.

The Battle of Britain veterans I met in the last century were a remarkable breed. It was a particular pleasure to meet Barry Sutton, who wrote an excellent book and a poem about the Battle of Britain, and Taffy Higginson, who both flew with Geoffrey on the day he was shot down in 1940.

Of course, the greatest thanks must go to Geoffrey and Pauline Page. Without meeting them in the 1980s this book would not exist.

They were an inspirational couple, intelligent, warm-hearted, and fun. When Geoffrey was described as 'even in the context of the *Battle of Britain he was the bravest of the brave*' it is, having met him, hard to demur from that view. I hope this book does both the pilot and the man justice.

# A Note On the Author

John Willis is one of Britain's best known television executives. He is a former Director of Programmes at Channel 4 and Director of Factual and Learning at the BBC. He was Vice-president of National Programs at WGBH Boston. In 2012 he was elected as Chair of the British Academy of Film and Television Arts (BAFTA).

He was educated at Eltham College and Fitzwilliam College, Cambridge where he read history. He started his career as a documentary maker and won a string of awards for his films, including Johnny Go Home, Alice – A Fight For Life, Rampton: The Secret Hospital, and First Tuesday: Return To Nagasaki.

He was Chief Executive of Mentorn Media - producer of Question Time for the BBC – and he now chairs the Board of Governors at the Royal Central School for Speech and Drama. He divides his time between London and Norfolk.